IN SE
H. V.

IN SEARCH OF
H. V. MORTON

Michael Bartholomew

Methuen

Published by Methuen 2006

1 3 5 7 9 10 8 6 4 2

Copyright © 2004 by Michael Bartholomew

The right of Michael Bartholomew to be identified as the author of
this work has been asserted by him in accordance with the
Copyright, Designs and Patents Act 1988

First published in 2004 by
Methuen
11–12 Buckingham Gate
London SW1E 6LB
www.methuen.co.uk

Methuen Publishing Limited Reg. No. 3543167

ISBN-(10): 0-413-77487-2
ISBN-(13): 978-0-413-77487-3

A CIP catalogue for this title is available from the British Library

Typeset by SX Composing DTP, Rayleigh, Essex

Printed and bound in Great Britain
by Bookmarque Ltd, Croydon, Surrey

CONTENTS

LIST OF ILLUSTRATIONS

PREFACE

I grew up during the 1950s in a nondescript London suburb. I now realise that, as a child, I was susceptible to the myth that the *real* England is not the England I actually lived in – the sprawl of semis, sodium streetlamps, municipal parks, and parades of dull shops. I was in some way made aware that the real England is the England of hedgerow and cottage, ploughman and shepherd, and that its location was somewhere out there, beyond the miles of tedious streets, deep in the green shires. I could just about reach the edge of the real thing by cycling through the suburbs and out into the scrubby fields beyond. On the few trips on which I was taken away from London, I caught glimpses of a somehow more authentic England from the windows of trains. There is something tantalising about the view of the English country-side seen from a train: enticing prospects are continuously promised, and then, at the last moment, withheld, as the train speeds on.

As an adult, I became interested in the sources of the myth that had shaped my view of the country that I lived in. I had not been a bookish child, but maybe I had imbibed, from the bits and pieces I was required to read at school, a sense of a place called England that didn't correspond with the place that I lived in. I remember, for example, having to do what was then called 'comprehension' on an extract from Hilaire Belloc on mowing a field with a scythe – a procedure that mystified yet intrigued me, as did the strange name of the author, which lodged in my memory. And I remember music lessons where we sang a song called 'Linden Lea' – rows of thoroughly urban children, warbling away about leaving the 'air of dark-roomed towns' and taking the 'homeward road' to where the 'apple trees do lean down low in Linden Lea'. Eventually, I found out who Hilaire Belloc was, and I found that 'Linden Lea' was an arrangement by Vaughan Williams of a poem by William Barnes. All three were purveyors of a very distinctive view of England. I began to browse around in second-hand bookshops, and found that between the wars, this essential, elusive

England had been the subject of a whole genre of books, with such titles as *England is a Village*, and *This Way to Arcady*, and *Forever England*. One particular author, H. V. Morton, turned up on the dusty shelves over and over again. He seemed to be the doyen of the genre. His *In Search of England* (1927 – with twenty-nine subsequent editions) was the defining book. The central proposition of the book is that England is neither omnipresent nor immediately discernible to its citizens. On the contrary, it is hidden; it has to be *sought*. As Morton presented it, England is the object of a quest, disarmingly undertaken by a narrator who, on a sunny spring morning, drives off, away from London, into the highways and byways in a little two-seater motor car.

For years, my slightly guilty taste for the arcadian fantasy to which books in this genre catered lurked deep in the background of my academic work as a historian. But there has developed over the past twenty years or so an impressive and vigorous sub-discipline of studies of 'Englishness' and of the ways in which our ideas of national identity are constructed. It eventually occurred to me that if I made a study of one aspect of the ruralist impulse in British culture it would not be a self-indulgence. And it further struck me that H. V. Morton, about whose life I knew nothing, would be a good starting point.

I began, therefore, to take Morton more seriously. It soon became clear that he was probably one of the most widely read writers of the inter-war period. He was as popular in his age as, say, Bill Bryson is in ours. A stroke of good fortune gave me access to Morton's private papers. They showed that there was a whole book to be written about him. The droll narrator of his books, it emerged, was an invention – a persona. Morton's travel books are not straight autobiography; they are narrated by an alter ego. Morton himself was a private man, a professional and skilful writer and journalist, living a life that he recognised at times to be rather sordid, but which was redeemed, he felt, by his writing. The documentation of his life is remarkably complete. His life ran from a childhood in the Edwardian England of bicycle rides through empty Warwickshire lanes, and on into the First World War, for which he enlisted, but in which he never saw action. It ran on into the 1920s, during which Morton, the successful newspaper reporter and author, strolled down Piccadilly to the Ritz in top hat and tails. It ran on into the thirties, during which decade he covered, unexpectedly powerfully, stories on urban poverty, and during which he also privately flirted with fascism. It ran on into the Second World War, during which he did his patriotic duty by joining the Home Guard, and by writing books that evoked the England of fields and villages that must be defended against the German onslaught, but also during which he was privately making entries in his diary that said how much he admired Hitler and how a dose of fascism would do Britain the world of good. His career, and his life went into a slow decline when the war ended, for he had no taste for the bare world of austerity and a reforming Labour government. He moved to South Africa, where he built a grand house, tacitly supported apartheid, and recorded, with a sort of grim satisfaction, the way in which, in his view, Britain during the 1960s was going to the dogs. Morton's life, therefore, spans a remarkable period, and the forty or so books that he wrote emerge from it in interesting and unexpected ways. My biography explores the gap that lies between the skilful, vivid pages of his many books, and the complicated, often disagreeable man who wrote them.

Has my study of Morton purged me of the myth of an essentially arcadian England? Do I now see it plainly as an elaborate artifice, a myth constructed and manipulated by writers as skilful as Morton undoubtedly was, and sustained to this day, seemingly incorrigibly, by magazines like *Country Living* and *This England*? Obviously yes, but I still cycle round the English lanes, and trudge the footpaths, faintly haunted by a residual shred of belief that I'll pedal round a bend, or plod over a horizon, and suddenly find myself in the England for which Morton searched, and which – because it is, after all, a myth – he never found.

Acknowledgements

My chief debt is to Marion Wasdell. By a circuitous route she came into possession of Morton's papers and has been determined to revive interest in him. The Morton who emerges from this biography is not quite the hero that she initially hoped for, but she has been a great help in bringing this book to completion, and is content to see him presented as he truly was. My next debt is to Linda Findlay, who also worked to get Morton's papers into order, and who knows about Morton's time in Hampshire during the Second World War. Other friends and colleagues have generously helped with research or comments on the manuscript. My thanks to: Robin Barraclough, Jan Bartholomew, Ian Findlay, Christopher Lawrence, Sue and Chris McDonald, Charles Perry, Jerome Satterthwaite, Wren Sidhe, Jo Wilcox and the late Ken Wilcox.

INTRODUCTION

Among H. V. Morton's papers there is a hand-written story about
mice, hedgehogs and cats, called *Night at the Wakan Rock*. The author,
whose name is neatly lettered on the cover, is 'Little Beaver'. The story
was written by Morton when he was a boy. He had chosen the animal
theme and the *nom de plume* 'Little Beaver' because he was then under
the spell of Ernest Thompson Seton, a writer of animal stories set in the
Canadian wilderness. Seton himself had used a *nom de plume* – 'the
Chief'. A copy of *Two Little Savages*, by the Chief, was one of the
young Morton's prized possessions.

About seventy years later, the elderly Morton – the accomplished,
successful author, living in a fine house he'd built in South Africa, near
Cape Town – started to write his memoirs. He drafted only a few rough
chapters, but he did recall his youthful enthusiasm for Seton. He
records that when he was eleven or twelve (this would have been
around 1905), his hero, the Chief, came to Birmingham, where Morton
lived, to give a lecture at the Balsall Heath Institute. The elderly
Morton recalled:

> I wanted the Chief's signature to *Two Little Savages* and, if possible, his
> photograph. I rehearsed my interview with him a hundred times. It was
> to be the most memorable day of my life. The moment came at last
> when I set off with my mother and faced that chilliest of sights, a
> platform empty save for a table, a chair and, upon the table, a tray,
> a glass and some water. What would the Chief be like? I had never seen
> a picture of him. But I knew how he ought to look. How would he be
> dressed? Would he be wearing garments of deerskin, beaded moccasins
> upon his feet? If so, how sorry I should be not to have come dressed as
> Little Beaver since my mother had insisted on an Eton suit. At last a
> large and smiling man, who was wearing a dinner jacket, stood before
> us and was introduced as 'our distinguished lecturer, Mr Ernest
> Thompson Seton, naturalist to the Government of Manitoba'. I was

aware that something awful was happening inside me. Little Beaver, stoic that he was, was not far from tears. This was not the man I had expected. This was not my favourite writer. This was just an ordinary man who might have come to tea and been jolly and asked what I was going to be when I grew up. This, in other words, was not the Chief I had worshipped.

So appalling is the gap between the ideal author and the real one that my mother had to urge me to go behind the stage with my book to be autographed at the end of the lecture. At length, I did so to discover the Chief in gay and laughing conversation with a group of young women. I stood there embarrassed, helpless, unseen. During a lull in the merriment, I made a timid movement in the direction of my now fallen idol, and though I think it likely that he may have noticed a small boy in the background with a book, he turned away to more attractive admirers; and who shall blame him? I was silent on the way home, and my mother, sensing that everything had gone wrong, did not ask any questions. So died Little Beaver.

In his memoir, Morton goes on to develop the implications of this mismatch between authors and their books. He writes that when, thirty years after his desolating encounter with the Chief, he himself began publishing, he was determined to reveal to his readers only what was actually printed on the pages of his books. There were to be no interviews, no photographs of the author on the dust wrappers, no promotional personal appearances. His decision to efface himself from the world outside the covers of his books, and to be known only through his writing, went back, he says,

to the Balsall Heath Institute and a small boy in an Eton suit. In many ways the author-reader relationship is the most perfect of human associations, an entirely cerebral marriage unmarred by physical contact, presumably the way angels communicate. So why alter it? In other words, in Little Beaver's experienced opinion, writers should be read but never, never seen.

Throughout his own life as a professional writer, Morton had applied the lesson that he'd learned at Balsall Heath pretty strictly: he rarely made himself literally visible to his readers, although, like Seton, he was more than happy to be surrounded by admiring, pretty young women. But if 'visibility' is interpreted more figuratively, a paradox emerges. Why did a writer who was so adamant about keeping himself out of the public eye write a memoir at all? Morton's sole bequest to posterity could easily have been the books upon which his fame rested. Why should he have risked jeopardising the angelic nature of the marriage he'd had with his readers by writing a memoir that would, inevitably, reveal a good deal about the man who wrote the books? That, after all, is the whole point of a memoir.

His publishers, Methuen, had been trying, for some time, to coax a memoir from their venerable author. He responded by writing draft after draft of his memories, reaching as far as the first forty years of his life, and then breaking off. He extracted and typed a reasonably fair copy from the vast mass of his scarcely legible notes. This typed copy, which I shall refer to as the *Memoir*, was never published. The *Memoir* itself, and the notes from which it was condensed, show that Morton was in at least two minds about the whole enterprise.

On one hand, the very quantity of material he wrote, and the care with which he drafted it, indicate that he wanted to produce a complete, publishable manuscript. He spent hours at his desk, writing, and he dreamed up at least fifteen different possible titles, his favourite perhaps emerging as *Fair Generally* – derived from *The Times*'s weather forecast for the day on which he was born. But on the other hand, he was sometimes suspicious of the very business of autobiography. For example, in a scribbled note that appears from nowhere in the middle of an entry recording his time in Fleet Street, he writes:

The point in writing autobiography is to strip oneself naked & expose all one's private life, which I am unwilling to do. Women have played the largest part in my life & anything I have done I owe to them, and not to men, yet not to do so is to evade the truth. Still, what is truth? We try to discuss it under the bedclothes. But, after all, is that the truth? I don't know.

And in another note he writes that his success as a Fleet Street writer was due to his having created a new personality for myself, a hard, tough, journalist type with no inhibitions who could walk into any office & say 'how much?' I believe that if the truth were to be known many a man & woman has made something of life by sheltering, behind an artificial fictitious character, their protective self, their alter ego. My other self worked beautifully. He rarely let me down.

Yet this description of himself is at odds with the more straightforward, urbane personality that he was projecting in most passages in the *Memoir*. Neither of these two notes survived into the typed version. And nor did another note, addressed, it seems, to yet another version of himself. This note quite accurately describes the overall character of the *Memoir*: 'By keeping myself in the shadow I also craftily avoid the danger of being too kind or too cruel to myself. I am not a leading actor but the chorus. Rather adroit, don't you think, if it comes off?'

So, the *Memoir* that wittily records Little Beaver's dismay at discovering the truth about the Chief also records version upon conflicting version of the truth about Morton himself. And Morton's abandonment of the project, as extreme old age overtook him, leaves us uncertain about whether he wished to see his *Memoir* in print before he died, whether he intended it to be published after his death, or whether he wanted it to be for ever suppressed – in which case it is unclear for whom he was writing. But finally, the decision to delve into Morton's autobiographical writings is mine, not Morton's. The dead do not care.

I have drawn extensively on Morton's diaries and letters, and so must ponder why I am trying to coax into the light a writer who was, at least sometimes, determined to stay in the shade. Perhaps it would not matter if his life turned out to be a straightforward, sunny amplification of the narratives of journeys and events that he presented in the travel books that delighted literally millions of readers during the 1920s, thirties and forties. But Morton's life was not like that. His devoted readers probably pictured him in the way that the young Morton himself had pictured the Chief. But if those readers had encountered the author behind the books, their idol, like Little Beaver's, would have toppled. There is, however, no virtue in toppling idols, just for the sake of it, especially when, as in Morton's case, the idol has, until the recent revival of interest in him, lain in decent and dusty obscurity on the shelves of second-hand book shops.[1] And in any case, what modern reader would be surprised to learn that the life of a writer was less edifying than his books?

The justification for overruling Morton and for moving freely between his books and his life is threefold. First, although travel writing has always commanded a huge readership, it has not, until fairly recently, been considered as a genre – as a body of work governed by powerful literary conventions. What at first sight seem to be straightforward, autobiographical chronicles of interesting journeys turn out to be artful, literary constructions. Customarily, travel books are written – as Morton's were – in the first person. This mode reinforces the reader's sense that he or she is reading the plain and simple truth: the success of the book depends entirely on the reader's being convinced that the events narrated really happened. Clearly, travel books are not presented by their writers as fictions. But on closer inspection, a travel book commonly turns out to have a structure closely akin to that of a novel. Unlike life itself, and most of the journeys we undertake, travel books tend to have plots, with beginnings, climaxes, resolutions and closures. They also have heroes – usually the narrator. Furthermore, when the narrator of the book is compared with the writer of the book, they often turn out not to be identical: the narrator is a literary persona, a version of himself or herself, invented by the author. There is nothing underhand in this process of invention. It is a necessary feature of first-person narratives. And explorations of this relationship between travel books and their authors are not undertaken in order to catch the authors out, so to speak, in cheap lies. Rather, their aim is to show how the genre of travel writing, one of the most durable and popular literary forms, works.

The second justification for looking closely at Morton's life and work relates to the extraordinary current interest in the question of British national identity, an interest that has registered itself at every level, from the popular to the scholarly, from the left and from the right, and from each of the four constituent nations of Britain (torturing the word 'nation', for the moment, to make it describe Northern Ireland). At least three related episodes in modern British history have generated this interest in the identity of the British. First came the dismantling of the British Empire and the subsequent immigration into Britain of black and Asian Commonwealth citizens. Secondly came Britain's membership of the European Union and the consequent debate about sovereignty. And thirdly came Westminster's enactment of various modes of devolved government for Scotland, Wales and Northern Ireland, hastening an end to the lazy assumption that 'Britain' effectively means 'England'. This has led to an extraordinary interest in myths of the British past – and I am using the word 'myth' here to mean not 'untruth', but a seductive, potent story that helps make sense of the lives of its adherents. Each British nation has its myths of identity. The English, for instance, have a universally recognisable version whose stock images and signifiers are those of royal pageantry, country lanes, the freeborn yeoman, thatched cottages, and the hedges and fields of a timeless English countryside – usually the southern English countryside. The market for this version of the English myth is perpetually buoyant. To take a couple of examples from thousands: the market for the myth sustains museums and stately homes that encourage in us the illusion that we are on a day trip to an arcadian past, and it sustains a popular quarterly magazine, entitled *This England*, whose readers are transported back to a lost world of corn dollies and billhook-wielding hurdle makers. The Conservative Prime Minister John Major (brought up in Brixton, an inner-London suburb) was in the grip of this myth when he characterised the England that he yearned for as an England of warm beer, sun-dappled cricket pitches and elderly spinsters cycling safely to evensong.

These myths have not reproduced themselves unchallenged. Starting in the 1980s, a formidable battery of scholarly studies has been assembled and has been firing away, from every angle, at the uncritical use of versions of the past to prop up untenable versions of the present, and, worse, of the future.[2] Predominantly, these studies have been politically radical, drawing attention to the inherently conservative nature of most national myths. But recently, Roger Scruton's doleful *England: an Elegy*[3] has emerged from the right wing.

Where does H. V. Morton fit into this discussion of national identity? He fits near the centre, for in writing, during the inter-war years, hugely popular books about England, Scotland, Wales and Ireland, he was an influential codifier and promulgator of enduring, cardinal British national myths. Morton's quintessential formulation of the myth of England comes on the first page of his most popular and influential book, *In Search of England*, published in 1927. He says that his search began when he was in Palestine, feeling ill and far from home. 'There rose up in my mind', he wrote,

> the picture of a village street at dusk with a smell of wood smoke lying in the still air and, here and there, little red blinds shining in the dusk under the thatch. I remembered how the church bells ring at home, and how, at that time of year, the sun leaves a dull red bar low down in the west, and against it the elms grow blacker by the minute. Then the bats start to flicker like bits of burnt paper and you hear the slow jingle of a team coming home from the fields . . . When you think like this sitting alone in a foreign country I think you know all there is to learn about heartache.

There will be more said about this formulation of the myth later in this book. For the present, it is enough to note that the 'home' Morton was so poignantly remembering was not a home he had ever lived in. He had been brought up in Birmingham and had moved from there straight to London. Plainly, his conception of 'home' had been shaped less by his own lived experience than by deep and enduring national myths. And the literally millions of readers who read Morton's version of the myth had their own notions of their national identity shaped by it.

Who were Morton's readers? He was supplying the huge market for books about Britain that had opened up at the close of the Great War in 1918, and which expanded enormously during the 1920s and thirties. This market was driven by a deliberate turning away from the years of slaughter in the trenches, and by the ready availability, in the post-war world, of paid holidays, hiking boots, bicycles, motor buses and cheap little cars (the Austin Seven was introduced in 1923). The drowsy country lanes of Britain lay open, effectively for the first time, to an urban people, sick of war, eager to discover the land that they'd been fighting for, and now with the means of reaching the quiet depths of the countryside. The British were passionately discovering Britain, and Morton was one of their most influential prophets and guides, supplying them with what one recent commentator has neatly termed 'motoring pastorals'[4] – records of journeys in a little car along the highways and byways, in search of the essences of England, Wales, Scotland and Ireland.

Morton did not stop at Britain. He went on to write half a dozen books about the Middle East. These books served the well-established market for accounts of the Holy Land, but they are much more than just pious tours round the famous Biblical sites. Indeed, they are not very pious at all: Morton never says what his own beliefs are. The books are driven far less by Christian conviction than by two of the standard impulses in travel writing, the impulse to show how un-British, how exotic, foreign places are, and to show how intrepid the narrator is. Morton's books on the Middle East are a counterpoise to his books on Britain.

The narrator of all of Morton's travel books is not the hard-nosed alter ego that he devised to conduct himself through the tough world of Fleet Street. Rather, the narrator is a witty, observant, learned, sometimes comically self-deprecating man who is as happy sharing his pouch of pipe tobacco with a wayside tramp as he is having tea with the owners of the grand houses he visits. This narrator is recognisable, in many respects, as the Morton who wrote the diaries and letters upon which I have drawn. But they are by no means identical, and Morton was self-aware enough to know that there was a difference. Yet another alter ego was at work. One revealing entry in his diary makes this plain. On New Year's Day in 1946 he was reflecting, somewhat self-pityingly, on what he considered to have been the demeaning life that he, one of the most successful pre-war writers, had been obliged to live during the war years:

Looking at the New Year Honours today, much as I despise them, I could have wished that I had a knighthood if only to bring the name of H. V. Morton, which is a kind of panache [i.e. a plume] of mine, something separate from myself that I have tried to carry with honour through life, again into prominence. It is very curious, that attitude to my name. I have let down Harry [the name by which Morton was known to friends and family] time without number and put him in the gutter, but H. V. Morton is someone I have tried to carry high in life. I have been Harry too long. I must climb out of the gutter and be H. V. Morton once again.

This brings me to my third justification for writing this biography – although 'justification' here is not straightforward. How can one justify inspecting the gutter that Morton alluded to? The world that Morton moved in, and the people who inhabited it have long gone. Nobody can now be hurt, save, perhaps, those loyal fans of Morton who hope that the narrator of the books will be the man himself. He wasn't. Morton's private life, his politics, his professional ambition, were all at odds with his writing, and they are gruesomely fascinating. To repeat, travel writing is not autobiography.

So, in the book that follows, my concerns are with H. V. Morton the travel writer, with H. V. Morton the purveyor of myths of national identity, and with the Harry Morton who invented this H. V. Morton.

A Note on Sources

As I have indicated, much of my information about Morton's life comes from the notes he made for his *Memoir*. The typed copy of it runs to just over 200 sides, but the quarry from which it was hewn is a collection of six foolscap notebooks, each in itself of around 200 sides, covered with undated entries. It is not possible even to arrange the notebooks in a clear chronological sequence, for he hopped about, back and forth, from decade to decade in successive pages and notebooks. Morton was into his eighties by the time he gave up writing his recollections and he may well by then have been suffering from short-term memory loss, for he wrote out versions of the same episode sometimes dozens of times, often almost identically, maybe having forgotten that he had already written it. His long-term memory is not entirely reliable, either. His recollections of the big events that shaped his life are vivid, but his dating of them is sometimes erratic. As a young journalist, he learned shorthand, but he wrote his books, his *Memoir* and his diaries in longhand, incorporating an occasional shorthand character. He seems never to have habituated himself to the routine use of a typewriter. His handwriting deteriorated seriously as old age overtook him. In the notes for the *Memoir* it is atrocious, and in many places indecipherable.

The extracts from Morton's papers that I quote are presented as if every word in the original were complete and clear, but in the originals he abbreviated lots of words and conveyed many by a hasty squiggle. Here and there I have had to make conjectures in order to reconstruct a passage, although never when I have concluded that Morton's general drift is unclear. I have added a few explanatory notes and queries of my own and have placed them within the quotations, but insulated by square brackets.

'The Blitz,' he wrote in his *Memoir*, 'destroyed nearly all my family portraits and photographs, diaries and letters.' This was a bit of an exaggeration. Certainly, there are big holes in the documentation of his life, but quite a bit from his early life escaped the bombs, and a great deal of post-war material silted up in the library of his house in Somerset West, near Cape Town. He lived for eighty-seven years, from 1892 to 1979, and diaries for twenty-five of those years survive. Morton tended to keep letters that were sent to him: four boxes of them have survived. He was a keen, expert photographer, and his library contains drawers-full of negatives and prints, almost all undated, uncaptioned, higgledy-piggledy.

I

1892–1913

'A BORN WRITER'

Henry Canova Vollam Morton was born on either 25 or 26 July 1892. The mild confusion arises because although his birth certificate says 26, Morton himself insisted that it should have said 25. 'My mother told me,' he wrote in the notes for his *Memoir*, 'that I was born on July 25 1892 . . . But Somerset House did not, and still do not, agree.' The place of his birth is not in dispute: it was Ashton-under-Lyne, in Lancashire.

His mother was a lowland Scot, born Marguerite Ewart. When she was pregnant with Henry, she fancifully believed that her surroundings would have an effect on her unborn baby, and so she chose reproductions of particular artworks to decorate her room. Among them were illustrations of the sculptures of the late-eighteenth-century Venetian sculptor Canova. When the infant Henry was born, in Morton's words, 'she landed me with the name of Canova, which I have managed to keep secret.' Years later, when Morton was writing his books on Rome, he offered lengthy reflections on two of Canova's productions, the scandalously nude sculpture of Napoleon's sister, in the Borghese Villa, and the, again faintly erotic, monument to the Stuarts in St Peter's.[1] Not surprisingly, he gives no hint that pictures of works by Canova were supposed by his mother to have shaped his character, or that he was named after the sculptor. As he grew up, his friends and family tended to call him 'Harry', although a few surviving letters to him are addressed 'Dear Canova'; evidently he didn't succeed in keeping the hated name entirely secret, although he always signed himself, and became known to his readers as, 'H. V. Morton'.

His father, Joseph Thomas Vollam Morton, was, at the time of Morton's birth, the editor of the local *Ashton-under-Lyne Herald*. In

later life, Morton went to great pains to trace his family ancestry and
was particularly intrigued to find out where the unusual name 'Vollam'
had come from. His father had told him that it was the maiden name
of his own great-grandmother, who had run off from Bath to India to
marry her sweetheart, Henry Morton, a soldier of the East India
Company. H. V. Morton could never verify this, but was pleased that
the name 'Vollam', with its romantic origin, had lodged itself in the
family. The Mortons had settled in India, growing tea, opium and
hemp. Morton's father was born there, the offspring of a marriage
between the son of the original East India Company soldier and a
woman whose name appears in the records of the wedding as 'Caroline
Smith', but who was also known, according to family tradition, as
Caroline Larkins, Maseyk, or da Maseyk. The true maiden name
of H. V. Morton's grandmother seems a trivial matter, but it was
important to him. In a letter to his own son John, in May 1977,
responding evidently to a request from John for the family's history,
Morton wrote:

> The extraordinary thing is that his [Morton's great-grandfather's] only
> son, my grandfather, within days of his father's death married a little
> Portuguese girl, said to be a great beauty. In the photo I possess she
> looks like a monkey whose laced pants are coming down. She was tiny
> and from her we inherit our Italian organ grinder look.

Much later, Morton's widow recalled that her husband used to say that
he was descended from Portuguese Jews. Morton's father left India as
a young man to enter Edinburgh Medical School. However, he could
not stomach the anatomy classes and left the university, turning instead
to journalism and settling permanently in Britain.

The Morton household in Ashton-under-Lyne seems to have been
prosperously middle-class. In old age, H. V. Morton wrote that his
earliest memories were of the sound of mill-girls' clogs as they clattered
off to work in the morning – although this seems to me a little too
stereotypical of the north of England to be certain: it's as if his infancy
was here being viewed by way of a Gracie Fields film. He also recalled
that his mother was a strenuous social improver,

known throughout the worst slums of Ashton as 'Cousin Maggie'. She
started a League of Good Conduct and founded a cot in the children's
hospital. The police were always calling on Saturday night to ask her to
go with them to streets which they patrolled two by two, and settle some
family dispute. This she never failed to do. She civilised the slums of
Ashton. As a small boy I can remember seeing our kitchen full of
crossing sweeper boys, their brooms in the scullery, sitting down to a
great meal of bread and jam or bread and dripping.

This recollection of the unabashedly paternalistic late-Victorian social
conscience in action again looks somewhat highly coloured, but, ever
the good journalist who checks his facts, the elderly Morton wrote, in
1970, to the Ashton-under-Lyne Town Clerk to see if there still existed
at the children's hospital the cot endowed by his mother, over seventy
years earlier. The reply, if it ever came, has not survived. Morton's
mother's social and political interests were wide. In notes for his
Memoir, he recalled that she was a militant anti-vivisectionist and an
anti-vaccinationist. But she did not, it seems, want the vote: 'It is
surprising,' he wrote, 'that she was not, when the time came, a
Suffragette.'

In 1897, by which time the five-year-old Morton had a three-year-
old sister, Margaret, the family moved to Manchester, where his father
had been appointed as the editor of the brand new *Manchester Evening
Chronicle*, founded by the Hultons, father and son, both named
Edward.* The elder Hulton had once worked as a compositor on the
Manchester Guardian, but had turned his hobby of keeping racing
pigeons to profitable account. He found that pigeons could get horse-
racing results back to newspaper offices quicker than could reporters,
who had to travel to telegraph offices in order to make their
transmissions. On the profits of the pigeon post system that he devised,
Hulton founded his own newspapers, including *The Sporting
Chronicle*. According to H. V. Morton, his father liked Hulton senior,
but 'could not stand his son', Edward Hulton junior. Hulton senior
had placed his son under the tutelage of Morton's father, from whom

---

* There was a Hulton newspaper and magazine publishing dynasty: Edward Hulton I (died 1904), his son,
Edward Hulton II (1869–1925), and Hulton II's son, Edward George Warris Hulton III (1906–88).

the son was supposed to learn the business of editing a newspaper. Not surprisingly, the teacher–trainee relationship between the editor and the proprietor's son did not prosper. Eventually, they fell out, and Morton's father left. This falling out was to have consequences for H. V. Morton himself twenty years later, when, according to Morton's *Memoir*, Hulton junior took his revenge.* Morton recalled two things from the five or six years the family spent in Manchester. One was his being taken to the newspaper's offices to see the pigeons come flying in with the racing results, and the other was of the death of Queen Victoria, in 1901.

From Manchester, Morton's father made another move within the roomy world of Victorian and Edwardian provincial newspapers. This time – in 1902 or 1903 – the family moved to Birmingham, where Morton's father took up a post as assistant editor of the *Birmingham Post*. From this period onward, the information about the young Morton's life becomes more plentiful. From 1909 he started keeping a diary, and his youthful entries can often be compared with the recollections of the same period made by the eighty-year-old who wrote the *Memoir*. I imagine that the elderly Morton had the diaries on his desk as he wrote: some of the information in the *Memoir* is plainly derived from them. But he never refers directly to the diaries or even says that he kept them. The diaries record the private feelings of adolescence and young manhood, along with the trivia of the daily round. The *Memoir*, by contrast, is a complex, imaginative re-working, chiefly of the external scenes of his youth, and only rarely of his inner, emotional life. Furthermore, the *Memoir*'s re-working is tinged with nostalgia, intensified not just by the lapse of seventy years, but also by the huge geographical distance between the Birmingham suburbs of his youth and the fine house near Cape Town in which he lived out his rather unfulfilling old age. He half remembers, half imagines a vanished Edwardian world of whistling errand boys, trams, draper's shops, Italian hokey-pokey (ice cream) sellers, music halls, straw hats, dancing bears, pretty shopgirls, and cycle rides along empty, dusty lanes.

The Morton family lived in a succession of four houses in Moseley,

*See below, pp. 58–9.

a leafy Birmingham suburb that was sufficiently in touch with the Warwickshire countryside for the residents still to call it 'the village'. Here is how the elderly Morton re-imagines it:

> The Edwardian village echoed to shouting and whip-cracking, to singing, whistling and laughter, to the thud of the dray horses harnessed to wagons with iron-shod wheels, to the brisk trot of the butcher's gig, to the sound of cab and hansom and the ring of bicycle bells.
>
> In addition to the noise of traffic there were many other sounds. There was music and singing from the ominous gutter: wavering voices accompanied perhaps by an accordion: there was the ever present barrel organ – the hurdy-gurdy – each one with its own beat, each one ready to break off in the middle of 'Goodbye Dolly, I must leave you', or 'Soldiers of the Queen, my lads' as the grinder ran into the middle of the road to pick up a penny flung from an upper window as a bribe for him to clear off, a hint he was always glad to take. There were the German bands of stout old gentlemen with Bismarck moustaches and peaked caps, sometimes with a Teutonic love of uniform with braided jackets, old boys who with their pom-pom polkas and waltzes were all believed to be spies to a man when the Great War came. The kind of organ which my sister and I liked best was played by Italians who often wore gold ear-rings. They were men of unreliable appearance but of ingratiating manners and, I now realise, were Neapolitans. They carried hand organs by a shoulder strap but when in action the instrument was supported on the pavement by a single peg-leg. Those organs were sweeter in tone than the hurdy-gurdy and the music, in comparison, was highbrow. Instead of 'I am the honeysuckle, you are the bee', they played 'O Sole mio', one's first introduction to Italian opera.

The elderly Morton, incidentally, had lost none of his lightness of touch as a writer: 'the ominous gutter' and 'men of unreliable appearance but of ingratiating manners' are examples of the dryly comic descriptions that made his books so readable.

When the young Morton does appear in a more central role in a passage of the *Memoir*, it is usually in a mildly comic, not a soul-baring role. For example:

The landscape had not yet entirely lost its rustic air. Opposite [our house] was a Georgian mansion called the Priory where Dr Horatio Wood lived . . . and the tops of his hay ricks might be seen above the wall in autumn. He visited his patients in a brougham driven by a man in a top hat who sometimes answered the door and might be seen at others wearing a green baize apron and polishing the silver. All I recall professionally of Dr Wood is that one afternoon a fish bone stuck in my throat and my mother rushed me across to him. He deftly removed the bone and charged my mother half a sovereign. When I got home the cook asked me what happened. 'He asked what kind of fish it was', I said. 'And what did you say?' asked the cook. 'I said salmon.' 'Oh, you silly boy', said the cook. 'If you'd have said kippers he'd have done it for sixpence.'

There are, however, a few passages in the hand-written notes for the *Memoir* that are more self-revelatory. It is characteristic of Morton that they were eliminated when he typed up the fair copy. These half-dozen or so passages concern his relationship with his father. 'My father, who was always busy and generally irascible gave me the impression that I was an unsatisfactory son,' he wrote. Morton thought that his sister, on the other hand, was considered by his father to have been his favourite, 'the apple of his eye'. Morton senior is sometimes presented as a remote, Victorian figure:

I remember him as a small, dark, incisive and stylish man who wore a black frock coat in winter and a grey one in summer. His departure in the morning was a ritual that never varied. As he appeared in the hall, a housemaid stood by the door while my mother took a silk hat, which had been polished with a velvet pad, and handed it to him, rather as an archbishop extends the crown at a coronation. My parent would take the hat, give it a quick final polish upon the sleeve of his coat, kiss my mother and my sister, wave a magisterial hand in my direction and step into a waiting hansom cab. With his departure, joy and happiness descended on the house. It was possible to shout and sing.

At other times, there is a warmth in Morton's recollections of his father. He compares him with Mr Pickwick, and sometimes with Mr

Micawber, for although the editorship of a group of Birmingham newspapers – which is what his father eventually achieved – conferred substantial status on him, he seems to have had an airy indifference to living within his means. Morton's notes even include a recollection of a call from the bailiff, an event that seared into him a lifelong fear of debt. His father's career took a steep dive in 1912. The newspaper group for which he worked collapsed, and he had to go to London to find new work. But even when living in new, reduced circumstances, he would, Morton recalled, always have a bottle of Clicquot or Chateau d'Yquem on hand for his guests, even if the room was shabby: 'He was a man unaware of his surroundings and would never have known whether he was seated on an orange box or a Chippendale chair.' Back in his prime though, in his respectable villa in Moseley, he could at times be a benign *paterfamilias*:

> Though by nature he was undomestic, my father was occasionally swept by brief home-loving moods when he was editing an evening paper and was able to arrive home, should the Press Club appear dull, at a reasonable hour. He would like to sit by the fire in an armchair, his feet in carpet slippers, a carved merchaum [*sic*] pipe in his mouth, and read to us. In that way I became acquainted before I was twelve with the names, at least, of Milton, Keats and Shelley (for some reason he never read Shakespeare) and with poets who were then modern, like Francis Thompson and W. E. Henley, both of whom he knew personally. He also read Dickens, Thackeray, Kipling and Conan Doyle, hot from the press, Meredith, whose novels he admired, and Lane's *Arabian Nights*.

Morton's recollections of his father are mixed. When he came to write his *Memoir*, he may have seen in his father rather more of himself than he liked. There was no parallel in their respective professional careers – the father's crashed, the son's prospered – but in the seedier aspects of their private lives, there may have been. There are hints that Morton senior did not treat his wife well. If so, like father, like son.

Morton's memories of his mother are invariably warm. He describes the way in which she converted the attic of one of their houses in Moseley into a studio, where, amongst the clutter, she enthusiastically painted, wrote stories for children, made rugs, and sculpted in plaster:

In the corner of the attic stood an easel on which rested a half-finished picture of the garden, not the real garden, but a slightly sinister scene over which brooded a tall Aubrey Beardsley figure, half man, half woman and neither aspect very attractive. Nearby, covered by a cloth, was a plaster bust of myself at the age of six with rose-bud mouth and a head covered with wavelet curls. That effigy existed until long after the first war when, battered and noseless, it was carried off at last on a handcart by a man who collected old bottles.

Mother and son were unaffectedly fond of each other. In his first surviving diary, written in 1909, when he was sixteen or seventeen, there are dozens of entries recording jaunts that they took together. They regularly went to the theatre, and sometimes performed in amateur theatricals. In a production of *Julius Caesar*, his mother played Portia and the young Morton played Mark Antony – in Roman armour of which he was very proud. On 5 March he writes: 'Well all I've got to say is that Mother is an absolute brick. She's a darling. She has actually arranged with Rileys to get me a ripping gramaphone [*sic*] which has been reduced from 6 guineas . . . I shall go balmy [*sic*] with joy when I get it.' On 23 March, after a visit by the entire family foursome to *Iolanthe* (his father clearly couldn't always have been irascible), they had 'a terrific lark' during which his mother squirted a whole soda syphon over him.

Visits to Moseley by Morton's uncle Willie – his father's half-brother – led to further larks. He gave the Mortons their first experience of the motor car, an experience that Morton recollects in the idiom associated with Mr Toad:

> My sister and I, hearing a series of explosions, would run to the window to observe Uncle Willie removing his goggles as he stepped from a motor-car that panted like a hot and angry dog . . . [He would suggest] that we should go for a 'spin', and my mother would always refuse. My sister and I would then blackmail her by hanging our heads and looking as if we were about to cry, until she said 'Alright, Willie, but you *must* promise not to scorch.' My mother, her hat tied beneath her chin, would sit next to Uncle Willie while my sister and myself occupied the seats behind [presumably, Morton's irascible father did not come along

on these jaunts], and, after some splendid explosions, the motor car would slowly advance to the road. In 1903 the speed limit had been raised to twenty miles an hour and that, to us, seemed like flying. Uncle Willie must have been a good driver since we never hit anybody, neither did horses shy away from us, but what I do remember is the rapidity with which in those days one left a suburb behind and found oneself in country lanes. Here Uncle Willie cast a great cloud of dust on the hedges, while the great car, it seemed to us, sweated and panted, until my mother cried sharply, 'Willie – stop it! You're scorching!'

The mutual fondness between Morton and his mother stayed strong, right up until the time of her early death, in 1918.

Morton's recollections of his sister are also warm, chiefly because she was a tomboy who was keen to follow her older brother about, joining in all his fantasies of the Canadian wilderness and the wild frontier. So unswerving was her loyalty to her brother that she once shot one of his enemies in the backside with an air rifle. When the victim's parents complained, Morton's father forgave his daughter, making a joke of it. Morton recorded the incident in his *Memoir* no doubt because it's amusing, but partly to show that he thought that his father was more lenient toward his daughter than he would have been toward the young Harry.

School figures prominently neither in Morton's *Memoir* nor his diaries. Little that it offered seems to have captured his imagination: the richest, most memorable days of his youth were spent at home, in the theatre, in the racy street market of Birmingham's old Bull Ring, and along the tranquil lanes of Warwickshire. Even allowing for the financial ups and downs of Morton's father's career, it would probably have been possible for Morton, the only son, to have been sent away to public school. But his mother was against it. His father told him:

While you were very young, the Oscar Wilde scandal broke [this would have been in 1895, when Morton was three] and your mother learnt of homosexuality for the first time. She then conceived the idea that every English public school was contaminated by homosexuality and was determined to shield her dear boy, and that he should be educated at home, which was, of course, quite impracticable.

Eventually, in 1905, at the age of thirteen, he was sent to King Edward's School, which was then in New Street, Birmingham, within easy daily commuting distance of Moseley. The building, erected in 1839, had been, by the time of Morton's enrolment, entirely blackened by soot from the trains in the nearby terminus: 'to my young eyes it was a perfect study in gloom.' He seems to have been neither actively happy nor unhappy there: he recalls, with equal detachment, a caning from the headmaster and the winning of Longfellow's poems as a prize. Later in life he acquired a copy of T. W. Hutton's history of the school and wrote on the wrapper, 'My school, where I learnt little except to enjoy Shakespeare.' The sharpness of this dismissal might have been partly a response to Hutton's own dismissal of Morton. In a section in which he records old boys who went on to do great things in the world of letters, Hutton promisingly begins a sentence, 'One reporter of the first rank the school did mother . . .', but it was not Morton he had in mind. He does give Morton a close second place, but casually devalues even that honour by writing: 'Of a later day and of hardly less distinction *in his own way* is H. V. Morton'. That is all Morton gets from the historian of his old school.[2]

Life outside school was more exciting than life inside its gloomy walls, and among the happiest times that Morton recalls, both in his diaries and his *Memoir*, are those he spent on his bicycle. Today, cycling is now enjoying a lively revival, but during the last third of the twentieth century it was in a slow decline. Bikes were either for those too poor to drive about in cars, or for a few enthusiasts who modelled themselves on riders in the *Tour de France*. But for Edwardians of all classes, bicycles offered a new and real sense of liberation. The length of a journey that they might undertake under their own steam was expanded fourfold, from around the fifteen miles that they might manage on foot, to the sixty that they could cover on a bike. The bicycle had started, in the 1870s, as a specialist, hand-built and somewhat dangerous item for well-to-do sporting young men, for whom the occasional spill from the high saddle of the penny-farthing was a routine, painful part of the sport. But by Morton's day, the bicycle had developed into a smaller-wheeled, reliable, safe, mass-produced item, available to thousands of Edwardians – men and women alike – who were eager to get out onto the empty roads and explore Britain. And the roads really were empty. The huge expansion of the rail network during the nineteenth century meant that most heavy goods, and most long-distance travellers, went by train. The scorching Uncle Willies and Mr Toads, in their newly-invented motor cars, were few and far between. The untarred roads were used chiefly for local journeys by pedestrians and horse-drawn vehicles, and so were wonderfully open to discovery by cyclists. Memoirs and photographs from Edwardians as diverse as Edward Elgar, Bertrand Russell, H. G. Wells, Flora Thompson (author of *Lark Rise to Candleford*), and Bernard Shaw, among many others, testify to the new pleasures to be had awheel.[3] In his diaries, the young Morton sometimes made notes about the books he was reading. It is interesting that one of the authors singled out is H. G. Wells. Morton read *Kipps, Love and Mr Lewisham* and *Tono-Bungay*, all within a few years of their publication. Maybe Morton identified with the young men in Wells's novels who pedal off in search of a better life. And he noted in his diary (8 April 1911) that *Tono-Bungay* (which contains an intense evocation of the England of the great houses) was 'a splendid work'.

The young Morton is a perfect example of a boy whose horizons expanded when he was given a bicycle:

The Warwickshire woods and meadows stretched away into green vistas with their farms and manor houses, their oaks and elms, their church spires and their black and white cottages. My joy for years had been the freedom conferred on me by my bicycle, upon which I set off on many a spring morning for Stratford-upon-Avon, twenty-five miles away, taking with me sandwiches which I ate beside the Avon, then offered the crusts to the swans. I can recall the road in some detail . . . It is not easy to explain to the young the layer of tranquillity that appeared to be spread over England in 1909, and a modern generation would find it difficult to believe that one could cycle for miles along roads and lanes meeting only a farmer in his trap, a shepherd with his sheep, cows moving across from one pasture to another, and loaded wagons drawn by two or more huge shire horses. The roads of England were the cyclist's paradise; never again will there be anything to match it. I think that to be seventeen and to be bicycling to Stratford-upon-Avon to see Mr Frank Benson [an actor-manager who promoted Shakespeare

festivals] as Mark Antony or Caliban or Hamlet was the most carefree
and delicious moment of my youth, indeed of my life.

'. . . Indeed of my life' is an extraordinarily high valuation for the
elderly Morton to have given, but it was heartfelt and authentic. His
bicycle was the means of uniting two of his passions, the Warwickshire
countryside and the theatre. It is no coincidence that later, when he
was writing the climax of *In Search of England*, and describing
the quintessence of the nation's landscape and culture, he sets it in the
Warwickshire countryside, close to Stratford, which he infuses with
the spirit of Shakespeare. Frank Benson, the actor-manager whose
performances so thrilled him, carried his influence over the young
Morton well beyond the stage:

> I met and made friends with Frank Benson, who was not yet Sir Frank,
> who organised the Shakespeare Festival with a company whose leading
> actors were generally ex-members of the O.U.D.S. [Oxford University
> Dramatic Society] We were made for each other. Benson's crackpot
> theories about Merrie England found an immediate response in me, and
> it now makes me squirm, or smile, to read the nonsense I wrote at the
> age of seventeen and eighteen under his influence and that of Cecil Sharp
> [the collector of folk songs]. I really believed that it was possible to put
> back the clock and persuade people to dance happily on the village green.

The note of embarrassment about his youthful ideals is plain, but this
recollection does indicate the potency of a particular conception of
English landscape and culture. Not surprisingly, and no matter how
daft the elderly Morton felt it to be, this is the conception that shapes
In Search of England.

The exalted passage that recreates, in old age, his youthful love of
cycling is from his *Memoir*. The short entries in the diaries he actually
kept as a young man tend to be more down to earth, but his pleasure
in pedalling out of Birmingham into the countryside is unmistakable.
Here is a sample:

> *8 April 1909*. Got up at 10 today. At 12 I started out on a most
> tremendous cycle ride. I arrived in Coventry at 10 past 2. Then I went

on to Kenilworth and got to Warwick at 10 to 4. Then I arrived in
Stratford at 5 o'clock PM. I came back home via Henley in Arden and
got home somewhere about 7.30 or 8. I feel half dead and thoroughly
tired out.

He had cycled over sixty miles. A couple of weeks later, he was cycling
off to Stratford again, this time to the theatre: 'I enjoyed *Coriolanus*,
immensely.' Such brief entries triggered memories in the old man who
wrote the *Memoir*, and he turned them into passages like this:

Not for many years have I sniffed what I always thought was the
unnecessarily foul stench of carbide [a chemical, a small lump of which,
when moistened and placed in a bike lamp, gave off an inflammable gas
that the rider set a match to]. But, were I to do so, I should see in the
mind's clear eye the pale circle of light from my bicycle lamp as it
wavered over the road on my return from Stratford-upon-Avon.
Pedalling along into the night, I passed through sleeping villages and
small towns which were fast asleep, and sometimes between hedges a
hare would run in the light for quite a way, and at last I would reach the
outskirts of Birmingham and home.

His bicycle led to exciting encounters, not just with shepherds, hares,
and Shakespeare, but with girls. His early diaries record the youthful
agonies of cycling around the streets of Moseley, hoping for accidental-
looking encounters with girls that he secretly fancied. In the spring of
1909, for instance, he fell for Irene, who is described in his diary
variously as 'ripping', 'lovely', 'exquisite', 'divine'. On 5 May he
lamented: 'I have cycled and walked miles and miles in hope of seeing
her, but have not been rewarded. It's awfully hard luck.' Further miles
in the succeeding weeks brought him no greater luck, and on 22 May he
cut his losses: 'As for Irene, I don't care a twopenny d. If she is so
inde-blooming-pendent I can be so as well.'

His manly bicycle maintenance skills led to another encounter:

5 April 1911. Coming out of the Midland Institute a delightful girl asked
me to light her bike lamp for her. I did. The glass of it was dirty, so I
cleaned it with a leaf torn from my notebook. She said 'don't clean it

with any £5 notes!' I said 'I'm afraid I haven't any,' and she retorted most charmingly 'Oh, no nice people do have £5 notes.' Puzzle: was she a socialist?

He prefaced this entry with a comment that foreshadows a stylistic trick he developed and used extensively in his later books: 'Had a nice little episode suitable for a "meeting" in a novel.' In his travel books, he would often engineer an encounter, of the sort that he works up here in his youthful diary, between his narrator and a pretty young woman.

The diaries show that he sometimes managed to have a girlfriend actually pedalling alongside him on his jaunts. Trips that combined cycling and courtship, however, had a drastic effect on the prose of his evening's diary entry:

> *11 July 1911.* This morning I got up at *6AM* ! and met Edith and we cycled out into the country and, bowered in soft trees, and bathed in warm sunlight, we leaned against a rude fence and watched the sun get higher in deep blue, cloudless heavens: this was absolutely Arcadian . . .

Arcadia wasn't the only place that interested him. It would be a mistake to picture Morton as a hater of the city – as a man whose soul was stirred only by fields and hedgerows. His 'Search' books, which were to achieve such huge success, chiefly celebrate rural Britain, but they are by no means systematically anti-urban. Morton loved cities, and not just the easy-to-love, obviously beautiful cities such as York, or Rome. His *Memoir* and his diaries show that he was exhilarated by the Birmingham city streets of his youth. Here is his recollection, from the *Memoir*:

> It was about this time [i.e. around 1910] that I began to miss my train home and to linger in Birmingham, highly dangerous conduct for anyone wearing a school cap. I cannot imagine why I was never reported. My two favourite haunts were in strong contrast, one improper, the other quite admirable. The first was the Bull Ring, the second was the Art Gallery. The Bull Ring, which had been the market place of Birmingham since the twelfth century was, when I knew it, tough, and mainly masculine, with a cloth-capped crowd

surging about the incline to St. Martin's church, crowding round the cheap-jacks, watching men writhing on the ground as they freed themselves from chains and handcuffs, listening to the patter of quack doctors, sandwiched in auction rooms where hideous china ornaments were knocked down to the highest bidder, entering the public houses, and circulating, a slow-moving, laughing, sneering and often quarrelsome gathering held there among those grimy streets, it seemed, by some kind of spell. It was impossible to mingle with the crowd without being offered some improbable object which had probably been stolen higher up the street. It was a good plan to empty your pockets before you went to the Bull Ring – not that I ever had anything in them worth stealing. A woman once told me that she once emerged from the Bull Ring with all four suspenders undone though she had never felt a thing.

The elderly Morton then stands back a bit and offers a weighty, romantic assessment of his own character, and recognises that the schoolboy in the Bull Ring and the distinguished author of the *Memoir* are manifestly the same person:

Looking back on the Bull Ring of 1907 with some amusement and a good deal of affection, I recognise in the schoolboy on the edge of the crowd a figure that has become familiar to me. It was in that place that I first became aware of the strangeness of mankind as I stood on the edge of the crowd with my books under my arm. How early in life one can set a pattern for oneself. For more than seventy years I have been standing on the edge of crowds, listening, wondering, observing, now in Rome, or in Athens, perhaps in Istanbul or Baghdad; the only difference is that I am wearing a hat and carrying a notebook. But I am just the same person in all essentials. One disguises oneself after the age of about twelve, but one does not change much.

It was not just the racy low-life of Birmingham that fascinated him. The Art Gallery was just as powerful an attraction, and it was there that a lifelong interest in antiquities – especially Roman and Egyptian – was kindled. An earnest entry in his diary for 30 May 1909 reads, 'I am determined to read up Egyptian and Babylonian history. I think it is most illuminative [*sic*] and the civilization marvellous.' One of the turning points in Morton's later career was his coverage, for the *Daily Express*, of the opening of the tomb of Tutankhamun, in 1923. The origins of his eagerness to go on this assignment, and of the journeys he later made through the Middle East are traceable to the Birmingham Art Gallery, where he was intrigued by a little statue:

> My interest settled, for a reason I can offer no explanation, upon an ancient Egyptian bust about half the size of life which I took to be – indeed it may have been so labelled – a priestess of Isis. I was vaguely conscious of its strength and vitality as though inside the granite, if cracked, would be found a spark, maybe a jewel or even perhaps something alive that had been alive there for centuries. I used to pop in and out just to visit the priestess and I was glad to find that I could buy a photograph of her . . . The work obsessed me and I began to write about it, trying to describe it, and in a moment of recklessness I posted one of these to (I would blush now if I could do so) *The Connoisseur . . .* [They] printed the article and sent me a cheque for thirty shillings or two guineas. And then, of course, my fate had been cast. To realise while still at school that you can make money by writing is a most dangerous thing.

The elderly Morton of the *Memoir* was trying to discern a pattern in his young life. And the pattern is one not of steady application to school work, with a place at Oxford or Cambridge in prospect, but of solitary, somewhat eccentric enthusiasms that were hitched up directly to the commercial world of writing for money. His fate – to become a professional writer – was cast, he says. This is neat, but he relies a bit too heavily on hindsight. The diaries he kept as a young man show that at times, he had quite different ambitions:

> *27 March 1909.* Went for a cycle ride in the evening. I waited up with Mother for Father and when he came home we had a very serious talk about my future. I want to be the greatest, or one of the greatest, actors the world has ever seen. Oh how I wish I knew if I should be successful if I went on the stage.

I doubt if his father was enthusiastic about this particular ambition. He thought that his son was drifting aimlessly. In the *Memoir* Morton often recalls how his father used to despair of him and declare that he would end 'in the gutter'. But the young Morton certainly took the theatre seriously. He was in the audience of every production that he could reach, from Shakespeare at Stratford, to music halls in Birmingham, and he was regularly on the stage himself in amateur theatrical productions.

I have already indicated the importance for Morton of Stratford, an enchanted place where all his youthful passions converged. But the young Morton's theatrical tastes ranged far beyond Shakespeare, and there were plenty of plays to be seen in Birmingham. The Edwardian years were a golden age for the theatre: it had not yet been challenged by the cinema, and nobody knew that the dislocating Great War was just a few years away. Morton recalled that there were three theatres in the Birmingham of his youth, often staging productions by London touring companies run by actor-managers. Their productions evidently impressed him vividly, for he was able to list dozens of plays that he saw, and describe the styles of performance of the leading actors – Beerbohm Tree, Forbes-Robertson, Fred Terry, for example. 'I remember them with gratitude,' he wrote.

The theatres of Edwardian Birmingham still put on plenty of Victorian melodramas, and Morton was a keen attender. He recalled the interplay between the villainous Sir Jaspers and the rowdy, but enthralled audiences: 'You come up here, Sir Jasper or no Sir Jasper, and I'll show yer!' Morton was no less keen on the music halls, where he saw what he calls 'a succession of great artists' – Harry Lauder, Vesta Tilley, George Robey, Florrie Forde. In his *Memoir*, he reflected on their technique:

The technique of the music-hall comedians had much to teach the short story writer and the journalist. That was the art of capturing the attention of an audience in the first moment. The capture had to be almost instantaneous because his time was short, and unless he held his audience from the start he was in danger of losing them for good. Though eccentricity played its part in the music hall, it was personality that held an audience in an almost hypnotic trance. The great artists created this feeling the moment they appeared, and it was wonderful, once the loud shouts and whistles of greeting were over, to be aware of that river of sympathy and approval that was flowing out from the audience to the performer. The antiseptic quality of English laughter was a wonderful thing to hear, gust after gust of it, sweeping away nonsense and pretence.

The supreme music hall artist, in Morton's view, was George Robey, and he gives a detailed account of his masterly technique. There is an opportunity here to compare, directly, the mature reflections of the *Memoir* with a youthful diary entry, for on 21 July 1909, he primly recorded: 'I went to the Empire and saw George Robey this evening. He was very vulgar.'

Morton's implied suggestion that he learned something of his own craft as a journalist from the music hall comedians – vulgar or not – may seem strained, but it is borne out, I think, by his writing. Characteristically, as we shall see, he opens his pieces with a gambit that is designed to hook the reader instantly into a rapport with the narrator. Not that this sort of opening can be learned only from music hall comedians, of course: writers have multitudes of ways of learning how to snare their readers. But it is interesting to see the elderly Morton reflecting on his own formative influences, and giving such a high place on his own list to the world of the stage.

Another, slightly bizarre theatrical activity is recorded in his diaries. In February 1909 he was away from school, following his grand-mother's funeral. He amused himself at home by making himself up, first as a bearded doctor, and then as a young lady, 'much to the delight of Auntie Norrie who said I would make my fortune on the stage'. In October, he made himself up as an old man, crept outside, and then knocked on his own front door to see if he could trick the household into believing that the visitor was not the young Harry. He succeeded: 'I was admitted and absolutely "took in" the nurse & the new cook.' In December he went further afield, succeeding in getting a housemaid to admit him, 'made up as an old major', to a house where he was due to pay a call. A couple of years later, in February 1911, he was confident and accomplished enough to go out into the streets in full disguise:

Had a great swank today. This evening was a students' night at the Royal. I, with difficulty, squeezed myself into a resemblance of a nice little girl – very lanky and with small hips! I got Parti [a friend called Partington] to come for me and we went down together. We raced about and had a great rag. We went up to the office [his father's newspaper office] at 10, past policemen, I in my costume showing a foot of delicate grey stockings and plenty of white petticoat. Mother came to the show late so I came home in the car [i.e. the tram] with her, Mrs Johnston and Mr and Mrs Buckham. I deceived Mr Towler completely when Parti introduced me as his fiancée!

This experiment in cross-dressing shouldn't, I think, be interpreted as a sign of some sort of tension within him about his sexuality, any more than his desire to pass himself off as an old major should be interpreted as a sign of anxiety about his youthfulness. Rather, I think that it illustrates an aspect of his personality that he himself identified in the recollection of his anonymous, schoolboy wanderings in the Bull Ring. He said that he had spent his life on the edge of crowds, looking in, as an observer. At the risk of over-analysis, could it be that his youthful experiments in disguise gave him a new vantage point from which to observe things? As I have already suggested, and shall argue more fully later, the narrator of his travel books was not, in any simple way, the man who wrote them. Morton had created a persona, and his facility in this creation could well have been developed as he watched plays, analysed acting and comic technique, trod the boards himself in amateur theatrical productions, and (if only rarely) went out into the streets dressed as somebody else.

Plainly, cycling, the theatre, and girls fully engaged his imagination. School did not. He worked only fitfully for his matriculation examinations, and in April 1909, when term ended at King Edward's, he left. He was sixteen. His final morning at school was, it seems, completely unremarkable. He drifted home, and spent the rest of the day in more congenial pursuits: he went out on his bike, and later went to the theatre with his mother.

7 April 1909. We broke up today. Well I suppose I am no longer a schoolboy! I feel awfully humpy about leaving now that the time has come. I went for a splendid cycle spin this afternoon & and in the evening Mother took me and Mrs Meakin to 'The Early Worm' at the Princes.

His 'humpiness' did not wear off straight away. After a seemingly aimless four months, he started to make earnest entries in his diary about buckling down to examination work again, with the aim of getting into Dublin University – which, he had been advised, was easier to get into than Oxford or Cambridge. But nothing came of it. He had finished school for good. It is hard to say whether he later regretted not having worked hard enough to go on to university. He was fiercely proud of having made his way entirely by his efforts as a journalist and writer, and, when he was working in Fleet Street, he was contemptuous of gilded youths who came swanning down from Oxford and Cambridge, expecting to sweep the newspaper world before them. In a perhaps exaggeratedly confident passage in the notes for his *Memoir*, he wrote, 'I count it as one of my life's greatest blessings that I never went up to university, simply because, instead, I learned a trade.' But then, on another page of the notes, he wrote, 'I have never regretted that I never went to public school, though I have had moments when I wish I had been at Oxford.' He wanted to be recognised as a well-read, learned man – which he was – but, when it suited him, he wanted to be seen as a man who was entirely at home in the compositors' shop, helping to put the night's edition of the newspaper to bed. This was genuine enough, but he was having to make a virtue of necessity: he was always uneasy about not having been to university. It is interesting that when Morton was touring England, searching for its essence, his chosen routes almost never took him to Oxford and Cambridge. He wrote no set-pieces on two cities whose place in the essential myths of England we might expect him to have celebrated, or at least to have examined. The one exception is Morton's brief, glancing account of Oxford, in *I saw Two Englands*, published in 1942. But even here, there is no purple passage on the colleges and dreaming spires. Indeed, the narrator, having arrived in the city, quickly sheers away from it, rather obliquely.[4]

His dismal performance at school, and his father's prophecy about his likely end, suggest that the young Morton was an inveterate slacker, but, in his own way, he was industrious and determined. His encounter with the Egyptian statue in the museum, for example, shows that when his imagination was engaged he could apply himself, and that he had a canny eye fixed on making money as a writer. However, his father, who by this time was editor-in-chief of the *Birmingham Gazette*, did not encourage Morton to follow him into the world of journalism. During the summer of 1909 he worked as a schoolteacher. He had been out of school himself only a few months, and did not turn seventeen until July of that year, so he was young and inexperienced to have been standing in front of a class – though I imagine that the pupils themselves were small boys. In June he noted, 'Miss Jones [the headmistress?] has offered me £1.10 to continue to teach till the end of term, which I am going to accept.' But schoolteaching was not the career his heart was set on. And his dream of becoming an actor was fading. Privately, out of sight of his father, he was writing, and was taking it seriously: '*29 May 1909*. Finished the article on camping. Went round and read it to Mr Buckley. He kindly told me its bad points and the stereotyped phrases I had unconsciously used.' As the year wore on, there must have been some sort of rapprochement with his father. Morton records paying more and more visits to the newspaper offices. As he later wrote, in notes for his *Memoir*, 'I gravitated naturally to the reporters' room of the *Gazette* where I began the fearful initiation of police courts, county courts, hospital out-patients departments, bazaars,' and of trying his hand at play reviews. Eventually, on 22 November, he opened his diary entry with. 'I start work tomorrow at the office' – with 'work' underlined twice.

Morton was encouraged to steer towards writing, rather than acting, by the music critic of the *Gazette*, Robert Buckley, the man who had given him helpful comments on his youthful literary efforts. In a scribbled draft for the *Memoir* that was discarded from the typed-up version, Morton wrote about Buckley, saying that he had been a major influence, and had inspired him to take his first trip abroad. He even went as far as to say that knowing Buckley, who is presented as a worldly, romantic, venerable figure, was his equivalent of going to university. Buckley was a graduate of Heidelberg University and was pro-German. He was a friend of the pioneer socialist Robert Blatchford, and apparently regarded himself as a socialist too, even though, as Morton recalled, 'he referred to the populace in general as "the muck".' Buckley lived, with his wife, not far from the Mortons' house in Moseley. The young Morton was a frequent visitor, and recalled:

> Buckley's stories of Germany and the continent were the first time I was
> filled with the desire to travel and see other countries. Indeed, it became
> an obsession. I bought and read travel books & dreamed of a day when
> perhaps I might see other countries and other people. I began to save up.
> I was consumed by a desire to see Heidelberg University & meet some
> Germans who had fought duels. The day came when I had ten golden
> sovereigns . . . One day, my heart beating with excitement, I took a train
> to Harwich & embarked upon a paddle steamer which thrashed its way
> to Amsterdam. Then I changed to another paddle steamer, Dutch or
> German, which smelt of cheese and was going down [i.e. up] the Rhine
> as far as Mannheim.

Morton's recollections are of a thrilling time, perhaps of the sort of journey that was to become the staple of his life as a travel writer. His recollection trails off though, leaving him on the paddle steamer churning its way upstream on the Rhine. Given the importance he seems here to have attached to Buckley and the trip to Germany that he inspired, it is odd that Morton did not complete his recollection of this episode and incorporate it, with accurate dates, into the *Memoir*. The surviving diaries from this early period of his life contain no mention of it. It is possible that he made the trip before 1909 – that is, before the first surviving diary was opened. If so, he could have been no more than fifteen or sixteen when he went. This is unlikely: he never refers back, in his diaries, to any foreign trip undertaken before 1909. More likely, he went in 1910 – a year for which no diary survives – when he was seventeen or eighteen and had just left school and started work on the *Gazette*. Whenever he went, the trip must have lodged in his memory as a significant episode, for, nearly twenty years later, it surfaced in an interview he gave soon after he had joined the *Daily Herald*.[5] Morton rarely gave interviews, and hardly ever opened up in public about his life, but he may have made an exception for the purposes of giving a boost to his stature as a new features writer on the paper. The journalist who was writing the profile had, it seems, coaxed old stories out of the reticent, and now famous writer. Morton told him of the trip to Germany, saying that the ten pounds he saved was 'a big sum for a schoolboy'. My guess is that a bit of poetic license had been applied to the anecdote. 'I set out alone for a Continental tour,' Morton told the reporter. 'I took a cheese boat down the Rhine. "Blued" every penny I had at Wiesbaden. And had to walk back to the Hook of Holland, penniless, and living on peaches that I stole from the walls.' It's hard to believe that this was all made up: the draft for the *Memoir* certainly describes a trip to Germany. But exactly how old Morton was when he went, and exactly what he did there, is not entirely clear.

Morton entered the world of full-time work on the *Gazette* in November 1909. Oddly, there is little sense of exhilaration or satisfaction in the diary entries that record the assignments he was sent on as a new cub reporter. His first few days in the press gallery of the police courts moved him only to make the somewhat po-faced observation: 'It was quite a novel experience to me and showed me what a thin mask so called civilization is, and that beneath all are the primeval cave man instincts and passions.' A couple of years, and no doubt hundreds of cases later, he wrote 'I am getting sick of the office work. I feel I could do good work and here I am stuck on police courts without end. It's disgusting.' (10 July 1911.) What did he want then? There he was, in a job conveniently supplied by his father, ungratefully complaining about the routines of the reporter's life.

There were, though, some commissions that excited him. Not surprisingly, these were connected with the theatre. The high point of his year was Frank Benson's Shakespeare Festival at Stratford. In the spring of 1911 Morton went down from Birmingham each day to cover it.

In September of the same year, now with a secure job and money in his pocket, he went abroad for a holiday. He spent a couple of weeks in Normandy with his friend Wilfred Partington, and wrote up a summary of the trip when he got back home. It is an unremarkable, though evocative record of two young men trying out their schoolboy French, flirting with waitresses, watching the swells going into the casino at Dieppe, observing the low life, bathing in the sea, getting drunk, and sharing what they considered to be hilarious private jokes. A snapshot of Morton in the waves is pasted into the diary. (See plate 1.) Memories of this trip may have passed through his mind when, later in his life, he made a list, running to over a hundred entries, of his sexual partners. Most of these partners are named, with just the woman's first name, but some are designated by the date and the anonymous 'wh' – presumably 'whore' – as in 'Wh – Paris 4.1.30'. The early entries on the list are not dated, but second on the list is 'Dieppe', and a bit further down, 'wh with Parti.' is entered. Morton's sexual life, as it developed, was complicated and relentless: it may well have got off the mark during his holiday in France.

In November 1911, back in Birmingham, and now probably reconciled to, or even enthusiastic about, the life of a newspaperman, he maintained his interest in acting by joining the company of Tom Taylor's *The Fool's Revenge*, to be performed at the Midland Institute. He played Serafino Dell'Aquila, a poet, and kept a cutting of a review of the play. The reviewer wrote: 'Another worthy study was the Poet of Mr. H. Vollam Morton, who showed a fine sense of character, and delivered Taylor's sonorous lines excellently.' The reviewer goes on: 'Miss Dorothy Vaughton made a pleasing Fiordelisa.' Four years later, Dorothy, the pleasing Fiordelisa, became Morton's wife.

He seems not to have been bowled over by Dorothy at first sight, but a day or two after the performance of the play, she playfully gave 'her poet' a bunch of violets, which he pressed in the pages of his diary: 'I have been chaffed a lot about Dolly. She is a nice girl anyhow.' A month later, in December, he heard, by a roundabout route, that she was keen on him:

> Downing told me on Sat. that Mrs Ross said that Dolly Vaughton was 'in love with that boy' (meaning me). Dear little Fiordelisa. Of course it can't be true, but even if it isn't, I somehow like to think of it. It's nice to be loved, or even think you are. I know.

It doesn't exactly look as if an arrow has pierced his heart. And when, a week later, they went on their first date together, his nightly diary entry was a good deal less than ecstatic:

Took Dorothy Vaughton to 'Dad' [?] at a matinee. We then had tea at
Kunzle's and I walked to Five Ways with her . . . She is a nice little girl;
an extremely nice little girl – with the 'would be artistic' temperament.
I think that these girls are very nice but I wonder if they are shallow if
you had to live with them. I think that they are what Bernard Shaw calls
'silly-clever'.

This severely critical initial assessment of Dorothy lasted only a few
weeks. Early in the new year of 1912, Morton was writing passionately
about her. But his passion was conveyed, right from the start, in rather
contrived, somehow slightly disengaged tones. From the outset of their
courtship, his diary entries strike an odd note. Here is the very first, and
it looks like a tryout for the sort of vignettes of racy life that he would
be writing for *Daily Express* ten years later:

16 January 1912. It was a girl's dressing room. Grease paints were
scattered about, and those wonderful, scented mysterious things – those
personal clothes of a girl – those exquisite loveable little blue-ribboned
things which profane eyes look not upon, were rammed into odd
corners. I stood in such a room tonight, and tied up the silk straps of
Columbine's shoes, and fixed black bows upon her arms. She came close
to me. I could smell the faint perfume clinging round her; her pretty
neck and shining shoulders, the scent of her hair and her slim black-
stockinged legs filled me with the romance of the scene. It was
wonderful. She pirouetted about the room and I helped to powder her
neck to tone down the paint.

This is the outstanding impression of Bernard Shaw's 'You Never
Can Tell' which I attended by request this evening. My Columbine was
Dorothy.

His romance with Dorothy developed steadily throughout 1912, but
old flames tended to re-captivate him, and new, brief conquests
distracted him. Only three days after his blissful visit to Dorothy's
dressing room, for example, he was escorting a girl who served in a
cigarette shop to her home, and coaxing a kiss from her: 'I like her and
go in and buy cigarettes I can't afford in order to see her. I hate her to
have to stand bold, with red little hands, behind that damned counter,

and hold a match to the cigar of every swine who comes along. It's devilish!' In February, he 'had a terrific time by a moonlit stream' with another girl – a girl with whom, next evening, he 'lay on soft straw' gazing up at stars that 'were throbbing in time to our heart beats'. Occasionally, he was seized with guilt and would make up for his lapse by writing pious, rather sloppy tributes to Dorothy, his 'White Soul', his 'little girl'. Their special place was the porch of a church, and on 27 February, and written in an attempted formal italic script, suitable for the solemnity of the inscription, he wrote:

> I have learnt one of the most beautiful things connected with me today. It almost brought tears to my eyes. I heard from Willie that Dolly was so impressed by our nocturne at the church that the dear little soul got up the next day in the cold, red dawn, walked to the church & took Communion. This is one of the most beautiful things I have ever known.
>
> I paid a pilgrimage myself tonight & dropped a red rose upon the spot where we stood and kissed.

Morton was conforming, almost to the level of caricature, to the stereotype of the man who, on one hand, characterises one, special woman as a devoted, trembling, little (there is always the diminutive) custodian of his soul, while, on the other, cannot resist the challenge to conquer every other woman who crosses his path. In later life, Morton stopped this ludicrous characterising of his wives, but he never gave up the challenge of conquering as many women as he could.

In early 1912, however, he was not formally engaged to Dorothy, and therefore perhaps felt himself entitled to continue to play the field. He oscillated between the mystical passion he said he felt for Dorothy and the more earthbound passion he felt whenever he caught the eye of a woman across a saloon bar or a shop counter. His inconstancy troubled him, as his diary indicates. On 11 March he spent a few minutes with Dorothy in what he called 'our own dream porch' – where they often dreamed of a little cottage with roses round the door. 'We had a great talk & a wonderful time. It is good to be alive.' The next day, his diary entry is just ten words long: 'Feel great today. All the world is full of song.' But on the day after that, the entry is almost as short, but very different: 'Feel damn bad. Went to see the doctor today. Am despondent etc. Got a bottle of medicine to take.'

A few weeks later, on 22 April , and recording his professional, rather than his romantic life, he noted, with evident satisfaction, 'Am off to do "special correspondent" work at Stratford. (Shakespeare Festival).' This was the sort of commission that Morton was to revel in: he was always more interested in being a features writer than in being a reporter. He much preferred being away from the office, staying in a hotel, working up a piece, or a series of pieces, on a topic of his own choice. His Shakespeare Festival assignment led to a highly pleasurable week at Stratford, and his week was made even more pleasurable when Dorothy came out by train from Birmingham to spend a day with him. Their romance had evidently blossomed. Here is Morton's record of the magical day at Stratford:

30 April 1912. Today, White Soul came to me. I was up early and hurried round to the station. At last, her train came – the 11.18 – & she stepped out of a carriage. O heaven itself. We bought some chocs at the request of the Golden Girl and went straight away to a wonderful wood by the Avon – Wiers Brake they call it. We were in heaven. However we had to come to earth & went to lunch at the Shakespeare Hotel where I had reserved a table. Benson was having lunch next to us, so I introduced him to Dolly & we had a very delightful talk. After lunch, as a matter of form, we went to Shakespeare's house. I hate show places & S's house is no exception to the rule. We then went again to Wiers Brake, & high up in a slanting pine wood from which we could see silver patches of the river right below us, we spent the afternoon. Never was afternoon so short or so beautiful since the world began. We lay far back till the wood flowers bent over us. We lay in each others arms and kissed and kissed until it seemed our souls met and mingled. White Soul let down all her hair and I twisted it round my neck and bound her to me by it. We confirmed our love a thousand times & were happy and sad by turns. At last the sun seemed to set in a red flash and we had to go. We had a quiet little dinner in my room at the Unicorn. It was fine to see this girl sitting beside me in her neat little blouse and skirt. It was great to help her to fish and asparagus & things & to see her lift a glass of water & drink. We smoked a few cigarettes & O, our kisses as we sat in the same chair. We made such fun of a 'Trophy of the chase' – a pair of bull's horns over the door – and criticised the ugly Victorian decoration of my poor, pokey little sitting room. O, how wonderful it was. Shall I ever forget leaning out of the window with her and looking out, at dusk, at the faint glow in the sunset sky. We had to run for the last train. I went to the hotel that night as though the sun, the moon & the stars had gone out & left me groping blindly in the darkness. My heart ached.

It is easy to see why, with memories like this, Stratford and the countryside around it became the ultimate destination of the journey dramatised in his most successful book, *In Search of England*, fifteen years later. But there is something slightly odd about this passage from his diary. The private recollections, by a young man of nineteen, of a passionate afternoon with his girlfriend are likely to be a bit overwrought, but then, they were not written with us in mind. They were, however, written for *somebody* to read, even if Morton couldn't have specified, as he was scribbling away, back in his pokey room at the Unicorn – if indeed he was writing it up then and there – exactly who he had in mind. What of such phrases as 'it was fine to see this girl sitting beside me . . .' or 'I went to the hotel that night . . .'? Aren't they a bit stagey, a bit calculated? It's as if there has been a significant lapse of time between the events and his record of them, even though the entry occupies its correct place in the diary's chronological sequence. (Morton used commercial, page-a-day desk diaries.) And his parenthetical explanation of what the 'Trophy of the chase' was tends to shift the tone of the passage from that of a wholly private record, in which such explanations would be superfluous, to that of a completed, polished anecdote. There is of course no obvious, naturally appropriate idiom for young men to drop into when they wish unaffectedly and authentically to set down in their diaries their feelings of love for their girlfriends. On their way to the page, feelings are always powerfully mediated by conventions governing their expression, and the more intimate the feeling, the more commonplace the record of it is likely to be. Even so, a sense of the uniqueness of the writer's feelings can break through the conventions. Does it here? There is no doubt that the passage expresses Morton's love for Dorothy, but it is written as if Morton was too self-consciously watching himself write it: the aspiring writer elbows aside the young man in love. Maybe his evenings in the theatre watching Shakespeare – the reason for his being at Stratford in the first place – had something to do with it.

But maybe there was something not quite right in his feelings for Dorothy. Their eventual marriage did not last, and its failure prompts a perhaps too forensic examination of the early years of their relationship. Hindsight can shed a glaring, distorting light, giving trivial problems the appearance of serious flaws. But even when knowledge of what was to become of his marriage is set aside, Morton's diaries from the years during which he was courting Dorothy suggest that their relationship was not securely rooted.

Despite his record of the idyllic day with Dorothy at Stratford, as 1912 wore on he was still confused about who he was actually in love with. This confusion reached a tragi-comic pitch toward the end of the year. Early in December, things were going swimmingly with Dorothy: 'Dolly & I are still happier than ever. I have called her "little wife" and we have dreamt of a dream cottage together . . . Really I am passing through the most glorious time of my life now.' But just before Christmas, an old flame flickered into life: Leslie, an old friend, and now a professional actress, turned up in Birmingham to play in pantomime. He met her in the moonlight on Christmas Eve and explained how deeply in love with Dorothy he was. Christmas Day, however, was 'the most miserable Xmas I can recollect'. And then, on Boxing Day, in a routine that was to be played out over and over again in his life: 'Like a fool went & saw Leslie again today & fell. I love Dolly, O how I love her, yet today I told Leslie I loved her too.'

The details of Morton's early love-life might seem to have little bearing on his developing career as a writer – less bearing, perhaps, than his trusty bicycle. But the pattern established in his early years did define his later life. In the long run, he and Dorothy were not suited to each other, and he eventually came to see her as a drag on the enticing prospects that the vivid metropolitan world was opening for him. His final, cruel assessment of her was much closer to the brisk, cool judgement he'd made of her after their first date than it was to the ecstatic praise that he'd poured out later in his diary. What Dorothy thought of *him,* as their relationship developed, is less clear. The few letters to him that survive from their courtship days show that she adored him, but she was, understandably, bitter when their marriage hit the rocks. Secondly, his sexual avidity may have left its trace in the seemingly blameless pages of his books. The primmest of readers could scarcely take offence at anything he published, but Morton often faintly eroticised his narrator's journeys by contriving for him the occasional wayside encounter with a beautiful young woman who is charmed by his wit and learning.

Putting Morton's tangled romances to one side, how was his career on the *Birmingham Gazette* progressing? As his satisfaction at being sent to cover the Stratford Festival shows, after three years at work on the *Gazette*, he was beginning to enjoy the life of the journalist. A month or so later, and back in the office, he noted in his diary, 'I am doing leaders now.' When his father was away, Morton was starting to take more responsibility for the paper. On 17 May 1912 he wrote, 'Am working hard bringing out the Gazette: I am getting on.' But less than a month later, developments on the paper brought his career lurching back to earth again. In his diary, on 5 June, he noted: 'The *Gazette* is rather crockey. A quarter of a column appears in the *Post* this morning of a Chancery Division action. I have hopes things will recover: if not – London.' The *Gazette* had been owned by Arthur Pearson. In 1908 he went blind, and a couple of years later, began to sell off his newspaper interests. This affected Morton's father profoundly, for he was a staunch Conservative, and the paper, after nearly foundering, was bought up by Liberals. Morton recalled that, as a youth, he had not realised that his father took his Conservative politics seriously. As a child, Morton had simply taken for granted his father's well-to-do connections, probably never even considering that they had a particular political colouring. He recalled being sent to the station to collect salmon and grouse that had been sent down from Scotland, during the shooting and fishing season, to his father by his grand acquaintances, and there are entries in his early diaries that indicate that his father would, from time to time, be invited to move, if only briefly, in exalted circles. For example, Morton noted, in August 1909, and with no sense of awe, that his father, mother and sister had been to tea 'with Lord Norton at Norton Hall'. Therefore, having taken, I suspect, only a casual personal interest in politics, Morton was brought up short when the *Gazette* ran into trouble and his father took a stand that led to a serious falling-out with the paper's new Liberal proprietors.

Morton made a number of attempts to write up this episode for his *Memoir*, but he never got it quite into focus: he never says whether there arose a question of where his own loyalties lay – to his father, under whose patronage he'd been given his job, or to the new proprietors of the *Gazette*. A month after the scare about the Chancery Division action, Morton received formal letters from the receiver of the company, saying that his engagement with the newspaper was in jeopardy and that he'd henceforth be employed only from week to week. That was in June 1912. Matters came to a head in November, when a new management swept in to carry out what would now euphemistically be called a major restructuring of the paper. As it was happening, Morton wrote, from the office, an account of events in a letter to his friend Partington. The letter appears not to have been sent, but Morton kept it folded up in his diary. He wrote, 'Last night after the first edition the gov. [i.e. Morton's father] took off his coat, ordered a taxi & got all his belongings out, leaving his desk void and inhospitable.' The letter goes on to say that the master of the chapel – that is to say the head compositor – came down, and exchanged tearful farewells with Morton's father, who then left, for good. Morton's letter then sets out to explain his own position, which turned out to be not as bad as he'd feared. His father had evidently spoken up for him to the new management, saying that his son was, as Morton jauntily reported to his friend, a 'born writer'. When his turn came for an interview with the new manager, Morton was asked, 'Now, what do you want to do for us?' Morton was confident enough to reply, 'Oh, literary and dramatic work is my ambition; also magazine work.' This is Morton's own, somewhat dramatised version of the interview, as related to his close friend, but if it is reliable, it indicates that Morton was now sure of his own abilities and wasn't begging to be taken back on to the paper in order to hack round the police courts and bazaars with his reporter's notebook. He convinced the new manager, who had read and been impressed by some of Morton's theatrical reviewing, that he should be retained. The upshot was that Morton was kept on by the paper, although the exact nature of his new post was not made clear. It seems to have worked out reasonably well, for on 10 December , he wrote in his diary, 'Am getting on well with the new Gazette people.'

Morton's father's career, by contrast, was wrecked, and he went off to London, leaving the family behind for the time being, to find new work as a journalist. He eventually re-established the family in London, although much more modestly than back in Moseley. Morton later wrote, in a draft for his *Memoir*, 'The circumstances of his fall from power, and the melting away of his important friends, made the greatest impression upon me and was one of the formative influences in my life.' His father's crash shook him up, even though he survived the wreck himself.

Morton himself did not, however, stay on for much longer with the *Gazette*. Unfortunately, his diary for 1913 has not survived, so it is not possible to establish the exact sequence of events. Morton chose not to enlarge in his *Memoir* on the reasons for his leaving the paper. Whether he jumped or was pushed is unclear. Unclear too is the nature of his family's domestic arrangements following his father's departure for London in search of work.

Sometime during 1913, at the age of twenty-one, Morton left Birmingham – and therefore Dorothy – behind, and set off, like Dick Whittington, to seek his fortune in London. He was now clear about what he wanted to do. He no longer dreamed of becoming an actor. He was certain that he wanted to be a writer – indeed, he already felt himself to be one – and he knew that to achieve his ambition he'd next have to establish a place for himself in Fleet Street.

2

1913–1919

SERVICE IN THE GREAT WAR AND FLEET STREET

I remember how I arrived in London in the year 1913 with £10 in the bank, with three crates of books, a basket chair, and a plaster cast of the goddess Isis.* No crusader ever cast his eyes for the first time upon the Holy city with greater awe and reverence than I, as, half way down Fleet Street, I saw the dome of St Paul's lifted above the railway viaduct† at Ludgate Circus. This was the arena in which I was to rise or to fall, and, being twenty-one, I had every intention of rising.

This is from Morton's *Memoir*, the chief source for this part of his life. He wrote a number of drafts of his crusading story. In one, the £10 in the bank becomes £20, and, according to an entry in his diary for 1915, he opened his first bank account only in January of that year. The elderly Morton's memory for fine detail was sometimes a bit shaky, and his recollections of the big events in his life are sometimes incomplete, but the *Memoir* does supply the broad outlines of his life during this period.

He took lodgings in Putney and began a dispiriting round of calls to all the Fleet Street offices, hoping to be able to impress editors with a scrapbook of cuttings of his articles from the *Gazette* that he'd assembled. He had no luck, often not getting as far as the editor's office. With money running low, he played his last card, a vague

---

*Presumably a copy of the statue that had captivated him in Birmingham Art Gallery and which he'd written up for *The Connoisseur*. He later noted that the statue turned out in the end not to be of Isis, but of a male scribe.
†Now demolished.

introduction to Andrew Caird of the *Daily Mail*, supplied by his mother, who knew the Caird family back in Scotland. He drew a blank there too. With hindsight, he said that by trudging round the newspaper offices, he was taking the wrong route: he would have stood a greater chance of success, he wrote, if he'd tried his luck in the pubs that journalists used: 'What I should have done was to have gone to the Falstaff, the Cheshire Cheese, the Cock, the Mitre, the Rainbow, the Old Bell or El Vino, and, having stood someone a drink, explained that I had been trained in the provinces and wanted a job.' Almost ready to admit defeat and return to Birmingham, he met – he could not remember where – Percy Watson, news editor of the *Evening Standard and St James' Gazette*. Later, this paper became one of the major London evening papers, but at that time, it was struggling along, largely feeding off stories generated by bigger papers. Watson could not offer Morton a regular job on the staff. The best he could do, in Morton's words, was to offer him 'the slavery of lineage' – that is to say, payment, by the line, for reports written by Morton and, if he was lucky, selected by the paper's sub-editors for publication. This is how Morton described the system:

> I would arrive at about 8 o'clock in the morning to find Watson already at work at a roll-top desk in a cloud of cigarette smoke. He wore a thin alpaca jacket and grasped a large pair of scissors. Around him lay the mangled remains of the morning papers. It was a typical scene in the headquarters of cannibalism – Fleet Street. The evening papers feed on the morning, and the morning on the evening. If either one or the other had ceased publication, the survivor would starve to death. Handing me ten, or more likely twenty cuttings, and the more the better, he would say, 'See if there's a follow up to any of this!' and off I would go.

If the stories took him on to the streets, rather than to the telephone, he was at a disadvantage, for he was completely ignorant of the basic topography of the city whose news he was now covering. But he was not a bumpkin, up from the depths of the country: he'd had three years on a paper serving one of the largest English provincial cities, and he speedily adapted to London, coming soon to know and love it as deeply as he loved the Birmingham Bull Ring and lanes of Warwickshire. His most pressing concern when he started on the *Standard*, of course, was not to stroll about the romantic streets of London, soaking up the atmosphere, but to earn some money, quickly:

> As soon as I got the hang of this cut-throat business I began to make £3 to £6 a week, but it needed luck and planning. The great thing was to start early and select three or four stories which the sub-editors would snap up for the first edition. If they were printed I could claim them as lineage. Then, an hour or two later I could fire a volley for the afternoon edition [and thereby earn more lineage] and, with luck, could save up the best and longest stories of all for the late night final. After a few months of this, when I was sometimes making £9 a week, I was taken on the staff at a salary of £6, which delighted me since I could now afford to take a day off.

In both his *Memoir* and his diaries, he very rarely bothered to mention the news stories that he covered. For example, back in Birmingham, his coverage of the sinking of the *Titanic* for the *Gazette*, in April 1912, was recorded in his diary chiefly because he had had to work all day and all night keeping up with the story. In the sparse diary entries that cover his early years in London, there are rather irritable ones here and there saying that he'd spent the day covering unenthralling events – a cat show, for example – but there is hardly any sense that, as a reporter, he was close to great events, or that he really enjoyed reporting the less great events that came his way. Newspapers constituted the world in which he'd always moved, and he loved the company of the professional, perhaps slightly cynical journalists that he joined when he left school. And he was very proud that, back in Birmingham, he'd learned the whole business of bringing out a paper; he even knew how to operate – unofficially – a Linotype machine. When he sought his fortune in London, he was proud and pleased to have got a foot so quickly on to the Fleet Street ladder, but he had no ambition to ascend it to the rank of chief parliamentary, crime or foreign affairs reporter, or to the rank of editor. He had no feel, or passion for politics or world affairs. His ambitions lay elsewhere, although in 1913 he couldn't have said precisely where. Notably, there is no evidence of an ambition to be a travel writer.

During his years on the *Gazette* and the *Evening Standard*, however much he chafed at the daily round of covering ephemeral stories, he was learning the trade of writing. Travel, and travel writing, came later. He was a writer first, and traveller second. Apart from the obscure, youthful trip to Germany, and his explorations of Warwickshire by bicycle, he seems to have had no burning desire to go off to see the world. When he left Birmingham in 1913, it was to go, with his file of cuttings, to Fleet Street, not to take to the open road with a rucksack on his back. It would be a mistake to picture him as an inveterate, restless traveller who returned home only to turn his travels into books. Rather, he was a frustrated newspaperman who was determined eventually to escape the grind of day-to-day reporting and find a way of writing features. But there is no indication that the young Morton, newly arrived in Fleet Street, and coming home bored by his day covering the cat show, was yearning to be out among the hedgerows in search of England, or to be bumping across Mesopotamia in search of Ur. As an increasingly accomplished writer, he was ready to turn his hand to *any* writing assignment that would release him from the treadmill of reporting mundane events, but there is no sign, in his early life, of an itch to be off into the wide blue yonder.

For the time being, he slogged away on the *Standard*. His father had finally got himself permanently installed in London and so Morton was able to quit his own temporary lodgings and move into the new family home, in Barnes. He was missing Dorothy, who was still living with her own family back in Birmingham. Despite his wobbling at the time of the visit from the pantomime actress, he seems now to have been sure that his future lay with Dorothy. They wrote to each other regularly and passionately, he went up to see her whenever he could, and he started saving for their marriage, although his prospects were still far too insecure for the date of a wedding to be fixed.

At the newspaper office, he was, he recalled,

> astonished to find that my colleagues, though older than those of my former paper in Birmingham, were livelier and more high-spirited. To me in 1913 a man of forty was venerable, and it delighted me as much as it surprised me, to see such elderly characters indulging in what I thought to be undergraduate ragging. The first day I arrived on the staff

I fell for the oldest London joke. Discovering a note in the rack for me marked as 'most urgent', I was asked to ring up a certain number and enquire for Mrs Lyon. When I did so, of course, I discovered I was speaking to the Zoo.

Practical jokes in the same vein, involving pencils made of rubber and glue on walking-stick handles, enlivened his induction into the Fleet Street world. His memories of that world are an odd mixture of amusement, pride and resentment. But his memories of London itself are unaffectedly warm:

> In six months I had come to know every bus and underground route in London. I discovered the inexhaustible pleasures of the museums, the art galleries, the parks, the changing of the Guard, the drama of the streets, the Thames slapping against the Embankment, Cleopatra's Needle. The streets of London were an inexhaustible delight and pleasure to me.

It is the verb 'slapping' that gives this otherwise unremarkable paragraph the bit of lift that we find in so much of Morton's writing. The *Memoir,* from which it comes, is incomplete and scrappy, but it is rarely dull.

'Nobody enjoyed a free Saturday in London more than I did in 1913 and 1914,' Morton recalled, and his warmest memories of all are those associated with G. F. Lawrence, an entirely self-taught antiquary who watched over archaeological digs on behalf of the London Museum during the week, and who ran a little shop in Wandsworth that opened only on Saturdays. Morton's first contact with the shop had been by post, when, as a schoolboy back in Birmingham, he had bought some small items from lists of antiquities that were circulated by Lawrence. When Morton arrived in London, the Wandsworth shop became a regular port of call, and as his finances improved, he built up a collection of Roman and Egyptian artefacts, based on his purchases from Lawrence. Morton wrote four glowing pages about Lawrence in his *Memoir.* Plainly, the antiquary made a substantial impact on Morton. The roots of Morton's travel books go back, I think, not to an innate wanderlust, but to Lawrence's shop, and before that, to the

37

Birmingham Museum, where he had been enthralled by the Egyptian sculpture. What drew Morton to foreign or new British places was not so much a compulsion to keep moving, or the allure of an unknown landscape, but a romantic historical sense of the people who had once lived there; and the older the traces of former cultures, the better. He recalled that, as a boy, when he had been able to afford to buy from Lawrence's list 'some fragment of the debris of a dead world', he would hold it in his hand and think, 'When this coin was minted Cleopatra was alive,' or 'when this bowl was made Boadicea had not burned down the first London.' Hence his attraction to Lawrence's shop: its Ancient Egyptian artefacts fed his boyhood fascination, and its Roman artefacts, and Lawrence's skill and knowledge, fed his developing sense of the history lying beneath the pavements he trod as he explored London. Many years later, in June 1975, Morton was interviewed for a book programme on BBC radio. He was asked about the origins of his books and he replied that he had been a 'rather lonely little boy' with a habit of 'wandering off alone, exploring things and discovering things'. Then, rather contradicting this memory of solitariness, but making an important point about his sense of the past and of place, he went on, 'my sister reminded me once that I was in the habit of stopping when we were out on walks and saying "Stop. On this very same place, if you dug down, down, down, you might come to a Roman." ' It was this sense, I think, that was nourished by his Saturdays at Lawrence's shop in Wandsworth:

> The little shop window displayed Greek and Roman coins lying in saucers, there were fragments of Greek and Roman pottery, lengths of mummy cloth, blue mummy beads, and I recall a perfectly preserved Roman leather sandal found twenty feet beneath a London pavement, and a shrunken black object like a bird's claw that was a mummified hand. All the objects were genuine and they were priced at a few shillings each.

Lawrence's shop was a port of call also for navvies who were excavating the foundations for new buildings in London and who had heard that Lawrence would pay them for ancient bits and pieces that they turned up:

It was a privilege to have watched, as I did so often, Saturday after Saturday, the arrival of navvies at West Hill. It was one of Lawrence's triumphs that he had managed to train some of them in rudimentary archaeology so that they knew roughly what to look for. They would arrive always wearing their Sunday best. Entering the shop, they would dump on the counter something wrapped in a red-spotted handkerchief. 'Any good to you, guv?' they would ask, as Lawrence asthmatically undid the handkerchief before distributing from his waistcoat pockets poisonous little cheroots to his visitors. His procedure never varied. Laughing and coughing, he would label all the finds with the date and the name of the street in the City beneath which they had been found. He had a number of boxes filled with scraps of Roman pottery labelled 'Cheapside', 'Leadenhall Street', 'Cornhill' and so on, from which he slowly over the months pieced together a vase, a plate, a bowl as new fragments were brought to him. He had five or six jigsaw puzzles going on at once, and only when there was no hope of further excavation did Lawrence patch up the missing parts of a bowl with plaster of paris mixed with burnt sienna. I spent many happy Saturday afternoons helping him to do this.

Morton's first books, it must be remembered, were not about the byways of rural England, but about London, and we can see the groundwork for them being laid during the Saturdays he spent in Lawrence's shop.[1]

After a year or so on the *Evening Standard*, Morton was saving hard for his dream home with Dorothy. In January 1915 he opened a bank account and deposited £2.10s. 'Doll has £7.10s in B'hm so we start with £10.' But the money was not coming in fast enough. He had hopes of promotion on the *Standard*, and was dreaming that he'd then be able to marry: 'O my little, little woman: we must walk hand in hand.' His devotion to Dorothy fortified him: he noted that he 'gave no loophole for advances' to a waitress – 'a devilish pretty girl' – who'd sat down beside him in a 'wretched café in Bishopsgate'. Then, on 2 February 1915 he jubilantly wrote in his diary:

Got a letter today from Beattie of the Daily Mail asking me to see him. I went. Was offered £7.7s and am mad with joy. Came out of Carmelite

House [the *Mail*'s offices] & ran, ran, ran. Sent wire to Doss. O! all our dreams can come true now.

Next day, the edge was taken off his joy, for Dorothy had not responded with a return wire: 'am very, deeply disappointed. I wonder if she understands what this means?' To Morton it meant status and security; he was moving into the editorial room of a big national daily paper.

The editorial room of Northcliffe's *Mail* was more solemn than that of the *Standard.* There were no practical jokes. The staff were ever fearful that the proprietor would put in an appearance and make some arbitrary, devastating decision. It was in many ways the world of the *Daily Beast*, brilliantly created, twenty years later by Evelyn Waugh in *Scoop*, published in 1938. Northcliffe could be as unpredictable as Waugh's Lord Copper. One night, Morton recalled, news was thin and they were having a hard time finding exciting stories. A south-coast journalist had filed a story of a local shipwreck in which the lifeboat, having safely taken off the crew, returned, through heavy seas, to rescue the ship's cat. The *Mail* ran the story and Northcliffe was impressed by it. He ordered that the provincial journalist who wrote it be brought to the paper and offered £1000 a year. With some satisfaction, Morton, who now, at the age of twenty-three, saw himself as an experienced old hand, wrote that the man, plucked from his seaside paper office, was quite out of his depth in Fleet Street, and had no idea of what to do when 'the whole world fired cables at him'.

What to do with him? He was obviously useless in the orderly chaos which surrounded the nightly accouchement of the *Daily Mail*, neither could he be paid off without loss of face. So he turned up on the minute every afternoon, hung up his bowler hat and stick and was willing to do anything, though there was nothing he could be asked to do. It was embarrassing for us to see him 'victim of a rich man's whim' as the old song so aptly puts it; also, we had become fond of him. He was gentle and without metropolitan guile. We admired him too for sitting in our wild beasts' den. He was not unlike a rabbit who had made friends with foxes. Eventually someone, taking pity on him, raided the book reviewers' room and provided him with a nightly supply of novels.

Someone else had a whip-round to buy a screen, and there the little man sat, reading in privacy, a pool of quiet in an ocean of turbulence like that which had originally cast him upon us. And when the time for his departure came, he said good-bye and went.

This was, it must be remembered, written in Morton's old age, and there may well have been a bit of embroidery in the telling of this tale of the eccentricities of a Fleet Street press baron, but what comes through clearly is Morton's pride in having made himself so thoroughly at home in that guileful world. He pictures his younger self as one of the foxes; he does not for a second consider that the young Morton, recently arrived from Birmingham, and the rabbit from the seaside might have had something in common. Morton evidently thought, probably with justification, that he'd covered a lot of ground in a very few years.

While this amusing episode was unfolding at Carmelite House, the Great War was raging in France. The war that was to slaughter millions, and then to cast a long, black shadow over the decades that followed, came into Morton's life obliquely and shaped it obscurely. There is a familiar pattern in the lives of writers who marched away to war in 1914. For some – Edward Thomas, Isaac Rosenberg and Wilfred Owen, for example – the war abruptly ended their lives. For those who survived – Robert Graves, Siegfried Sassoon, Edmund Blunden, for example – the war left a mark that could never be expunged.[2] Morton did join the army, and *In Search of England*, which he published in 1926, is in many ways the archetypal, post-war record of a soldier, home from the trenches, going off to try to locate and define the country that he'd been fighting for. But it is hard to find out what Morton actually did during the war. Only one diary, the one for 1915, survives, and even that has most of its pages blank: he gave up keeping it soon after he was offered the contract at the *Daily Mail*. More promisingly, a photograph album kept by Morton during the war vividly documents some of the episodes in his military career. But his *Memoir*, and the hundreds of pages of notes that he made for it, refer to his war years only glancingly. And nothing in the forty or so books that he published after the war, and scarcely anything in his later diaries and letters, even where there is an obvious opening for him to have enlarged on his war years, fully describes what he did while he was in uniform.

His *Memoir*, for instance, which gave four pages to Lawrence the antiquary, gives barely two, rather inconsequential pages to his own war years. He wrote that he 'wished more than anything to be in khaki, because all my contemporaries and friends had enlisted, and I longed to get away from helping to sub-edit the *Daily Mail*'. He was, however, rejected twice when he tried to enlist in the army. (In an odd little note randomly scribbled in his 1929 diary, he remembered the number of army rejections as three, not two.) In notes for the *Memoir* he says that a 'weak chest' was the reason for his rejection. He put his infirmity down to his having hated games at school, and therefore to his not having developed a strong constitution, but a weak chest – whatever this vague diagnosis might have signified – did not prevent him, as a schoolboy, from cycling sixty miles in a day, so it is not clear what the army doctors who rejected him had found wrong with him. His repeated rejection mortified him, and he tried to get himself fit by joining a gym in Regent Street and exercising under an instructor. 'I pranced about in white shorts and rubber shoes for months, lifting weights, doing breathing exercises and ending up with a coldish shower, all before I went on duty' at the *Mail*. Unexpectedly, his father was able to offer him a bit of help. Only one of Morton's father's circle of rich acquaintances had stayed in touch with him after his move from Birmingham to London. This was Lord Willoughby de Broke. According to notes made for the *Memoir*, Morton's father discussed his son's plight with His Lordship:

'Can he ride?' asked Willoughby de Broke.

'I have no idea,' replied my parent, 'but I don't think so'.

'Well', said W. 'tell him to take some riding lessons & get into the army & after six months apply to be sent to the Cavalry Training School. If he passes and gets his commission, I'll take him into the Warwickshire Yeomanry.'

So that is what I did.

During the autumn of 1915, while Morton was trying to enlist in the army, his long and occasionally erratic courtship of Dorothy came to a conclusion. On 14 September, they married, at St James' Parish Church, Edgbaston, Birmingham. (See plate 2.) Morton's diary is blank from February onward, and the *Memoir* is entirely silent about his marriage, so we have no way of knowing his state of mind as the wedding approached. The only personal record from the time is the remains of a sprig of white heather, tucked into the diary at the page of their wedding day. One possibility is that with the war looming over the couple, they married in haste. But this is unlikely: the surviving diary entries from the time of his move from Birmingham to London indicate that he and Dorothy were deeply serious about each other and were planning to marry as soon as they could afford to. Maybe the war concentrated their minds and forced the pace of their plans, but they would, I think, have married anyway. I doubt, though, whether the newly-weds had time to set up home together. My guess is that Dorothy stayed at the family home in Edgbaston, while Morton went off to war.

Morton eventually enlisted on 10 December. The file containing his service record, preserved at the Public Record Office,[3] includes a medical report that gives no indication of why he had had such a struggle to get into the army: at five foot eight inches, with a thirty-two-inch chest, 'slight varicose veins', and a 'fair' standard of physical development, he was plainly no superman, but equally plainly, he was no less fit than thousands who were being swept up into the war effort. He remembered the day of his enlistment vividly:

I was given a uniform made for a larger man. The brass buttons were green, like uncleaned saltcellars. My boots appeared to have been made of iron. I had no idea how to wind my puttees. I emerged with my kit bag on my shoulder and orders to report to a unit on the south coast. This gave me one night in London. I must have appeared a terrible sight as I sat in the tube on the way out to Barnes. Perhaps people thought I had gone mad in the trenches, but I tried to look heroic. When I reached home my mother was just finishing dinner in the small front room. I decided to make an entry. Pulling myself together and setting my cap straight, I appeared, wrongly dressed everywhere, but with a noble expression. My mother rose as if she had seen a ghost and said: "My son, you look wonderful! Come back with your shield, or on it!* In that moment of sublime bathos I went laughing into her outstretched arms.

The few pages that Morton wrote about his war years tend all to be in this vein. It is as if they are a leisurely, comic introduction to a story that will soon turn to tragedy as the writer reaches the mud, squalor and slaughter of the trenches. But Morton's story never gets that far: he never went beyond writing drafts of versions of his impressions of his six months' basic training, and then his time at Cavalry School. There is not a word about actually engaging the enemy.

'My six months as a private,' he wrote, 'were among the most hilarious I have ever spent. I have never laughed so much in my life.' Then, having completed his basic training, and now under the influence of Lord Willoughby de Broke, he transferred to the Cavalry School at Netheravon, on Salisbury Plain. At Netheravon, while the fighting was bogged down in the trenches in France, men were being trained to make the sort of glorious charges of mounted cavalry that trench warfare, barbed wire and the machine gun had made obsolete. Morton's ludicrous training programme had survived from another century. De Broke's first question to new subalterns, if Morton's memory of it is to be believed, is beyond parody: 'And good-day to you, sir. May I ask if you are familiar with the works of Surtees?'†

As this recollection of de Broke shows, Morton recognised that his cavalry training was absurd – he described it elsewhere as 'grotesque' – but he couldn't deny his attraction to the glamour of it all. His most complete record of Netheravon is contained in a letter he wrote to a friend, in June 1962: 'I joined the Army in the first war in a mounted regiment as if I were going to fight Napoleon. I was given a sword, a bandolier, a pair of spurs.' So, in a war where the breakthrough would depend on the development of the tank, Morton was being trained, among other things, to trot, without stirrups, while holding a drawn sword. In one regimental charge across Salisbury Plain, Morton's horse

---

* This is what the mothers of Spartan soldiers were supposed to have said to their sons when they went off to war. Mothers desired their sons either to return triumphantly bearing their shields, or to return dead, their bodies borne upon their shields.

† R. S. Surtees (1805–64) was the writer of comic novels about fox hunting, featuring Jorrocks, a hard-riding, impecunious enthusiast.

died under him and he had to carry his saddle miles back to camp, balanced on his head. But the glamour of the cavalry was irresistible: 'It was worth joining the cavalry to hear the chink of one's spurs on the pavements of Piccadilly.' And there was nothing like the feeling of

> riding ahead of a troop of cavalry on some wonderful spring or summer morning, glancing over the hedges, giving the sign to trot or walk, and turning in the saddle, to look back and see one's men, riding two by two, their chin straps down, their carbines knocking in the leather buckets, the horses tossing their heads.

He successfully passed out of the Cavalry School, 'blossomed forth in well-cut riding breeches and beautiful brown field boots by Maxwell', and was commissioned, as de Broke had promised, in the Warwickshire Yeomanry. The glamour of jingling spurs then steadily faded as his regiment was ordered to undertake more mundane duties.

Morton was fortunate. There is no question about his eagerness to serve, but he was lucky not to have been taken into the Yeomanry earlier. According to the historian of the regiment, H. A. Adderley,[4] between August and December 1915, a detachment was sent to Gallipoli, where, despite their training as cavalrymen, they were used as infantry and suffered heavy losses. Morton is listed in Adderley's appendix as second lieutenant, 28 November 1916, and lieutenant, 28 May 1918. The Yeomanry's movements, from the time of Morton's commission with them, registered a steady decline from their cavalry status. The earliest photographs in Morton's wartime album are of camp at Wrotham, Kent, in June 1916, showing lines of bell tents and lines of horses. In August, the regiment was posted to Essex, and, a few months later, as Adderley tersely puts it, 'the horses were taken away and Bicycles substituted, the Regiment being transformed into a Cycle Unit of four companies.' Morton's album has photographs of the last of the horses, and the first of the bicycles. In September 1917 the Warwickshires were posted to Colchester, from where detachments were sent, from time to time, to France. Morton's photographs from this period are not of France, but of tennis parties, sports days, deckchairs on lawns, a meeting of the fox hunt, an archaeological dig in Roman Colchester and boating trips with Dorothy on the river at

Stratford while he was on leave. (See plate 3.) At Colchester too there were amateur theatricals. Morton wrote 'a musical farce' called *The Bounder of Baghdad* and staged a public performance of it at Sawbridgeworth, in aid of the Red Cross. One photograph is of an oriental stage-set with four members of the cast posed in front – with Driver Watts as a fetching Fatima. The photograph album's records of preparations for warfare are, by comparison, sparse. Morton's duties were evidently concerned with signals. He is pictured with heliographs and reels of cables, and a photograph of the 'Special Signals Company' shows them parading with bicycles and motorcycles. (See plate 4.) At the foot of a copy of standing orders, tucked into the album, Morton signs himself 'Lieut. O.C. Signals, 2/1st Warwickshire Yeomanry'.

Adderley says that the regiment formed part of a 'Special Brigade' that was

to be sent overseas under secret orders on an expedition, the purpose of which was at that time undisclosed. The German offensive in March 1918, however, caused the abandonment of the scheme. It was found necessary to call for large reinforcements for the army in France, and a considerable number were taken from Colchester including many of the Special Brigade which was thus broken up.[5]

Whether Morton was part of the 'Special Brigade', and what its mission was, is unclear: his movements are difficult to track, and some strange, fragmentary comments written by him in old age are hard to interpret.

In November 1917, a couple of months after his posting with his regiment to Colchester, he went down with influenza. In the autumn of 1918, and in the spring of 1919, a succession of vicious flu epidemics swept through Britain, killing thousands; Morton seems to have been struck down during an early visitation by the virus. A medical board report in his service file, dated 22 November 1917, says that he had been taken to hospital on 7 November and that he would not be fit for service until early in January 1918. Another medical board report, from the new year, dated 1 February 1918, certifies that 'he has recovered', and orders him to report to his unit for general service. What influence this bout of nearly three months of ill health had on his military service is not clear. The *Memoir*, and the notes made for it, make no mention of his illness. They do, however, record Morton's recollection of a visit to Colchester made in 1918 by his mother to say goodbye to him before he set off on a mission.

While at Colchester, Morton's mother was herself taken ill and had to go into a nursing home. Morton recalled her asking: 'Do you know what I should like more than anything? – a glass of champagne.' Morton bought a half bottle of Clicquot and left it with the nurse while he went off for the day to attend to his signals duties. On his return, the matron told him that, during the day, his mother had been looking forward to her glass of champagne. As a nurse had poured it out for her, his mother had risen from her pillow, 'then suddenly, as if in surprise, said "oh" and fell back dead'. This vivid account of his mother's death comes in a scarcely legible note that Morton made for his *Memoir* but which was eliminated from the typed version. In another note, he says that her death 'was one of the bitterest moments of my life'. His account of her death is followed by an account of his attempts to get in touch with her, beyond the grave:

> My mother had no fear of death. We had an agreement that if I were killed in the war she would go to seances & mediums, & we arranged a system of passwords & other safeguards which would save us from fraud. When I was demobilised I haunted spiritualistic circles and although 'your mother' often 'came through', never once did she give the password, which we both knew so well. I gave up after that, after testing the leading medium in London & incidentally wasting a lot of money.[6]

There is an odd reversal here. After the war, there was a vogue for spiritualist attempts by bereaved wives and mothers to get in touch with husbands and sons who had been killed in action. Morton's, though, is an attempt by a soldier who survived the war to get in touch with his mother, who had died in a Colchester nursing home.

Morton's mother's death certificate gives 16 April 1918 as the date of her death, gives 'mitral disease of the heart' and 'bronchitis' as the twin causes, and gives Colchester as the place of death. The date and place are important, for they give one fixed point in Morton's undated, and somewhat vague – maybe even evasive – recollections in his *Memoir*.

What was the special mission on which Morton and the Warwickshires were engaged? Adderley's history of the regiment says that the project was aborted in March 1918, but Morton's scattered, fragmentary recollections were that he was expecting to be sent abroad soon after his mother's farewell visit to him, in mid April 1918. One of these recollections runs: 'My mother came to Colchester to say goodbye to me because I was [then a?] signals officer to a unit that was to rush the mole at Zeebrugge.' The Zeebrugge Raid was a dashing action, carried out under the command of Admiral Keyes, to destroy the German submarine pens in the Belgian harbour. Submarines had been attacking allied shipping, and with the land war bogged down in France, Keyes was hoping that a naval attack that put the enemy's submarines out of action might raise the nation's morale. The approach to the harbour was to be blocked, and the mole was to be stormed by a landing party. The attack took place on St George's Day, 23 April 1918, with great heroism and great loss of life. Was Morton part of it? The historian of the raid, Philip Warner, makes no mention of men from the Warwickshire Yeomanry. Indeed he says that although there were early plans for the army to be involved, in the event, Keyes, who wanted the expedition to be a wholly naval affair, had his way.[7] It seems highly unlikely, then, that Morton went on the raid. But even in his notebooks, Morton seems to have been unable plainly to say as much. The nearest he came was an entry in one of the notebooks from which the *Memoir* was quarried. The entry reads: 'My mother came to say good-bye to me in 1918 when I was due to go on the Zeebrugge Raid, but I never w'. Not only did he break off before he completed the word that, presumably, would have been 'went', but he crossed the whole entry out.

Elsewhere, Morton made two more tantalising references to the Zeebrugge Raid. One is in his *Memoir*, at a point where he is recalling a trip he made to Germany, after the war, in 1920.* The ferry on which he crossed to the continent docked at Zeebrugge, and, again in a crossed-out passage, he wrote of the docks as 'the scene that might have

---

*See below, pp. 56–8.

been my grave'. He adds not a word of explanation. The other reference comes from one of his books, *The Call of England,* published in 1928. The narrator is in Liverpool, standing on the Pierhead watching the shipping. He watches a ferry approaching 'with a cargo of pretty girls' across the Mersey from Birkenhead, and speculates that it might be the *Daffodil* or the *Iris,* 'which took such a different cargo one dark night under the bloody mole at Zeebrugge'.[8] He does not enlarge. I doubt if his readers would have remembered, ten years after the war (if indeed they had ever known), that these two Mersey ferries had been commandeered for use in the raid. Morton makes his narrator deliver this cryptic reference to the ferries, I think, because the Zeebrugge Raid was of great, though unexplained importance to him personally. But to the average reader of the book, the short passage would have meant next to nothing.

Morton's demobilisation came on 4 March 1919, at Chiseldon, not far from his old cavalry training haunts on Salisbury Plain. Waiting for his release, he seems to have been depressed. He recalled: 'I had no wish to write again. I had lost interest in newspapers, indeed I had the impression, which comes to one at various stages in life, that what had gone before had happened to someone else.' This loss of interest in his career as a writer seems to have been profound, for, while he was waiting for demobilisation, he filled in an application to join the Indian Cavalry. He was, he recalled, 'attracted to the idea of a gay life in a warm climate with good pay and prospects of promotion'. But despite this plan for a complete change of direction, and despite his rejection of the idea of a career in writing, he was, at the same time, fishing around for a place back in Fleet Street. He had written to a friend, and the friend had showed the letter to Percy Watson, the man who, in 1913, had given Morton his first Fleet Street job, at lineage rates, on the hard-pressed, low-budget *Evening Standard.* The fortunes of the paper had picked up during the war: it had been bought, in 1915, by Edward Hulton II. Watson offered Morton a job, at £400 a year (£500 in another of Morton's versions of the story, and eight guineas a week, according to a more reliable diary entry in 1919), and petitioned the War Office for Morton's immediate demobilisation so that he could start work.

Back at Chiseldon, Morton was faced with a choice that would determine the course of the rest of his life: to India with the Cavalry, or back to Fleet Street? In his *Memoir* Morton makes the most of the dramatic possibilities inherent in his having to have made such a stark choice. At the time, the choice may have appeared to him to have been a real one, but I doubt whether the Indian Cavalry stood much chance against a job with a London newspaper, however much Morton grumbled about the life of the reporter. Here is how he dramatises his interview with his colonel, which took place in a wooden hut, buried in snow – like a set from Chekhov or Tolstoy, as Morton points out:

'I have here' said the colonel, 'a telegram from the War Office ordering your immediate demobilisation. And here I have your request for a commission in the Indian Cavalry.'

'Yes, sir, I wish to withdraw it.'

'You wish to withdraw it?' There are moments when to echo a person's remark in a certain tone of wonderment implies not only devastating disapproval but also the probability that the person so addressed is not quite sane. It was one of those moments.

I explained that since I had applied for a commission in the Indian Cavalry I had been offered a civilian job and had decided to leave the Army. I could not tell him of the weeks spent with others of my own age and rank who, now faced with a return to civilian life, were half glad, half scared to death.

'And so you wish to return to civilian life?' said the colonel. 'By the way, what were you doing in civilian life?'

'I was a journalist.'

The colonel had suffered many a shock since he had been obliged to deal with temporary gentlemen, and now he winced and ground out his cigarette as if it tasted of arsenic.

'And you wish to go back to be a journalist?'

'I do.'

'Here' said the colonel, holding up the application papers for the Indian Cavalry, 'you have an honourable career and the life of a gentleman, and here,' he contemptuously waved the telegram, 'you have – what?'

In his dramatisation of his demobilisation interview, Morton makes fun of the colonel's snobbery, but there is something about the notion of the 'temporary gentleman' that resonates less comically than he perhaps intended. For all of his life, Morton was divided about how he wanted to be seen. On one hand, he liked the image of the anonymous, *déclassé* newspaperman, in trench coat and trilby, notebook in hand, skilfully levering a story out of an unpromising situation and taking it back to the inky office. On the other hand, he was attracted to the image of the acknowledged gentleman – the man he had felt himself to be when, in his immaculate breeches, boots and cavalry tunic, his spurs clinking, he had sauntered down Piccadilly. The war had temporarily made him a gentleman, and a commission in the Indian Cavalry would have made the change permanent. I think that what he hoped, as he left Salisbury Plain for Fleet Street, was that these two images might become one. Perhaps journalism might lead to some more enduring sort of writing which, in turn, might give him another route to the alluring world of the gentleman.

Morton left the interview with his colonel, said goodbye to the few acquaintances he'd made at the camp, and floundered off through the snow to the station. He was soon on a train, bound for London, and back to Fleet Street. His first civilian night was spent at the Langham Hotel, wrapped up in his 'British Warm' service greatcoat, giving himself up 'to anguish and doubt'.

> Any exhilaration I might have expected on getting out of the Army was absent. I felt lost, out of step and as bewildered by the size and indifference of London as I was when I came up from the provinces. I had married during the war and I now rang up my wife, Dorothy, in Birmingham to say that I was a civilian and suggested that she should come and find a flat. Still wearing a British Warm, I went the next morning to the offices of the *Evening Standard*.

What conclusions can be drawn about Morton's war service? Adderley's book on the history of the Warwickshire Yeomanry ends with an appendix listing the regiment's officers. The list distinguishes between those who served with the regiment overseas, and those who did not. Morton's name is among those who did not. The most reasonable conclusion, therefore, is that Morton, having dutifully and honourably enlisted in 1915, was never ordered into action. Maybe his spell of illness kept him out of one particular mission, and maybe he was never fully fit, but why he was required to stay in England throughout the three years of his enlistment, when there was such a shortage of troops for the battlefields, is a mystery.

The Great War defined a whole generation. For those who saw action and survived, nothing was ever the same again. For those who evaded the war, their reluctance to enlist was something to keep quiet about. Morton found himself in a curious half-way house. It is pretty conclusive that he wanted to serve his country. Why else would he have tried so hard to get himself fit enough to pass the army's medical board? Once in uniform and under King's Regulations he could not pick and choose where and when he'd fight. And the savagely high death rate of officers on the Western Front produced a ruthless demand for replacements. It is remotely possible, although there is no evidence, that the discreet patronage of Willoughby de Broke kept him out of the firing line, but it is unlikely. Morton seems to have been washed into a backwater of the war, where he slowly circled in the eddies at Colchester, waiting for orders for action that never came. His one chance for death or glory was snatched away by illness, or by a change in the plans for the operation, or both. At all events, his period of war service was a time that Morton chose not to recall in much detail. He seems, more than anything, to have found it somewhat embarrassing.

3

1919–1926

THE ESTABLISHED WRITER

The *Evening Standard* had gone up in the world a bit since its takeover by Hulton, but the atmosphere, and the staff, had not changed much during the six years that had elapsed since Morton, freshly arrived from the provinces, had first worked there: 'As if I had not been absent for a day, Percy handed me a cutting with the usual "See if there's anything in this."' Despite the fact that he'd freely chosen the life of a journalist over the life of a gentleman cavalry officer, Morton was not elated. In his *Memoir*, he recalled how dismal seemed the prospect of once again trudging off to follow up story after dull story. The one that Percy Watson had given him required him to trek out to White City, in west London, on a dull, drizzly day, to cover a sale of army surplus equipment: 'could anything have been more dreary or less worth writing about?' he wrote. The recollection of this early assignment strikes a note that was sounded regularly, throughout Morton's Fleet Street career: he alternated violently between loathing and loving the newspaper world. Almost simultaneously, he hated what he was having to do, and yet was proud of what he was able to do with the unpromising materials presented by routine reporting. In the case of the White City army surplus dump, he found himself suddenly brightening up, as he travelled back to the office:

I realised that I wanted to write about the dump – about anything. My alter ego, H. V. Morton, the journalist, absent for so long, had suddenly and unexpectedly returned to me and I knew that my three years training in that extraordinary trade had not been forgotten. 'Yes,' I said to myself (or rather H. V. Morton said to me) 'there *is* a story in this frightful dump if only you can get it past the subs.'

The article he wrote cruised safely past the sub-editors and was published on 11 March 1919, just a week after his demobilisation from the army. Morton intended to reprint the whole article in his *Memoir*, though not, he said, because he looked back at it as a particularly good example of his writing, but

> simply because it is probably the most important thing I ever wrote. It set the pattern for the slightly off-beat story which was to tide me over until I could do more developed work; and, above all, it saved me in the meantime from the worst drudgery of the reporting room.

The piece is whimsical and overwritten. Its central idea is that if only the 1,200,000 army boots at the White City dump could speak, they could tell a tale or two: they are, as the headline of the article proclaims, 'Boots that creak history'. The boots could tell of marches that reach 'to the sandy limits of Kut and reach to the walls of Bagdad [*sic*]; they tread the desert where the Sphinx watches, and they extend to the ruined pillars of Ctesiphon, where "only the lizard and the lion keep court." ' The article goes on to explain that the authorities at the dump are grading the boots and selling them off, and that there is a brisk market in country districts, where farmers and labourers buy them. 'It would be interesting to know if Hodge, the ploughman, homeward plodding his weary way, ever feels uplifted by the thought that his right boot may have explored the muddy maze of the Hindenburg line, while his left boot – if it has any squeak left in it – could tell him a strange story of the long white road that leads to Galilee.' The stylistic elements that Morton was later to deploy so skilfully are here laid on clumsily. The range of exotic reference is strained and ostentatious, and the attempt at lofty wit falls to earth: who was Morton to patronise Hodge, who probably knew enough about the muddy maze of the Hindenburg Line to last him a lifetime?

The return of Morton's alter ego had produced only an unmemorable piece, but Morton was right to see it as an early example of the sort of article that, when he'd fully mastered the style, would eventually get him out of Fleet Street and into hard covers. There was still a long way to go, though. In notes for the *Memoir*, he recalled a rather poignant discussion with an old journalist on the *Standard*, to whom he'd opened his heart. Morton had confessed that he felt that he was getting nowhere: 'I felt I was wasting my time writing drivel & wished I had stayed in the army.' 'I was writing smart Alick stories which I detested.' The old journalist T. H. Crosland, who had lost his only son during the war, took a fatherly interest in Morton and gave him advice about his writing. Morton's ambition was becoming clearer. As he described it in the *Memoir*: 'my ambition was to write myself out of Fleet Street into independence.'

Meanwhile, he developed a technique that would make his work as a reporter more endurable: he wrote up his reports of some of the events that he was covering before they had taken place. There are two entries in his 1919 diary where he notes why he did this. One reason was his pride in the quality of his copy. If he stayed punctiliously at an event until it concluded, and then wrote up his report, he might have had to telephone it back to the office, and, like all reporters, he hated the way in which the prose that he'd painstakingly written would sometimes be mangled by the copy-taker. One way to avoid this was to write the report before the event was over, and deliver it to the office personally. Thus, on 5 July 1919: 'Did the march of the London troops for the E.S. [*Evening Standard*], a column which I wrote without seeing the procession, which is always the best way.' Another reason for his unscrupulous practice was to increase the pleasure he might derive from the occasion he had been sent to report. On 16 July he noted that he'd recently been sent to cover two royal garden parties at Buckingham Palace. The first was a disappointment: he'd had to leave the party before it had really got going, in order first to write his story, and then to get to a telephone and dictate it to a copy-taker. He was not going to make the same mistake twice: 'The second party was a huge success. Determined to enjoy it, I wrote my account of it beforehand. It was in type before the guests began to assemble in the Mall!' Freed from the nuisance of having to report the actual event, he was able to mingle with the guests, among whom was Lord Willoughby de Broke, his old commanding officer. 'He was more at home at a garden party than in command of a yeomanry field day,' Morton noted in his diary. The royal host of the garden party, George V, was described by Morton as 'the rather pathetic little bearded man in the grey top hat'. But this rather ungallant characterisation of his monarch is tempered a little by Morton's continuing: 'my instincts are all Royalist and I rather wish our Kings could be real leaders again.' This is a casual, off-hand comment, but it indicates that Morton was not a natural democrat. He never systematically formulated his political views, either privately or in print, but they remained consistent with this seemingly bland expression of royalism, coupled with a fondness for 'real leaders'.

His status as a journalist on the *Evening Standard* steadily rose. In late January 1920 he was sent to Holland, accompanied by a photographer, to interview the Kaiser, who, following his nation's defeat in 1918, had fled to Holland, where he was living in seclusion in a country estate, between Arnhem and Utrecht. The chances of Morton's actually being given an audience with the Kaiser were vanishingly small: he had no letter of introduction and no experience of the niceties of European diplomacy. None the less, the pair set off across the channel with high hopes. The photographer was James Jarché. He later became famous as one of the foremost documentary photographers of the inter-war period, but at this time he was, like Morton, just beginning to make his way in Fleet Street. The two hit it off straight away, and they became lifelong friends.* The closest they got to the Kaiser was to stand on the outside of the high wall that surrounded the estate, listening to the sound of what a local resident told them was the Kaiser's daily exercise. In the words of Morton's report for the *Standard* on 2 February: 'While thousands in all parts of the world are asking "What is going to happen to him?" this white-haired man of 61 goes on calmly sawing wood on the other side of a 12 foot wall.' Sixty years later, recalling this incident in his *Memoir*, Morton gave rein to his impulse to connect events from different eras. Reflecting on the Kaiser's somewhat eccentric exercise programme, he wrote: 'how extraordinary to think that the arm that was able to saw [one of the Kaiser's arms was congenitally withered] had held the dying body of his maternal grandmother, Queen Victoria.' And then, again

*In 1933, they collaborated on a series on slum housing for the *Daily Herald*, later published as *What I Saw in the Slums*. See below, pp. 145–7.

in a typical, endearing, parenthetical query, he pondered, 'And why did Edward VII allow his nephew to support his dying mother?'

Back in 1920, and undaunted by their failure to get remotely within interviewing and photographing range of the Kaiser, Morton and Jarché – who had to lug with him the extremely bulky and heavy photographic equipment of the early 1920s – pushed on into Germany, staying in the most expensive hotels that they thought that the *Standard* would pay for, and sending back reports every day.

Most of Morton's reports have the witty, somewhat languid tone that was to characterise much of his later writing. In his report on 9 February from the border crossing between Holland and Germany, for instance, he advises: 'If you think of spending a holiday in Germany camouflaged as a business trip, let me advise you to be content with Bournemouth.' He dutifully interviews important people – the man who was to be Germany's *chargé d'affaires* in London, or a Hamburg shipping magnate, for example – but his reports come alive when he is telling the *Standard*'s readers about the high life in Berlin and its melodramatic contrast with life on the streets. In the 25 February edition he writes of a smart hotel in which the champagne is flowing:

> Outside, in the light of the tall lamps, a starved, white-faced ex-soldier, shivering in his field grey, hawks shoelaces; limps towards the enamelled door of a limousine, into which, with a flash of silk stockings, a jewelled and furred example of Berlin's newly rich enters, remarking, sympathetically to her cavalier, how hard it must be for the poor who have not yet received their coal ration!

The flash of silk stockings was to enliven many of Morton's later pieces. The reports he sent back from Germany in 1920 are chiefly in this vein, but one or two give a glimpse of a path that Morton chose not to tread very often. He was at his happiest and most confident when writing vignettes of social life, but he recognised that something politically momentous was happening in Germany. The value of the mark, for instance, plummeted while he was there. He saw the significance of a ruined post-war German economy. He told his readers that Germans were not militaristic and arrogant; rather, they were apathetic, 'demoralised – not defiant and nationalistic'. Commercial men, he reported, had suffered a 'moral collapse'. His conclusion, albeit somewhat tacitly expressed, was that if the allies pressed too hard for war reparations, they would destroy what was left of Germany. In his 26 February dispatch he quotes a businessman to whom he had spoken: 'If you are not very careful, you will draw not indemnities but blood.' Morton here was uncharacteristically shrewd and prescient. He rarely offered political analysis of this sort. He always preferred personal, idiosyncratic stories: international affairs rarely aroused his professional interest.

Morton knew enough by now of the newspaper world to realise that he wouldn't be received back in the London office as a conquering hero. He came back to 'the tepid approval, so usual in Fleet Street, of those who were afraid that more robust praise might provoke a request for a rise in salary'.

The recollection in the *Memoir* of his trip with Jarché to Germany was fondly written. But the next incident at the *Standard*, despite four or five attempts by the elderly Morton to rough out a recollection, never made its way to the typed version. This memory, by contrast, was evidently painful. On 18 October 1921, he was sacked. He had spent the morning among cows and milkmaids, covering a dairy show at Islington. On returning to the office he plucked a letter from his rack. It contained three months' salary and a letter of dismissal. He recognised that among his faults were over-confidence and complacency, but he couldn't believe that these were the cause of his sacking. Abrupt dismissals were (and are) common in Fleet Street, but, understandably enough, Morton felt insulted and humiliated. Eventually, by asking around, he assembled a story that would account for the treatment he'd suffered, although he could never establish the exact provenance of the story. He heard that the proprietor of the *Standard*, Edward Hulton, had asked his editor if the 'H.V.M.' who wrote for the paper was related to the Joseph Vollam Morton who used to edit the *Manchester Evening Chronicle*. When he was told that they were father and son, Hulton, according to the story that Morton heard, said, 'Get rid of him at once.' Back in 1902 or 1903, Morton's father had resented the way in which the same Hulton, to whom he was then supposed to be teaching the business of editing a paper, had, instead of submitting to instruction, tried to lord it over him.* The final straw had been placed on the breaking back of this relationship between editor and proprietor's son when Morton's father had returned one day to his office to find Hulton sitting in the editor's chair with his feet up on the desk. Morton's father had ordered him out. Now, in 1921, Hulton had come into his own as the proprietor of the *Standard*, and could take revenge by proxy: he fired the son of the man who, twenty years earlier in Manchester, had ordered him out of the editor's office. Morton never met Hulton, but the resentment he felt at being fired by him did not diminish as he got older. He kept, as a memento, details of a dinner that was given for him by the staff of the *Standard* when he left. In 1978, the year before he died, he added a note to it: 'This was a dinner given to me by the staff of the *Evening Standard* when I was sacked by that unpleasant oaf Sir Edward Hulton. He hated my father and visited his hatred upon me. I was very upset.'

Morton was not out of work for long. In November 1921, a month after his sacking by Hulton, he was taken on by Beaverbrook's *Daily Express*, then edited by Guy Pollock. Morton's salary was now eighteen guineas a week – more than three times as much as the £6 he'd been paid when he'd first been taken on to the staff of the *Standard*, back in 1913. Within a year of his new appointment, he was promoted to Literary Editor of the paper, a promotion, he recalled, that sounded grander than it really was. But it took him into the *Express's* circle of writers – as opposed to reporters. Two particularly colourful figures were D. B. Wyndham Lewis (Bevan Lewis), creator of the 'Beachcomber' column, and Lewis's successor, J. B. Morton, the writer with whom the column is most famously associated.† I imagine that Morton felt that he was starting to make real progress when he began to associate with such writers: he writes very warmly about them in the *Memoir*. His sketch of J. B. Morton is particularly interesting, for it describes him as the sort of man that readers of Morton's own *In Search of England*, which started life as a series of articles for the *Express*, might well have imagined H. V. Morton himself to be.

J. B. Morton was an admirer of Hilaire Belloc, the writer who

---

*See above, pp. 3–4.
†Names are confusing here. D. B. Wyndham Lewis is not Percy Wyndham Lewis the vorticist painter, and J. B. Morton was no relation of H. V. Morton.

59

celebrated the 'South Country', the downland landscape of southern England, and particularly of Sussex. Morton recalled a moment in the *Express* office:

> I remember one morning in 1922 when, hearing a banging and a great clatter approaching, Bevan [Wyndham Lewis] turned to me with a sigh and a shrug to indicate that Johnny Morton was approaching. Soon our door was flung wide. Before us stood a short, sturdy young man with a fresh complexion, wearing old army breeches and a pair of dirty field boots. His eyes were blue and angry, his hair was tousled and he had not shaved over the weekend. He grasped his 'great staff' Durendal [named after the sword carried by Roland, the hero of a French medieval romance] which he now flung with a clatter into a corner of the room. 'Hallo hogs!' he shouted, addressing us in a voice that would have carried across Trafalgar Square. 'While you have been sweating in this filthy city I have been walking the roads of Sussex – I and Durendal!' He paused. 'And,' he said, pointing a toe, as if he were about to dance a minuet, 'we have also walked the roads of Kent!' He then began to dance, thumping and banging in his great knee boots, while he sang at the top of his voice,

> 'All the bluebells rang with joy as we came into Kent.'

Johnny Morton was a more rumbustious character than the narrator of *In Search of England*, and I am not suggesting that he exerted much of a stylistic influence on H. V. Morton, but it is interesting that Morton, who at this time seems to have been entirely metropolitan in his tastes – save for a liking for exciting trips abroad – should have been impressed by a man who brought the dust from the lanes of the English countryside into the Fleet Street office. The lanes of Morton's own youth in Warwickshire, and his bicycle, had been left behind, seemingly without a backward glance, when he went up to London. *In Search of England* appears to spring from a deep, abiding love of the countryside, but there is scarcely a sign of this passion in Morton's life during the years that run up to its publication. He certainly did want to travel, but the sort of journeys he had in mind were not of the rucksack-and-freedom-of-the-open-road sort: he preferred the luxurious trips financed by his employers. For example, a diary entry made back in March 1921, when he was still working on the *Standard*, records his delight in having managed to wangle a foreign trip – this time with Dorothy: 'We are going to Italy! Have got free tickets to Bologna & think I can work passes in Italy. Hurrah!'

In London, though, his delight was to be counted now among Beaverbrook's 'young lions'. He recalled dinners at the Savoy, given by the proprietor for his young staff. At one such dinner, he 'was greatly helped through the evening by mixing Bollinger with Clicquot and never refusing a passing refill of Mumm'. Even half a century later, when writing these reminiscences, Morton was plainly keen to show how he'd been rising in the world during the 1920s. And in the diaries he kept at the time, whenever he took Dorothy out to dinner, or was himself wined and dined, he proudly noted the vintage of the wines he drank. But his pride and pleasure in being part of this brilliant world were always balanced by outbursts of hatred for it. He noted in his diary on 24 February 1921 that only two things were of interest to him at that moment. The first was 'a general loathing of journalism. At times I simply hate it.' He goes on savagely to characterise journalists, but the characterisation maybe fitted Morton himself. Perhaps there was a touch of self-loathing in his observation about the world of journalism: 'It is full of clever half-educated men with a distorted sense of value.'

The second thing that he recorded in this diary entry balances his hatred of journalism: 'I have had a big revival of interest in Roman archaeology . . . This love of mine for Roman things burns fiercely and seems to light up everything while the fever lasts. I dream of writing a novel about Roman London.' His boyhood passion for the ancient worlds of Rome and Egypt had never waned. He was still as keen as ever to add to his collection of antiquities. He haunted the London antiquarian shops, and, as he grew more affluent and well-connected, he started meeting professional scholars of the topics that fascinated him. He got to know, for example, Sir Flinders Petrie, the archaeologist of ancient Egypt, and Sir Ernest Budge, keeper of the British Museum's Egyptian collection. Morton's next major foreign assignment came as a direct result of his growing expertise in the history and archaeology of Ancient Egypt. In January 1923, he was sent by the *Express* to cover the

opening of Tutankhamun's burial chamber. The trip was tremendously important to Morton, and he devoted a whole chapter in his
Memoir to his recollections of this great international news story and of
his part in it. The importance for Morton was threefold. First, it was
only by an extraordinary stroke of good luck that he was sent on the
assignment. Secondly, the assignment finally proved to Morton and to
his editor that he could operate at the highest and most competitive
levels of journalism. And thirdly, it gave him the chance to visit the
Middle East, a region that was eventually to produce some of his best
travel writing.

The story starts back in 1907, when the rich amateur archaeologist
Lord Carnarvon teamed up with the professional Howard Carter and
started excavating in the Valley of the Kings in the hope of finding a
royal tomb. Successive yearly digs brought nothing sensational to the
surface, but hope of a breakthrough was kept alive. The Great War put
a temporary end to their excavations, but in 1917 the pair resumed, and
toiled on, with their band of labourers, for a further six years. When the
1922 season began, in November, Carnarvon was in England, but
Carter had made a start. He soon stumbled upon an entrance leading
down into what would turn out to be the Tomb of Tutankhamun. He
left the entrance sealed up until Carnarvon could be cabled, and could
complete the lengthy train, boat and ultimately donkey journey that
would bring him back to the Valley of the Kings. When Carnarvon
arrived, together they broke through the sealed door and found
themselves in a rubble-filled passage that ended at another door. This
door gave on to a room piled high with objects associated with the
burial. Two life-sized statues guarded a section of plastered wall,
behind which, it was confidently guessed, the royal tomb itself lay. For
the time being, they went no further: they left the wall to the tomb
intact. They were staggered by the riches they had already discovered
in the anteroom and decided that they had better proceed cautiously.
Carter went to Cairo to commission the construction of a steel door
that would protect the entrance until arrangements for the systematic
study and emptying of the antechamber and the tomb itself could be
made. Carnarvon returned to England.

A report of the breakthrough in the Valley of the Kings reached the
Times, 'by runner to Luxor', and Morton was thrilled by it, although at

that time – late in 1922 – the *Express* was intending no more than to have its man in Cairo keep an eye on the story. The editor, Guy Pollock, certainly had no intention of sending Morton, the paper's Literary Editor, off to Egypt. To satisfy his own interest, Morton went to the British Museum to discuss the significance of Carter's and Carnarvon's work with Ernest Budge, and recalled, 'It was a wonderful story and I walked through the December streets of London with my head full of Luxor and the tomb.'

Meanwhile, Carnarvon was trying to free himself and his beloved project from the clamour that the world's press was starting to send up. In the hope of keeping reporters at bay, he struck a deal with *The Times* to give them exclusive rights to the coverage of the opening of the tomb. It was agreed that *The Times* should send the distinguished war correspondent Sir Perry Robinson to cover the story. Any other paper would then be free to buy the story from *The Times*. As Morton put it in his *Memoir*,

> The offer split Fleet Street and, beyond Fleet Street, the Press of the world. Some newspapers were willing to subscribe to the *Times* service, but a great number refused to do so, either because they thought the monopoly incompatible with the freedom of the Press, or because they feared that Sir Perry Robinson might be a bit heavy for their readers.

The upshot was that the *Express*, the *Mail* and the *Morning Post*, followed quickly by Reuters, decided to send reporters to Luxor and to offer rival subscription services to that offered by *The Times*. Morton was still not remotely being considered by Pollock to represent the *Express*, but at the last minute, the reporter who was chosen could not go. Morton seized his chance. He wrote a leader on mummification to show Pollock that he knew what he was talking about, and then dashed home, packed up his precious collection of Egyptian antiquities, brought them back to the office and displayed them before Pollock. He concluded his presentation by writing Pollock's name for him in hieroglyphs. Three days later, to Morton's 'inexpressible joy and astonishment', Pollock appointed him as the *Express*'s man in Luxor. Morton's boyish enthusiasm, and his eagerness to impress his editor with his exhibits, shine through the account that the eighty-year-old wrote up for his *Memoir*. Plainly, he regarded the Tutankhamun assignment as one of the high points of his career.

His next stop was a tropical outfitter's on Ludgate Hill, one of the many shops in London that kitted out the men and women who ran the British Empire. 'It was a proud moment for me when I strode in and announced that I was leaving for Cairo in two days' time.' Naturally, a solar topi, or pith helmet, was one of the first essential items to be recommended.

Leaving London in January 1923, he made his way to Cairo, via Calais, Paris, the Orient Express to Venice and Trieste, and then a ship to Alexandria. Throughout the journey he wondered if he were really up to the job, but his self-doubt was dispelled when

> one day in the afternoon I went on deck and laughed with sheer delight as I saw upon the horizon a shining white line which was Alexandria. My adventures were beginning. How splendid it was to be alive! There came to me across the water the smell of Egypt, a hot dusty, minty smell. Perhaps Herodotus and Strabo had been aware of it; perhaps Alexander, Caesar and Antony had known it. I watched fascinated as the palm trees took shape and the sun dipped lower. During the train journey to Cairo, darkness fell. I remember with what delight I watched the green canalscape of the Delta pass, with its palm groves, its dusty cavalcades of donkeys, its towns and villages, the wood smoke hanging in the air, then suddenly, apparently in the middle of a field, a felucca with a huge lateen sail like a stranded moth.

Again, this is from the *Memoir*. The elderly Morton evidently could still turn out an agreeable paragraph, although the manuscript shows that nothing came without effort; every sentence has been revised and revised again. In this example, two of his characteristic stylistic modes are in play. First, he sets his impressions against a lengthy historical timescale, peopled with ancient heroes. His childhood habit of wondering if a Roman had ever stood precisely on the spot in Moseley that he himself stood upon never left him. And secondly, he gives his descriptions of places a lift by using an unexpected adjective – like 'minty' to describe the smell of Egypt – or by devising a vivid simile – the Nile felucca's sail is compared to the wing of a moth.

At Luxor, Morton became friendly with two other journalists who were trying, like him, to outwit *The Times*. According to the *Memoir*, the trio, Arthur Weigall of the *Daily Mail*, Valentine Williams of Reuters, and Morton, decided to work together. Weigall was an Egyptologist, Williams was an expert foreign correspondent, and Morton described himself as 'an active and willing dog's-body'. Each of them represented a large number of papers that had subscribed to the services that they were offering, in competition to *The Times*. Morton proudly noted that he represented over ninety papers himself. It was clear, though, that Carnarvon and *The Times*, with the co-operation of the Egyptian authorities, had made a very tight deal. The actual royal tomb had not yet been opened, and the trio, along with the rest of the press, were kept away from the excavation site. They were obliged to watch from a distance as load after load of fabulous items, interred for three thousand years, was carried up from the tomb's antechamber into the blinding light. Protests from the press eventually made the Egyptian authorities relent a little, and, once a week, reporters were allowed into the antechamber. Morton's visit to the half-cleared room thrilled him. He wrote about it in his *Memoir* as if it had happened not half a century earlier, but half an hour. He recalled wandering among the three-thousand-year-old clutter, marvelling at the incongruity of a dismantled chariot, stacked there ready for any journey the dead pharaoh might need to take, and at the poignancy of a discarded funeral bouquet, disintegrating into dust now that the twentieth century air had reached it. Summing up his experience, he wrote:

> I climbed up into the sunlight. I had expected my feelings to be those of a privileged amateur Egyptologist, but, oddly perhaps, I did not think much of Egyptology. Instead I was awed – stunned is almost the word – by the liberty I had taken with Time. As I saw the objects piled up, boxes on chairs, chariot wheels, alabaster vases and lamps of alabaster, mummified ducks and various foods for the king for his long journey into the shades, I thought of the hands that had placed them in just that order thirty centuries ago. No hand had touched them since. And during that time, Athens and Rome had come and gone. Nothing stranger would ever happen to me.

He had written another version of his visit to the tomb's antechamber for his *Through Lands of the Bible*, published in 1938. I shall come to this book in its turn, but in order to exhibit Morton's vivid way of conveying the lapse of long passages of historical time, a fragment will be useful here. In the antechamber, standing either side of the entrance in the wall that protected the actual tomb, were two life-sized statues.

> It was a queer experience to stand beside the two guardian statues of the king and to know that when Alexander the Great was born they had already been there for over a thousand years, grasping their thin wands of office, and that their incredible vigil had lengthened to nearly two thousand years by the time William the Conqueror set foot in England.[1]

Morton wrote not for professional historians but for a huge popular readership. It was touches like these, that brought to life aspects of the passage of time that professionals take for granted, that made him successful.

Luxor was alive with rumours about the date and time when the wall into the actual tomb of Tutankhamun would be broken down. The trio of Morton, Williams and Weigall monitored them all, including those that they elicited themselves by means of hefty bribes. One rumour was that the tomb would be opened at night, in the hope that spectators would be absent. The trio elected Morton to mount a night watch at the site. This was quite a dangerous undertaking, for the site was on the western bank of the Nile, across the river from the hotel. Tourists were advised not to go to the western side of the river after nightfall. Two people had recently been murdered there. Understandably, Morton never forgot his anxious night under the stars, and, wrote two accounts of it, one in *Through Lands of the Bible*,[2] and, half a century later, another in his *Memoir*. From the far shore of the river, he and his donkey boy, who was armed with a large club, set off up into the hills overlooking the tomb. They watched the fires of the guards slowly burn out and, as midnight approached, concluded, from the sleeping silence of the encampment around the entrance to the tomb, that no activity was planned for the night. But Morton felt that he had to stick it out: 'I lay there, it seemed, for uncountable ages, listening to the night sounds of the Theban hills: the far-off yapping of jackals by the Nile; a sudden inexplicable, soft scurry or scamper among the rocks, a desert rat maybe, perhaps a night adder . . .' Then, in this passage from the *Memoir*, he used the characteristic device of slight self-deprecation, or loss of dignity, to modify the picture of intrepidity that he'd been building up:

> It was at that moment that my donkey, perhaps catching my mood, lifted its head and sent out over the hills a wavering hee-haw, laden with sorrow and loneliness. I was appalled. I expected to see the guard turn out at the tomb. I expected thieves and murderers, with whom the desert was reputed to be infested, to locate us with ease. But how to silence the donkey? Its owner confessed himself helpless. Whipping off my braces, we tightly tied the jawbones of the ass.

Using one's braces to bind the jaws of a braying donkey, in the face of the helplessness of the local 'boy', is an example of a recognisable trope in travel writing, and one that Morton relied on. The scene is exotic, the traveller is brave and resourceful, the anonymous, 'helpless' native is patronised, and the traveller himself takes pleasure in the revelation of his own, comic, momentary loss of dignity.

The tomb was opened, not secretly at night, but with advance notice, on Friday 16 February 1923. Valentine Williams, the Reuters member of the trio, was hoping to get the news of the opening back to London for the evening editions. He succeeded. He got his cable away first, and thereby scooped *The Times*. Williams's plan was meticulously prepared. It required guile, fortified by bribes, and the reconnoitring of the fastest possible route from the tomb to the cable office in Luxor. This in turn required a new car, bought especially for the purpose of carrying him from the tomb to the river (with a string of donkeys posted along the route to the river as a backup). Then, a hired felucca was deployed to carry him across to the eastern bank, from where a Model T Ford, one of its wheels, in the absence of a tyre, newly shod with rope, stood ready to take him and his cable to the office. In London, Lady Carnarvon learned of her husband's success in finding Tutankhamun's sarcophagus when she saw the *Evening Standard* that night. The anti-*Times* trio then composed and despatched their overnight cables for the Saturday morning editions of their papers, and finally, ordered champagne to be put on ice, and dressed for dinner.[3]

The headline story on the front page of the *Daily Express* for Saturday 17 February 1923, by 'H. V. Morton, Special correspondent', makes the very most of the chiefly second-hand information that the trio had gathered. Morton's report concedes that he was not actually at Carnavon's side when the wall to the tomb was broken down, but it gives readers a strong impression that their special correspondent was, in all important respects, in at the kill. (See plates 5 and 6.)

Obviously, when the elderly Morton came to write up his recollections of his first major international news story, he made the very most of his role in the events at Luxor. And in an interview with a writer who visited him at the Cape, when Morton was in his eighties, Morton was keen to regale his visitor with a detailed account of the events at Luxor that had unfolded half a century earlier. He gave, for example, memories of devious meetings with officials who could be persuaded to reveal what was going on in the excavations. The Tutankhamun story, Morton said during the interview, was 'the greatest story I ever covered'.[4] Not surprisingly perhaps, the account written by Williams does not give Morton quite the star billing that Morton gave himself. There is, for example, not a word about Morton's risky night vigil in the desert.[5] And in any case, the recollections of two reporters of an episode in the history of Fleet Street rivalry seem now to be a bit anti-climactic. By and large *The Times* defended its monopoly, and Morton got no story that was denied to the other reporters. But the trip to Egypt made an enormous impact on him. It confirmed that he could hold his own, professionally, with heavyweight journalists, covering a major international story. But perhaps more important, it gave him a new taste for travel. He had, of course, been abroad before, but Cairo, Luxor and the Valley of the Kings were altogether different, not just because of their obvious, exciting exoticism, but because they gave him the opportunity to experience the very sources of the culture whose relics he had been avidly collecting since he was a boy.

'I stayed on at Luxor,' he wrote, 'until the season's work was ended and the tomb was covered in again. Unable to resist a longing to see Jerusalem, I returned to England by way of Palestine.' Strangely, with his head full of Tutankhamun, and with the exciting prospect of seeing Jerusalem before him, this detour sowed a seed that three years later would grow into a series of articles for the *Daily Express*, which in turn would be published as *In Search of England*. Perhaps, though, it is not so strange. Maybe the most intense feelings for home come to those who are alone and thousands of miles away from it. And these feelings are doubly intense if the exile is ill and doubtful of ever seeing home again. The much-quoted opening of *In Search of England* dramatises such feelings:

> I believed that I was dying in Palestine. There was no woman to convince me that the pain in my neck was not the first sign of spinal meningitis . . . In the black depths of misery, I climbed a hill overlooking Jerusalem . . . and, turning as accurately as I could in the direction of England, I gave way to a wave of home-sickness that almost shames me now when I recollect it . . .
>
> There rose up in my mind the picture of a village street at dusk with a smell of wood smoke in the still air and, here and there, little red blinds shining in the dusk under the thatch. I remembered how the church bells ring at home, and how, at that time of year, the sun leaves a dull red bar low down in the west, and against it the elms grow blacker by the minute. Then the bats start to flicker like little bits of burnt paper and you hear the slow jingle of a team coming home from the fields . . .
>
> I took a vow that if my pain in the neck did not end for ever on the windy hills of Palestine I would go home in search of England, I would go through the lanes of England and the little thatched villages of England, and I would lean over English bridges and lie on English grass, watching an English sky.[6]

This is Morton at his most potent and I shall return to his highly charged evocation of England later. I set it out here, in advance, so that I can explore the interval between the experience that Morton recalls, and the publication of the book that it inspired. There are no diaries against which his artful recollection of his illness in Palestine can be checked. All we have to go on is the dramatised version from *In Search of England*, and some notes he made, in old age, for his *Memoir*. In these scarcely legible notes he wrote: 'The genesis of a book is often interesting if the writer can really trace the first moment of generation. In this case I am able to do so.' He says that he caught a cold while on a train crossing the Sinai desert on his way to Jerusalem. This put him on his back for a couple of days in a hotel. He was, he goes on, in no fit state to absorb impressions of the city that he'd come so far to see. He spent his few days there feeling very feverish, wandering about, and sitting in a Greek taverna, eating, and drinking ouzo. His notes broadly confirm the account with which he brilliantly opened *In Search of England*, although they are not as highly coloured. He says that in the feverish, hallucinatory state produced by his cold, he really did have a vision of England, and that he promised himself, there and then, that if he recovered and got home again, he would 'travel about England, of which I knew nothing, except Warwickshire within a cycle ride of Birmingham'. Incidentally, no vision of his family, equivalent to his vision of England, is recorded in his notes, and there is not a word about the political condition of Palestine, then under the British mandate. It must be remembered, though, that he was drafting a memoir of his literary, not his personal life.

These recollections, and the first page of *In Search of England*, set up an expectation that as soon as Morton got back to England, he would have pulled on his boots, seized his walking stick, and, like his colleague J. B. Morton, set off down the dusty lanes in search of the vision he'd had in Jerusalem. But he did nothing of the sort. He returned to the *Daily Express* office and resumed his love-hate relationship with metropolitan journalism. His energies were directed not toward a search for the England of thatched cottages and jingling teams of shire horses, but, often less than whole-heartedly, toward the routine assignments that came his way from the editor. Morton did, I think, have a memorable vision of rural England when he was ill in Palestine in 1923, but it was not so all-consuming that he was driven to put everything in his life to one side while he pursued it. First and last, he was a professional writer, trying to make a living, and he was able, as it were, to file that vision of England away for three years while he got on with other, more pressing work, and then bring it out again to provide the brilliant opening to his most famous book.

When he returned to the *Express* offices from his trip to Egypt and Palestine he was, as he put it, 'innocent enough to expect a pat on the back' for his coverage of the Tutankhamun story. His expectation was not fulfilled, for there had been a palace revolution while he had been away. As a consequence, his welcome back was distinctly offhand. Guy Pollock, the editor who had sent him to Luxor, had gone, and had been replaced by Beverley Baxter. This had led to a shuffling of seats further down the line of command, and Morton found his old desk occupied by a new man. Morton's contract with the paper was still intact, but he found it difficult to settle back into the *Express* world.

> My Via Dolorosa led eventually back to the Big Room [where reporters and editorial staff worked] . . . to hours of hanging about, of sitting on the edge of desks, of chain-smoked cigarettes, of perilous invitations to pop over to the Falstaff [a public house], of too frequent cups of strong tea and eventually of sudden, feverish activity. What almost broke my spirit was the pointless and unconstructive character of my life. It was impossible to do anything with the great amount of spare time except to wait about, and the future gnawed at me . . . I sometimes think that my subsequent life was founded on a flight from the Big Room.

The spasms of contempt for the whole world of newspaper journalism that periodically racked Morton were not always entirely concealed from his new editor: in his *Memoir* Morton recalled that he took a savage sort of pleasure, during editorial conferences, in rubbishing the morning's edition of the newspaper, especially if his colleagues were, in his opinion, too pleased with it. This could hardly have endeared him to Baxter.

However, as usual, Morton's spasms of contempt were balanced by periods of immense satisfaction with the world in which he was now able confidently and suavely to operate. He continued to enjoy the well-financed trips abroad that came his way:

> Weeks of boredom were forgotten in a sudden unexpected trip abroad with the excitement of being plunged into some foreign crisis or pageant. And it was done in the greatest comfort: the Palace Hotel or the Ritz in Madrid, the Continental in Paris, the Excelsior in Rome, the Danieli in Venice and Bertollini's in Naples.

And along with the excitement and luxury went a certain style that Morton found irresistible:

> When I was new to the game an old foreign correspondent gave me a tip. 'My boy,' he said, 'always keep a silk hat and evening clothes in the office in case you're sent abroad in a hurry. No foreign police cordon can resist an Englishman in silk hat, white tie and tails.'

Glamorous in a different way was a trip to Klosters, in the Swiss Alps, to write about the experience of taking a mountaineering course run by the Swiss Alpine Club.

He complained to his diary and to Dorothy that he was not earning enough money, and, from time to time, he gave way to bouts of hatred for the whole world of newspapers, but he was now being sent on more interesting assignments, and was getting his name printed alongside some of his articles. In his *Memoir*, he veered between expressions of pride and expressions of frustration when he tried to deliver a judgement on his years as a newspaper man. Here is one of his rosier reflections:

> The 'Gay Twenties' were a wonderful time for me, a time of hard work, which I enjoyed, a time of constant movement and variety. I never knew in the morning when I came on duty whether I should be describing Crufts or catching the Channel boat on my way to Paris. When there was no obvious story to cover I found my own themes, contributing an almost daily article on some topical event which was signed 'H.V.M.' and became a popular feature of the paper. Reading some of them now, I regret a certain vein of facetiousness in some of them which I would not pass today; but then I am fifty years older.

One of the jobs he was given at the *Express* was to write a new gossip column, which he signed 'Dragoman'. (The Arab guides and translators that Morton had used in Egypt were known as 'dragomen'.) Beaverbrook enjoyed the column and it became an established feature in the paper. The authorship soon passed from Morton and was eventually handed to the young Tom Driberg, who, writing under the name 'William Hickey', made the column even more popular and durable.

Despite his outbursts against the newspaper world, Morton was doing well professionally. A number of his Fleet Street contemporaries published autobiographies during the 1930s and their references to Morton show that he had a considerable presence on the *Express*. The editor, Baxter, with whom Morton was to have a stormy relationship, recalled, rather inscrutably, that Morton was 'a young man of subtle charms with a mind that was Western in its penetration and Eastern in its foundation. He was as sensitive as a schoolgirl and as shrewd as a Rothschild.'[7] This seems not to have been intended as a compliment. Even his praise of Morton's writing – 'delicate and full of feeling' – looks a bit faint. What Baxter's characterisation perhaps hints at is that he had detected the Anglo-Indian strain in Morton's ancestry, was guessing at a Jewish strain, and was using both in what would today be seen as a subtly racist slur. Other Fleet Street contemporaries were both more forthright and affectionate than Baxter. S. P. B. Mais, then a junior member of staff on the *Express*, was awed by the hierarchy of the paper's big room:

One corner of the room was partitioned off into a tiny cupboard in which sat three 'star' reporters, each armed with a typewriter. Their names were H. V. Morton, J. B. Morton, and Bevan Dominic Wyndham Lewis.

H. V. Morton was a thin, tall, quiet man with a deathly pale face and a passion for Egyptology . . . In those days he was sent out on all the biggest stories and invariably came back with the least fuss and the best results. He was, and is, entirely devoid of arrogance, haste, bluster, or any of the attributes that we are apt to associate with the 'Star' reporter.[8]

Morton evidently made such an impression on Mais that Mais recollected him as a tall man. In fact, as Morton's army medical report shows, he was of no more than average height – five feet eight inches, although he was thin and pale. (See plate 7.) It is notable too that Mais recalled Morton as being 'devoid of arrogance'. This is the exact opposite of the view that Baxter took. But Mais, of course, was not Morton's editor.

Finally, Collie Knox, who, like Mais was a junior on the *Express* during the 1920s, recalled the awe he felt when

such gods as H. V. Morton and Hannen Swaffer descended from their
thrones and entered the news room. With longing eyes I gazed at them.
For here indeed were names with which to conjure. They were in receipt
of more money per week than I earned in a year. I followed these men
with envious eyes as they stood surveying the room. Lords of all they
surveyed.

Knox said that as a young reporter he had wanted to be 'a second H. V.
Morton', and he defined what he thought it was that made Morton's
stories distinctive. He also says something about the strained relations
between Morton and Baxter. According to Knox, Morton would

> attend a national ceremony with every other newspaper star writer, and
> he will notice that a shy little woman in black with a medal ribbon
> pinned on her breast is sobbing in a corner. While the other writers will
> concentrate on the obvious highlights, the pomp and splendour, Harry
> Morton will hang his story on the little woman in black. Instantly she
> will stand out as the central figure and she will live before the reader.
>
> I know that Baxter had a few tussles with 'H.V.' If he did not think
> that a story was worthy of his time or his talent, he would refuse to go
> out on it. Baxter once said that he would rather deal with a tempera-
> mental prima donna than with H.V. when he was in that mood.[9]

Plainly then, despite his feuds with Baxter, Morton was collecting
admirers and was becoming established as one of the *Express*'s star
writers. His domestic life, by contrast, seems not to have been a great
success. He and Dorothy had established themselves in London, first in
a flat, and then a house, both in Dulwich. Their first child, Michael,
was born in 1919, and two further children followed within a few years
– Barbara in 1922, and John in 1926. Morton wrote about his marriage
neither in his *Memoir* nor in the voluminous notebooks from which it
was extracted. If he had lived long enough to see the *Memoir* in print,
his readers would have learned next to nothing about his personal life
– nor indeed about his political or religious views, or anything else not
strictly related to his career as a writer. But the few diaries that survive
from this period of his life, and a few, scattered, oblique recollections
in his notebooks, offer occasional glimpses of the private life of the

young journalist who was starting at last to make real headway in Fleet Street.

As the money started to come in, he and Dorothy could start to enjoy the West End world of the Bright Young Things:

> Life seemed to me almost too good to be true. A Savile Row suit cost 12 guineas, & there was so little social malice that we could, and after the theatre did, stroll on a summer's night along Piccadilly in white tie and tails wearing a silk hat, one's partner in evening dress, & no-one turning to look or comment.

The arrival of the babies diminished Dorothy's opportunities to go out, and although there are diary entries that testify to a contented family life in Dulwich, Morton was beginning to seek pleasures elsewhere. The partner on Morton's arm as he strolled down Piccadilly was not always Dorothy.

His liaisons seem at first to have been casual, and they are registered in his diary by such comments as 'arrived home feeling rather cheap', and by entries on the following days that record lavish spending on Dorothy – on clothes, or presents. Judging by the dates that are sometimes scribbled alongside the names of women in his list of sexual encounters, he was maintaining an energetic programme of extra-marital sex during the 1920s, and as the decade wore on, some of his casual liaisons turned into more systematic, calculated affairs.

Between 1924 and 1927, he had an intermittent, seemingly deeply-felt affair with a woman called 'Theo' – presumably a shortened form of 'Theodora'. The affair was conducted in Paris, in Cannes, in London, and in Bath. He recorded its progress in a notebook – although 'recorded' is too neutral a word to convey the mode in which he wrote. It looks as if he composed the notebook entries in four or five bursts, each intensely evoking his meetings with the woman. He artfully sketches in the background, writes passages of dialogue that give much more explicit voice to the woman's presumed feelings than to his own, and uses the present tense, as if he is reliving the events he's recording. For example, in Paris they are in the back of a taxi, looking for a hotel where they can pass as a couple: 'I feel the naked flesh of her leg where the stocking ends. We long for one another, O passionately.'

They book in to the hotel: 'Two large bare impersonal rooms reeking of old scent & the ghost of lechery. We blush & feel beastly & laugh & pass it off.' The notebook indicates that, despite the sexual desire, there was in Morton's heart something that Graham Greene said all writers must have – a 'splinter of ice' that keeps one part of them cold and detached enough to turn experience into literature. In Paris, temporarily apart from the woman, and despite the seemingly all-consuming physical passion of the encounter, he cannot resist the sort of observation that later would characterise his books: 'Slept fitfully in a room overlooking the Rue St Honoré with the window open. O noise: people singing, chattering, noisy engines & those characteristic French motor horns, some an octave of sharp agonised sound apart.' Morton is no Graham Greene, and the notebook entry was not turned into great literature, but it was a stage on the road to his emergence as a writer who could deftly establish place, mood, and character.

In 1925, Morton's affair with Theo was given an unexpected boost when a quite unrelated event gave him the chance to meet her in France again. The event was a strange coda to his sacking from the *Evening Standard* by Hulton, back in 1921. Morton scribbled, almost illegibly, this coda in one of the rough notebooks for the *Memoir*. While he had been busy establishing himself in his new job on the *Express*, Hulton had become ill and had retired, after selling his newspaper interests. One Saturday night in March 1925, Morton was phoned up by his new proprietor, Lord Beaverbrook, and asked if he could go at once to the south of France to deliver a supply of capsules of the newly-discovered drug insulin to Hulton, who was dying of diabetes. He was advised to carry the capsules discreetly, lest he be taken for a drug smuggler. Morton thought it odd that he, who 'detested newspaper Caesars', should have been asked to drop everything and transport medicines that might save the life of one. But the prospect of a trip to Cannes was irresistible: 'I gladly agreed to do this, and within an hour, a motor cyclist brought me a small parcel, a return ticket on the Blue Train & a wad of five pound notes.' The impulse to overcome his dislike of Hulton may have been fired by more than the wad of notes and the prospect of a trip to the French Riviera – although these would probably have been enough. It seems that he took the chance that this assignment presented him with to arrange quickly an assignation with his mistress: the notebook that records Morton's steamy affair has some entries made between 2 and 5 March 1925 that speak of a trip with Theo to Cannes: 'The Blue Train . . . My sleeping car over the rear wheels & she there in the dark saying goodnight . . . In my arms.' Money, a luxurious train journey to the Mediterranean and a few days with a mistress were, it seems, sufficient to suppress any qualms about the nominal purpose of the assignment – the saving of the oafish Hulton's life. In any case, Morton's journey could not have made much difference, for Hulton died a couple of months later, on 23 May 1925.

The woman with whom Morton had this affair appears as number eight on his list of sexual encounters. There are another hundred or so that follow her. Morton was becoming an accomplished, compulsive adulterer. He even devised a little symbol that he would draw in the margin of his diary to record encounters, although many were the result, not of his personal magnetism, but of cash payments: he picked up prostitutes and probably visited brothels, often when he was abroad on newspaper business. But the particular woman recorded in the notebook must have been special, for fifty years later, in 1974, and out of the blue, the eighty-two-year-old Morton wrote in his diary that he had spent the day re-reading all her letters. 'She was a lovely talented woman & the first to encourage & praise my work.'*

It is significant that the proprietor of the *Express*, Beaverbrook, should have phoned Morton and requested him to undertake the delicate mission to Cannes. Morton had got to know Beaverbrook personally a couple of months earlier, probably during the autumn of 1924. The year, Morton recalled, had been a bad one for him and he had been looking around for ways of escape from the Big Room at the *Express*. He had heard that both the Bishop of London and the Prince of Wales were looking for press secretaries. He considered applying, but in the end decided not to. In the *Memoir*, he says that towards the end of 1924 he was as near as he ever got to giving up: 'Even the unexpected jaunt to Paris, or to Cannes, had lost its attraction.' Then, a chance encounter with his proprietor led to a sharp upturn in his fortunes.

Morton's recollection was that on a gloomy evening, as he was

---

*See also below, p. 83; p. 100.

rushing through the *Express* building, he bumped into Beaverbrook. In the conversation that followed, again according to the rather manicured-looking account that Morton wrote for the *Memoir*, he told his proprietor, 'I am wasting my time and your money.' This risky gambit produced not the sack, but an invitation to spend a day with Beaverbrook and his guests at Cherkley, his country house in Surrey. The visit, probably sometime in November 1924, was highly productive for Morton. (Incidentally, there is no mention of Dorothy in Morton's account of the visit to Cherkley: Morton went alone, it seems.) Somewhat to his initial embarrassment, Beaverbrook asked him to accompany him to his dressing room, where, while Morton told his tale of frustration at the trivial tasks he was being obliged to perform at the *Express*, the magnate was solemnly stripped by his valet and reclothed in a fresh outfit. Morton told his proprietor, 'I want to write.' This plaintive request produced not scorn, but an enquiry as to what Morton wanted to write about. Bearing in mind the apparently urgent, passionate vow to go in search of England, made to himself when he was ill in Palestine, it is reasonable to suppose that, at this most propitious moment with Beaverbrook, Morton would have explained this vow and asked for the resources to begin his search. But when he was asked what he wanted to write about, he recalled: 'I had to think quickly. There could not be the slightest hesitation. "About London", I replied.' Beaverbrook agreed to Morton's request, with the stern proviso that if, after a trial period of a fortnight, the series on London was not working, he would be fired. Beaverbrook also told Morton that if jealous rivals at the paper tried to sabotage the series, he should apply to him for protection. The personal support of the proprietor for Morton's project was a tremendous asset. Morton went home content. It had been a very fortunate encounter. Morton's working relationship with Baxter, the editor of the *Express*, was poor: it was, therefore, extremely useful for Morton to know that if he fell out with him he could appeal over his head to the proprietor.

On Monday 8 December the *Express* launched the first of Morton's articles in a series called 'The Heart of London'. The series became very popular with readers. Even so, it was just as well that Morton had Beaverbrook's backing: a hard-pressed editor might well have relegated the column to an obscure part of the paper, or terminated the series altogether. Morton watched over the production of his series zealously, and only once had to appeal to Beaverbrook to have an article's privileged place in the paper protected. He recalled that his vigilance over his precious series

> meant that I had no life outside the office for nearly a year. I would go up to the case room every night and wait to see the page containing my story in type locked up and sent down to the foundry before I would put on my hat and coat and go home at about 11 pm.

This could hardly have enhanced his domestic life with Dorothy and the children.

His London pieces for the *Express* occupied a right-hand column on page nine, a slot in the paper that Morton was to monopolise for the next few years, building up a tremendous following from the paper's readers. The column, decorated with a little line drawing, declares that its aim will be, day by day, to capture for the reader's inspection 'some common thing' drawn from 'this sea of emotion called London'. His first catch was a pair of lovers, leaning over the parapet of the Embankment, gazing at the river. He does not speak to them, but spins from his observation of them an entirely fictitious story about their hopes and fears. It is a pretty slight piece of writing, but it got Morton off the mark, and on most succeeding days there would be a piece from him, describing what he had found as he roamed around London. He presents to his readers stories about cabmen, chorus girls, Billingsgate porters, Kensington Garden nannies, down-and-outs, Harley Street doctors. He describes places – the Royal Mint, a night club, a city church, a Bloomsbury boarding house. Each piece, and dozens more in the same vein, is a vignette of some aspect of the variegated life of the city.

In his *Memoir*, Morton recalled a piece entitled 'Madonna of the pavement' as the piece with which he opened the series. In fact the Madonna piece came much later, but it is typical and will serve as a specimen that might be looked at a bit more closely. Its subject is a destitute family that Morton had encountered in High Holborn, but to which, like his couple on the Embankment, he had not spoken. The man slouches along, and the woman, a baby bundled in a shawl at her breast, straggles along behind him. The baby stirs and the woman pauses to look down at it:

> I tell you that for one second you ceased to pity and you reverenced. Over the tired face of chiselled alabaster, smoothed and softened in a smile, came the only spiritual thing left in these two lives: the beatitude of a Madonna. This same unchanging smile has melted men's hearts for countless generations. The first time a man sees a woman look at his child in exactly that way something trembles inside him.

The sentiment is mawkish, and the expression of it is trite and complacent. More than that, under the guise of sentiment, a set of highly dubious assumptions, compressed into a very small compass, is paraded. Pity for the poor may be suspended if they exhibit spiritual qualities. Poverty can have an aesthetic appeal. The children that women bear are, in some unequal sense, the father's. The poor are accorded more attention if one of their number happens to be a beautiful woman – 'She had once been pretty'; her smile 'with all its rich, swift beauty . . .' Morton was certainly not breaking any new political or moral ground here; a great deal was casually being taken for granted.

However, Morton's column seems to have been just the sort of thing that readers of the *Daily Express* in 1925 wanted – and it must be said that most of the pieces were better than the unpromising 'Embankment lovers', or the 'Madonna of the pavement'. He wrote, in his *Memoir*, 'Soon my letter-bag, rather than any virtue my writing may have had, made me virtually invulnerable. If anyone had tried to extinguish me I could have snubbed him with my daily post.' Morton was still working in Fleet Street, writing what he had no reason to believe would be anything other than ephemeral pieces. But at least he was no longer at the beck and call of an editor who would choose his assignments for him and send him rushing off to wherever the news story happened to be. The London pieces gave Morton an opportunity he'd longed for: he could roam the streets of the city, looking for the out-of-the-way, the comic, the poignant, the historic, the exotic, the ceremonial. The impulse that he'd had as a schoolboy to slip away from school and wander among the colourful crowd at Birmingham's Bull

Ring was at last finding its adult, professional expression. The initial fortnight's probationary run of London pieces was successfully completed, and the series was extended. Two further series followed. In his *Memoir* he paid tribute to Beaverbrook:

> I have always thought of him as the founder of whatever fortune has come my way. His decision to back my *Heart of London* for a fortnight, then his response to my appeal when the series was threatened, helped to establish me in the position I held for years as a privileged writer on the staff. But I doubt if he ever read a word I had written.

Once Morton had got the hang of producing a daily piece on London, he was sometimes able to stockpile a week's output and turn his mind to other things. He was still restless. He decided to write a novel. Together with a colleague who also had literary ambitions, he rented a basement room in the Temple – one of the Inns of Court, near Fleet Street. They bought a kettle, tea and a tin of biscuits, and earnestly went there, when time permitted, to write. Morton worked on what he recalled as 'a picaresque London love story'. His colleague worked on a play. The project petered out, before Morton had completed chapter one, when a burglar broke in and made off with the kettle, tea and biscuits, but disdained to steal the manuscripts. Much later, during the Second World War, Morton wrote his one and only novel. It is an interesting, frankly propagandist piece, written for the War Effort, but it indicates that Morton was astute, back in 1925, when he recognised his limitations and abandoned the idea of becoming a novelist.*

Like many journalists, Morton craved to get his writing between hard covers. The novel-writing project went nowhere, but he was surprised and pleased when he received an invitation from E. V. Lucas, the chairman of Methuen, to go and see him. Lucas, himself a highly successful travel writer, proposed to Morton that a selection of his London pieces should be published as a book. Morton jumped at the offer, and, in June 1925, *The Heart of London* was issued.[10] Two problems, both of great significance for Morton's new career as an

---

*I, James Blunt. See below, pp. 190–1.

author, had to be overcome as the little book went through the press. The first was the cover price. Morton was appalled to find that Methuen were planning to issue the book at six shillings. He thought that this was far too expensive and would put off large numbers of his potential readers. He therefore took the matter up with Methuen's managing director, C. W. Chamberlain. Chamberlain, who was to become a lifelong friend of Morton's, agreed to cut the price to three shillings and sixpence, and to double the print run to 10,000. Morton was shrewd enough to have recognised that his own interests would be served better by a low cover price – and therefore a small royalty per book – coupled with a high volume of sales, than by a large royalty per book, from a smaller volume of sales. It was a policy that served him well, throughout his publishing career.

The second problem had to do with copyright. The book was not far from publication when Morton, who had no experience of such matters, was horrified to learn that the copyright of his London pieces belonged not to him, the author, but to the *Daily Express*. This meant that royalties from the book, big or small, would flow not to him, but to the newspaper. How could he persuade the *Express* to make over the copyright to him? There was neither financial nor legal incentive for them to do so. He devised a clever but risky stratagem. The newspaper happened to be undergoing an economy drive. Morton chose this moment to go to Baxter and ask for a £10-a-week rise, knowing that he had no chance of getting it. It would have been an increase of nearly a third over the £23 he was then receiving. Baxter 'just laughed & I pretended to be most upset and disgruntled'. Morton's masterstroke (at least in his own version of events) was to follow through with an affectedly casual request to Baxter that, if he couldn't have the rise, could he instead have the copyright both to the articles that he'd already written, and to those that he would write in the future, for the paper? Baxter 'laughed again. "Of course."' The *Express* management sent Morton a letter that confirmed Baxter's offer, and Morton kept the letter for as long as he lived. He attached a note to it in 1969, when he was seventy-seven, giving the version of the encounter that I have set out here, and also saying 'This is the most important letter I have ever received; it also marks the most improbably skilful act of business I ever performed.' It also explains why Baxter's recollections of him were chilly.

The way was now clear for the publication, in a cheap, though not a mean format, of the book that was to launch Morton's highly successful career as an author. The book was issued on 11 June 1925 and was dedicated 'To S.D.W.' In the private reminiscence that the elderly Morton wrote in his 1974 diary about his affair with Theo in France, in which he noted that she had been the first to encourage and praise his work, he concluded: 'My first book, *The Heart of London* was dedicated to her; "to S.D.W." – semi-detached wife.' Whether or not he had another interpretation of these initials with which he could satisfy Dorothy, can only be guessed at.

The book was a great success, and Methuen followed it up by issuing, in the following year, another collection of their new author's *Daily Express* London pieces. *The Spell of London* was published on 11 February 1926. Five months later, on 10 June, Methuen published, in their 'Little Guide' series, Morton's *London*. Less than a couple of months after that, on 29 July, they issued another collection of Morton's London pieces, entitled *A London Year*. And finally, in Morton's bumper year of 1926, they issued yet another collection of Morton's pieces, under the title *The Nights of London*, published on 11 November.[11] So, in exactly seventeen months, from 11 June 1925 to 11 November 1926, Morton published five books. He had finally hit his stride, and had been taken up by a clever and congenial publisher.

The dust jacket of the second edition of Morton's guide book, *London*, published in 1927, carries advertisements for three of his other London books. The sales figures given show that a total of 73,000 copies had been sold in the couple of years since their publication. And, judging by the number of editions that were issued as the 1920s and thirties rolled by – twenty editions of *The Heart of London* by 1941, for example – demand remained high. Why were they so popular? One of the London books is a special case. Although Morton became a travel writer, and went on to publish forty books, only one, his contribution to the Methuen 'Little Guide' series, is formally a guide book of the sort designed for tourists to carry around with them in their pockets as they explore a new city. It is a workmanlike book. The inquisitive delight Morton had taken, ever since he arrived in London in 1913, in walking the streets, in reading about the history of the city, and in spending his Saturdays with Lawrence, the antiquary of Roman London, had paid off. The little book efficiently supplies two things: first, it gives potted information about the history, the museums, churches, galleries and administrative structure of the city; and, secondly, it gives a gazetteer that lists places of interest alphabetically. It is not hard to see why this book should have become a steady seller.

Morton's other London books, however, are collections of his ephemeral, often whimsical newspaper articles, written under the pressure of daily deadlines, and held together, within hard covers, by only the vaguest of unifying themes. It is not easy to see why they caught on and stayed in print for twenty years. The subject matter, although often a bit thin, does offer the reader one of travel writing's fundamental satisfactions – that of being vicariously taken to places that he or she is not likely personally to be able to visit. And although quite a few of the pieces look as if a hard-pressed Morton was struggling to make a visit to a bus garage, or a Post Office sorting room, sound enthralling, he does go to some interestingly obscure places. He reports back from a fur auction, a Whitechapel boxing match, a sitting of the Judicial Committee of the Privy Council, a film agent's office, a river police boat at night, a Chinese Fan Tan gambling den, and many more, often juxtaposing visits to the seamiest side of the city with visits to the exclusive haunts of the wealthy. The political implications of these reports of encounters successively with the very rich and the very poor are never brought into the open. If there is an implicit, controlling political standpoint, it is one from which the deserving poor are presented sympathetically, but which entails no criticism of the overall rightness of the status quo. Morton's political analysis was never profound, and rarely went very deep.

The narrator that Morton had devised for these pieces is recognisably a development of the voice that he was experimenting with in the piece on the White City army surplus dump, five years earlier, and which was beginning to reach a polished form when he sent his dispatches from Germany back to the *Evening Standard* in 1920. The narrative is always in the first person, usually in the present tense, and commonly addresses the reader personally, as 'you'. ('I tell you that for one second you ceased to pity and you reverenced.') The tone is generally light-hearted and amusing, save for occasions when the narrator is describing the great state occasions, or the sites that symbolise the city and the nation: then the tone is hushed and reverent. The narrator wears his considerable learning casually, and is often winningly self-deprecating. He wants to show himself, on one hand, as an intrepid voyager to the lower depths, and on the other, as a swell who is perfectly at home in the most exclusive of places. In some passages he manages to do both at once:

> I dined in a smart West End hotel, exchanged a silk hat for a cap in the cloak-room, and in half an hour was enjoying one of London's strangest contrasts – Limehouse.
>
> As I walked on through dark streets it seemed impossible that the grill-room I had left, with its elegant women, its discreet string orchestra, its air of assured comfort and well-being, could exist in the same world with these gloomy avenues, like a slum in hell, through which shivering lascars shuffled, hugging the shadows, while Chinamen with their mask faces and their sharp eyes peered from dim doorways into the night . . .[12]

Some of the people he describes in his pieces are acutely realised as individuals, but, by and large, Morton relies on stock characters, as he does in this opening to his report of a visit to a Limehouse gambling den: the Chinese men that he meets have 'mask faces'. Cockneys are invariably chirpy: at the State Opening of Parliament, they shout witty and irreverent catcalls as the peers process into the House of Lords, but they instinctively doff their caps as the royal coach goes by.[13] And in transcribing cockney speech, Morton uses the stock locution 'wot', instead of 'what', as if in some way it more accurately conveys the sound cockneys, and only cockneys, make. Jews, who appear chiefly in their roles as market traders, are pictured as bringing a touch of the Orient to the East End city. A beautiful Jewish girl he observes in the street market, Petticoat Lane, is fated, the narrator says, to lose her 'lithe grace' as the years advance, and become fat: 'That is the burden of the Jewess.'[14] American tourists who appear in the pieces are from a limited stock of stereotypes. They tend to be either pretty young women, eager for guidance from the urbane narrator, or crass, middle-aged couples who are wheeled on by the narrator to register either vulgar incomprehension, or awe, at the great antiquity of what they see, compared with the shallow newness of their own country. At the Trooping the Colour ceremony, for example, the narrator points out to an American that the saddlery of the Grenadier Guards was given to the regiment by the Iron Duke: ' "My!" says the American. "This thing's alive; it's got roots! No wonder you people feel these things in your throats, and I'm mighty glad to have seen this – it helps to explain . . . means something . . . Tradition . . . And I guess . . ." ' [15]

Methuen negotiated deals for the publication of Morton's books in America, and they were very popular there: his banal, patronising characterisation of Americans seems not to have damaged his sales. Why not? Maybe Morton disarmed his readers by drawing them, so to speak to his side. It was open to his American readers not to see themselves in the insulting caricatures: they could take comfort in knowing that *they*, at least, were not like the vulgar Americans Morton depicted.

But despite all this mundane stuff, there does emerge from the London books a powerful sense of the vitality and variety of the city. They are a positive celebration of the place, written by somebody who wasn't counterfeiting his first-hand knowledge, and who genuinely loved the history and the feel of its streets. Moreover, here and there, there are original insights into urban culture. For instance, his analysis of the social conventions that apply at a suburban dance hall would not have looked out of place in a report from the Mass Observation Unit of the 1940s. The narrator notes that the conventions are quite unlike those that apply 'in all the smart hotels and dance places in London'. In the suburban dancehall that he visited, the sexes come together only during the actual dances. As soon as the music stops, the girls move off to one side of the hall, 'like a collection of bright little humming birds on one long perch', and the young men move to the other. The two groups, segregated by tacit agreement, eye each other suspiciously. 'There is no friendliness, no companionship, no dancers have apparently brought partners, each dance is the signal for the men to raid the humming birds, and the end of each dance is the signal for them to abandon them.' [16]

But the really memorable passages from the London books are those in which Morton goes into the exalted mode that was to make his reputation as the delineator of Britain and of its national character. No passage exhibits Morton in this mode better than his piece on the Tomb of the Unknown Warrior, in Westminster Abbey. Taken as a whole, the London books do not reach formal conclusions about the ultimate significance of the scenes and places that are described. The books are simple assemblages of vignettes of a varied, cosmopolitan city. But in his piece on the Unknown Warrior, he rises to a grand statement of the tomb's significance. The Warrior, the narrator writes, 'lies not only at the heart of London, but also at the heart of England, here in magic earth'. Morton's later searches for the essences of Britain characteristically took him to the depths of the countryside: it is significant, therefore, that in this early formulation of a key British myth, his locale is as urban as it could possibly be. As a location, Westminster Abbey, despite its venerable, medieval origins, would seem to rule out reference to the green shires, with their familiar range of potent symbols. But, in a small tour de force, Morton unites the middle of Westminster and the English countryside: the Unknown Warrior sleeps in 'the silence of a mighty church, a silence as deep and lovely as though he were lying in some green country graveyard steeped in peace, above him a twilight in which the stored centuries seem to whisper happily of good things done for England'.[17] Symbolically then, the soldier is lying simultaneously in London – albeit an ancient part of London – and in a country graveyard.

The green country itself came into view when, towards the end of 1925, Morton started on the project that had its origin in Palestine in 1923, and which was to result in his most famous book, *In Search of England*.

4

1926–1927

IN SEARCH OF ENGLAND

Towards the end of 1925, when his series of London articles for the *Express* came to an end, Morton started to devise his next project for the paper. He decided to implement his long-deferred plan to go in search of the England whose image he had conjured, three years earlier, in Jerusalem. His new series was announced on the front page of the *Express* on 23 April 1926. The half-column announcement, illustrated with a photograph of Morton (a practice that he generally disliked), says that in the forthcoming series, the paper's star writer 'leaves London in a two-seater motor-car, and goes out at random into England to discover people and places'. The carefree tone of the articles that followed give the impression that the writer, stirred by the coming of spring, impulsively set out from London on a heedless, casual journey along the highways and byways. But in reality, the project was the result of some shrewd manoeuvring. The feeling of carefree impulsiveness that gives the series of articles its charm was highly calculated.

Morton's relationship with Baxter had not improved. They were, Morton recalled in his *Memoir*, 'like two wary dogs walking round each other waiting for trouble'. Morton had had a great deal of support from Beaverbrook, but he knew that the proprietor could not be expected invariably to take his side in every disagreement he had with the editor, so he had to approach Baxter circumspectly. The idea was to get him to agree to a plan whereby, at the paper's expense, Morton would drive off into the blue, with no arranged route, and send back articles describing what he'd seen. 'In other words,' Baxter said, when Morton broached the idea, 'you want a holiday.' It is not certain that Baxter uttered these precise words, for they come from one of the half-dozen versions of the interview that Morton scribbled, fifty years later. No doubt he polished up his recollection of the encounter so as to show himself off to advantage, but it can be relied on, I think, to indicate how chancy, at the time, were the prospects of the enterprise that was to result in not only another popular series of newspaper articles, but also one of the most widely-read books of the inter-war period. In addition, Morton's recollection establishes where the title for the book came from.

Baxter was not at all impressed by Morton's plan. He suggested an alternative. Morton should restrict his tour to the coastal resorts and send back articles for a series on 'The Seaside Girl'. Morton thought the idea vulgar, and said that vulgarity wearing a top hat is no less vulgar than it is when it wears a cap, and that a girl from Eastbourne is the same as a girl from Torquay. This set off a row in which Baxter accused Morton of being uncooperative. The row was interrupted by the ringing of Baxter's telephone. As he took the call – which, Morton speculated, might, coincidentally, have been from Beaverbrook – Baxter waved Morton away, terminating the interview angrily with ' "All right then! Have it your own way. Go in search of England." '

In planning his quest, Morton knew that he was stepping into a tradition of writers, stretching back to Celia Fiennes and Daniel Defoe in the early eighteenth century, who had journeyed around Britain, recording their impressions of the state of the nation. In the announcement of his forthcoming series, Morton had likened himself to William Cobbett, whose *Rural Rides*, published in 1830, had captured the feel of rural England just before the pace of urbanisation and industrialisation irreversibly accelerated. Cobbett, who travelled on horseback, for there were as yet no trains, recorded a tour around a pre-industrial England. Morton's own journey captured another moment of transition. The countryside was still substantially as it had been when, as a boy, he had cycled out from Birmingham into the quiet Warwickshire lanes. What was different in 1926, and what was as decisive in the transformation of Britain as the coming of the railways, was Morton's mode of transport, a little two-seater car. The motor car had developed from the garish, exploding contraption driven by his Uncle Willie, into a neat, fairly reliable little vehicle that could safely take its passengers into the deepest, remotest parts of the countryside. Britain lay open to discovery by any family that could raise the couple of hundred pounds that a small car cost. And Morton was the first to show them that an essential England, the England that he had conjured into mind when he was ill in Jerusalem, was there, waiting for the Austin Sevens, the little Fords and Morrises to come chugging up the lane. In notes made for his *Memoir*, Morton looked back and realised that he had been fortunate in chancing upon this moment in the history of British car ownership:

> For the first time in history these panting and efficient little machines were beginning to take individuals and families all over England, inaugurating a new age of discovery, called, in the typically deceptive English way 'motoring'.* Probably nothing like it had occurred since the days of medieval pilgrimage.

But most of Morton's readers did not own cars. What did his articles and his book offer to them? Maybe the reassuring knowledge that an essential England is out there, and that he had located and described it, was all his readers needed: it would still be there if ever they could afford a car. And even though the 'motoring pastoral' format gave prominence to his chosen mode of travel, it did not rule other modes out. Trains and buses were perfectly adequate means of getting out and about: J. B. Priestley, for example, went on the trip that resulted in his own *English Journey* (1934) by motor coach. And readers of Morton's book who used bicycles, or who preferred to walk, or even who were content to sit at home in their armchair and simply read, could all picture themselves, with a bit of imaginative modification, as the person to whom the book was addressed.

The growth of motor traffic during the 1920s and thirties could not be accommodated on the network of roads that had served a far less mobile, horse-drawn society. Morton later glimpsed the conclusion that has, in the twenty-first century, become a grim commonplace: the very act of driving to visit a precious landscape contributes to the degradation of that landscape. But back in 1926, the high spirits of the narrator of *In Search of England* were not dampened by premonitions

---

*In fact, the verb 'to motor' had come into use by 1896. See *OED*.

September 1911. Morton, aged 19, frolics in the sea on the Normandy coast during the holiday he took with a friend.

Morton and Dorothy, at around the time of their marriage.

Dorothy, Morton's first wife, photographed by Morton while on leave, sometime between 1915 and 1918, at one of their favourite places – Stratford upon Avon. The spire in the background is that of Holy Trinity church, burial place of Shakespeare.

The opening of Tutankhamun's tomb in 1923 – Morton's first big break as a reporter.
This photograph was taken by the *Times* photographer. Under armed escort, treasures
are being removed from the tomb. The figure leading the way is the official archaeologist, Howard Carter. The figure on the extreme right, furtively shadowing the party and
taking surreptitious photographs, is Morton. When the photograph was published in
The Times, Morton, the interloper, was cropped from the image.

Opposite Lieutenant Morton of the Signals Unit on his motorcycle – a comedown from
his cavalry charger, but perhaps preferable to the bicycles to which his company had
been reduced.

Daily Express

LATE LONDON EDITION

NO. 7,125. LONDON, SATURDAY, FEBRUARY 17, 1923. ONE PENNY.

TO-DAY'S WEATHER: UNSETTLED.

Our Free Insurance: £14,800 Paid This Year.

PHARAOH'S COFFIN FOUND.

WONDERFUL TREASURES IN THE SECRET CHAMBER AT LUXOR.

GOLDEN SARCOPHAGUS.

DEAD KING GUARDED BY A GIANT CAT.

The romantic secret of the tomb of Pharaoh Tutankhamen in the Valley of the Kings at Luxor was revealed yesterday when, for the first time in three thousand years, the inner chamber of the tomb was entered.

Every expectation was surpassed. Within the chamber stood an immense sarcophagus of glittering gold, which is almost certain to contain the mummy of the king. Wonderful paintings, including that of a giant cat, covered the walls. A second chamber was crowded with priceless treasures.

AWE-INSPIRING SIGHT.

By H. V. MORTON,
"Daily Express" Special Correspondent.

LUXOR, Friday, Feb. 16.

ONE of the most wonderful sights ever witnessed by Egyptologists was seen by the excavators of Tutankhamen's tomb to-day when the inner chamber was opened and they peered into the darkness.

Around an immense sarcophagus lay a mass of precious objects—vases, [illegible], statuettes, and boxes with the dust of thirty centuries on them. The light of three powerful electric torches flickered like white moons in the pitch darkness, illuminating sections of the painted walls, where the weird gods of Egypt were pictured tending the soul of the king on its journey to the shades.

SILENCE.

Although twenty persons were present there was not a sound in the dim tomb when the lights were focussed on the break in the wall leading to the death chamber. Hearts beat fast as the excavator-

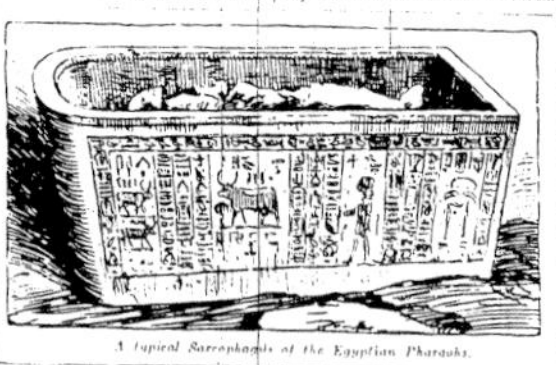

A typical Sarcophagus of the Egyptian Pharaohs.

in-chief was bidden to look at that which no human eyes had seen for 3,000 years.

No matter how little superstitious a man may be, the act of breaking the rest so carefully guarded through the centuries must cause an emotion which time can never efface. Lord Carnarvon was pale as he stepped slowly into the darkness and was lost in the shadows of Ancient Egypt.

The chamber is high, and measures fourteen feet by fourteen feet. In addition to magnificently painted gods of the underworld, bands of hieroglyphic inscriptions cover the walls. The paint is as bright as when it was new.

It was impossible to move at once the great lid of the sarcophagus. Inside there is probably another coffin, and inside this a third, in which it is believed the body of Tutankhamen lies decorated with his jewels.

GIANT CAT.

The only people to enter the chamber were Lord Carnarvon, Mr. Howard Carter, whose twenty years' work has now been crowned with success; M. Lacau, Director General of Egyptian Antiquities; Soliman Pasha, Under Secretary for Public Works; and Lady Evelyn Herbert, Lord Carnarvon's daughter. The others stood looking through the broken wall.

As the lights flashed on the sarcophagus it was seen to be all gold, glistening and sparkling. The little band of five, treading softly on the dust of ages, stood awestruck before the image of a giant cat, beautifully painted, which has kept vigil over the coffin of the king all these years.

Near the sarcophagus was a canopic jar containing part of the mummified body of the king.

When the party had recovered from the wonder of the first room, another surprise was in store for them. On the right hand was an opening leading to another room stacked with funeral furniture in indescribable confusion. Among the most remarkable objects were three more war chariots standing upright, decorated and gilded, just as when they were placed there by the burial party thirteen hundred and fifty years before the Christian era.

A box of ivory and ebony may hold manuscripts which will throw light on

Special Luxor Pictures on Page Eight.

this period of ancient history, or may contain Ushabti figures placed there in accordance with the ancient Egyptian belief in their magic power to work for the dead king in the underworld. It is not possible to walk in this room owing to the mass of valuable objects which it contains.

These facts now definitely establish the discovery of the tomb as the most important ever made in Egypt. It appears that the tomb robbers of a later dynasty did little harm, and robbed the tomb with great discretion.

Will the body of King Tutankhamen be found untouched when the third coffin is opened? If so, it will be the first time that an unrifled royal body has been found in Egypt, and it will be possible to know for the first time how a king of the eighteenth dynasty was wrapped after death and the exact disposition of the magical amulets placed to safeguard him in the other world.

In the first flush of the amazing discovery it is impossible to give any details regarding manuscripts. Archaeologists the world over will await them with eagerness. As Tutankhamen may have lived in the period of the Exodus, perhaps there is buried with him an account of Israel and Biblical times from the Egyptian standpoint.

Possibly also a full account of Akhnaton and his revolt from idolatory will be discovered, as well as an account of his Utopian city of Tel El Amarna, whither he removed his court, and where he preached Christlike doctrines.

GREAT SECRECY.

The peep into the mummy chamber of Pharaoh took place amid the greatest secrecy. Not one tourist was present, and no correspondent—not even those favoured by the excavators—entered the tomb.

Preparations for the opening began at half-past eight this morning. Impressions of the seals on the inner doorway were taken by Dr. Alan Gardiner and Professor Bearsted, of Chicago. The glaring electric lights were tested, and the last of the timber work was made ready.

The party of twenty arrived at 1.15 for the great event. The door of the outer chamber was reopened at half-past one. Cane chairs were taken into the tomb for the visitors, the men removed their coats—for the heat in the heart of the sepulchre is intense—and at last the party entered.

A dramatic time of suspense and excitement followed.

The seats were placed in rows facing the walled-up mummy chamber, and the

(CONTINUED ON PAGE SEVEN.)

BRITISH RHINE ARMY.

WITHDRAWAL IF FRENCH PLAN IS ADOPTED?

CONFERENCE ENDS.

"Daily Express" Lobby Correspondent.

NO result was reached at the Anglo-French Downing-street conference yesterday on the request of the French Government for free railway facilities in the Cologne area.

It was pointed out to the French delegates that if these facilities were granted it would not be possible for the British troops to remain on the Rhine.

TWO HOURS.

The conference was in progress for a couple of hours, and as it was felt that no definite conclusions could be reached without further reference to the Government in Paris, the French delegates, M. le Trocquer and General Payot, returned last night.

The rectification or readjustment of the line which the French now urge they should take over is well to the west of Cologne, and runs to Neuss, leading to Dusseldorf. The French urge that these facilities are essential to them, and that the readjustment they require will limit the responsibilities of this country in that area. F. J.

A House of Commons debate in which Labour M.P.s attacked France is reported on Page Four.

POET'S MIDNIGHT FRENZY.

WILD SCENES IN ISADORA DUNCAN'S ROOMS.

"Daily Express" Correspondent.

PARIS, Friday, Feb. 16.

Isadora Duncan and her husband, Serge Essenin, the Russian poet, have been in Paris only a few days, arriving from New York in a "dry" steamship. She is now in retirement at Versailles, having been forced to leave the Hotel Crillon, and he is on his way to Moscow, after being locked up for wrecking her apartment in the hotel.

Isadora Duncan.

He arrived, filled with temperament, in the apartment at 2 a.m., and after a few dramatic words that sounded like the mad scene in any one of Gogol's plays, he began to throw the entire contents of the room at her. Four policemen interrupted him in the middle of his task.

"THIS IS THE END."

"I can manage him," cried the dancer, executing a nimble step to dodge a missile. As he was dragged out, on his way to the lock-up at the Mairie, she exclaimed, "This is the end of it all." Both her eyes were blackened.

An hotel guest in a lower room, says the "New York Herald," Paris edition, heard a crash, and thought that the clumsiest waiter on earth had accomplished his masterpiece. He ran upstairs, and found that the poet had smashed windows, chairs, tables, and mirrors.

A passenger who was with them in the George Washington said that the poet and dancer stayed in their cabin throughout the trip, and that Essenin's pent-up thirst overcame him as soon as they landed at Cherbourg.

RELICS OF THE SOMME.

BRITISH SKELETONS IN A WOOD.

AMIENS, Friday, Feb. 16.

Many bodies of British soldiers, most of them little more than skeletons, have been found during the clearing of a wood in the devastated area round Albert.

Many have been identified by means of their Army discs.—Reuter.

Neither the War Office nor the Imperial War Graves Commission has yet received any information regarding the identity of the soldiers. A War Office official said last night: "There are anything from 50,000 to 60,000 British soldiers who fell in the war whose bodies have never been traced."

U.S. BATTLESHIPS TO GO.

WASHINGTON, Friday, Feb. 16.

President Harding has transmitted to Congress an estimate for the appropriation of £4,500,000 to meet the costs of scrapping American battleships under the programme agreed to at the Washington arms conference.—Reuter.

JOCKEY BADLY HURT.

J. Phillips, a jockey, was badly thrown by the fall of Sainte Helene in the Novices' Steeplechase at Hurst Park yesterday, and is suffering from severe concussion.

Two doctors and a nurse are in attendance.

TUTANKHAMEN.

His coffin was found in the Luxor tomb yesterday.

CITY EQUITABLE SENSATION.

ANOTHER ARREST IMMINENT.

The "Daily Express" understands that another sensational arrest is imminent in connection with the failure of the City Equitable Fire Insurance Company, Ltd.

Gerard Lee Bevan, chairman of the company, fled from London on February 8, 1922, by aeroplane for Paris. He was brought back to England on August 17 and sentenced at the Old Bailey on December 5 to seven years' penal servitude for fraudulent conversion and obtaining money by false pretences.

BATTLE HONEYMOON.

IRISH "DE WET" AND HIS BRIDE IN A TRAP.

"Daily Express" Correspondent.

BELFAST, Friday.

Mrs. Bofin, a beautiful colleen, married to "General" Bofin, the "Irish De Wet" less than a week ago, defies volleys of Free State bullets, shell bursts, and bombs in order to be by her husband's side during the battle now raging in the Arigna Mountains, Co. Leitrim.

Bofin and a band of rebels that dwindles hourly before the Free State onslaught are trapped in a ring of steel.

For three nights the rebels have had no sleep. Aeroplanes hover over them all day signalling their movements to the Free State cordon. Field guns bombard them with high explosives.

Their "general" and his gang have lived by loot for weeks. They made wassail nightly in their fortresses, and for diversion sallied into the countryside to blow up bridges.

One man who mined a great bridge single-handed spent the remainder of the evening celebrating his feat in the taverns of a near-by town.

When he set off to walk back to his cave he apparently forgot that the bridge had gone.

Next morning they found him drowned in the water in the chasm his mine had made.

MORE WASTE!

The British taxpayer was called on yesterday to provide another £813,000 for Mesopotamia—£350,000 for defence and £463,000 for railways.

These two items have cost him £9,979,000 since last March.

Details on Page Seven.

CHEAPER LIVING.

The average level of retail prices on February 1 was approximately 77 per cent. above that of July 1914, states the "Ministry of Labour Gazette."

This is 1 per cent. lower than the percentage for January 1 last and 11 per cent. below the figure for February 1, 1922.

FRAU WAGNER'S POVERTY.

"Daily Express" Correspondent.

BERLIN, Friday, Feb. 16.

Among the innumerable victims of poverty in Germany is Frau Cosima Wagner, widow of the famous composer, who is reported to be in great need.

DR. O'HIGGINS AVENGED.

SONS TRACK DOWN HIS ASSASSIN.

DYING WORDS CLUE.

"Daily Express" Special Correspondent.

DUBLIN, Friday.

DR. THOMAS O'HIGGINS, father of Mr. Kelvin O'Higgins, the Free State Home Secretary, has been avenged by two of his sons.

I understand that the sons, one a doctor and the other a private in the Free State Army, have traced to his lair and seized the leader of the rebel gang who slew their father in his home at Stradbally, Queen's County, on Monday.

"I KNOW YOU."

The prisoner is a man named Byrne. Dr. O'Higgins, the moment before he was shot, said in his wife's presence, "I know you, Byrne, and from the way I often helped you I think you should be the last to attack this house!"

Byrne, seeing that he was identified, pulled his cap over his eyes and ordered his subordinates to fire. Mrs. O'Higgins saw and heard all that took place. Her husband fell dead at her feet. His blood stained her dress.

The sons at once determined to track down Byrne.

For four days they have pursued him clue by clue, from one hiding place to another.

Dr. O'Higgins was the coroner of his district, and the doctor, friend, and counsellor of scores of families. The whole countryside rose to assist his sons in securing his murderers.

Byrne is now in custody, and it is believed that other members of the gang also will be soon under lock and key.

THIRD REVOLVER BY POST.

EXPLOSION IN A LONDON SORTING OFFICE.

A third revolver, packed so that a cartridge would be fired when the parcel was opened, has been found in the sorting-office in Coborn-road, Bow.

The package, addressed to a young woman in Poplar, was handed in at one of the Bow sub-offices. As it was handled by the sorting-office staff a cartridge suddenly exploded.

No one was injured, but several sorters narrowly escaped being hit. The bullet was afterwards found embedded in a desk.

Scotland-yard detectives examined the wrapper and the handwriting on the parcel, and afterwards took a statement from one of the assistants at the office where it was handed in.

The police believe that the person responsible for this outrage is the person who sent similar packages to Mrs. Hobbs in Clerkenwell and Mr. Childs in Forest Gate.

The detectives have so far failed to trace John Santiall, whom they are anxious to interview concerning the case.

STOP PRESS.

DEBT BILL CHANGE.

WASHINGTON, [illegible]

The Senate [illegible] adopted an amendment to the Debt Funding Bill providing for Congressional [illegible] of President's approval of the settlement [illegible]

Reuter.

PRISON DRAMA.

"Daily Express" Correspondent.

BERLIN, Friday, Feb. 16.

An attempt was made to-day to free Max Hoelz, the notorious Communist robber and murderer, who in 1920 terrorised South Saxony. He is now imprisoned in Breslau. A band rushed to the prison gates, overpowered the warder, and seized the keys, but they were overpowered by the reinforcements who came to the aid of the officials.

FRENCH COAL STRIKE.

"Daily Express" Correspondent.

PARIS, Friday, Feb. 16.

Members of the French Communist mining syndicate have gone on strike. In the north the movement is general, while in the south it is partial. The numbers of strikers is computed to be 100,000.

The strikers claim an increase in wages of 10d. a day.

HOUSES NOT DECONTRO[LLED]

RENT RESTRIC[TION] TWO-AND-A-HAL[F]

CABINET P[...]

Far-reaching new Governme[nt] building and rent control were an[...] Griffith-Boscawen, Minister of He[alth ...] first speech of his by-election cam[paign ...]

Chief points of the new schemes are:

RENT RESTRICTION.

Extension of the Rent Restriction[s ...] and a half years.

Middle classes are not to be sacri[ficed ...] the higher-rented houses next Ju[ne ...]

BUILDING.

A limited State subsidy per new ho[use ...]

Subsidy to enable building societie[s ...] thirds of the value of a house t[...]

State aid to be limited to working [...] type.

These and other proposals will be em[bodied ...] to be introduced in the House of Common[s ...]

MIDDLE - CLASS [...]

SIR ARTHUR GRIFFITH-BOSCAWEN said that the Government were still considering the two very difficult problems of rent and housing, and had not yet decided their policy, but they were determined to solve them.

He could, however, say two things with certainty. One was that, although the present Rent Restrictions Act came to an end next June, the Government had decided that rent restriction must continue for a further period. A Bill would, therefore, be brought in for this purpose.

Sir A. Griffith-Boscawen.

TOO FEW HOUSES.

Secondly, there was to be no sacrificing of the interests of the middle classes. The Government could not, therefore, accept the proposal for the gradual decontrol of houses which would entail the higher-rented houses coming out of the Act next June.

The interests of the middle classes would not be neglected. They had suffered too much already as it was.

With regard to the housing question, the Government would like to see a complete return to normal conditions, with no rent restriction and no State housing scheme, but they recognised that at the moment this was impossible.

People said: Why not rely entirely on private enterprise? He wished they could, but private enterprise, although it was to some extent supplying the villa type of house, would not and could not under present conditions supply the

(CO[NTINUED ...])

A dramatically-lit portrait of Morton, taken (in York) at around the time of the publication of *In Search of England*.

A Bullnose Morris from the mid-1920s. A model like this carried Morton on the tours that led to his *Search* books.

Opposite The front page of the *Daily Express*, Saturday 17 February 1923, with the Tutankhamun report sent in by 'H. V. Morton. Special Correspondent'.

The dust jacket of *In Search of England* (1927), featuring a painting by Alfred Taylor.

of what would be the consequences of mass car ownership. One of the fantasies spun by the book is that each of its thousands of readers could be at the wheel of a little car, bowling through empty lanes, on the way to meet folk who would greet them as honoured travellers, rather than as grudgingly acknowledged tourists.

Unfortunately, Morton's *Memoir*, and the surviving diaries, cover the period of his journeys around Britain only patchily. Because he wrote his newspaper articles and books in the first person, it is tempting to assume that they are the equivalent of diaries and that they can be used as straightforward chronicles of his life. It's a risky assumption, for although there is no doubt that he did undertake the journeys, there is considerable doubt about the manner in which he travelled, and about the incidents and places that he wrote about. For example, did he always, as the narrative voice of the books indicates, travel alone? On many of his later trips he certainly had companions, although they are invisible in the texts. Maybe there was a companion sitting in the passenger seat for some parts of his early journeys too.

The series opened on 26 April 1926. Standing in the shadow of St Paul's Cathedral, the narrator suddenly hears the whisper of Spring. ' "Take off those stupid gloves and that black coat and that sorrowful face and make love to me! Run to me on an open road in wind and rain and sun and catch me, if you can." ' The narrator quickly regains his balance after this over-exalted, rather hysterical beginning, and explains to the reader that he is about to fulfil a vow that he'd made to himself while ill in Palestine. Then comes that famous evocation of the essential England that will be the object of his quest – the village of thatched cottages, of plough-teams plodding home, their harnesses jingling, of the smell of burning oak logs.

> This village has no name. It is a village which many a townsman has seen in lonely foreign places, for it is the essence of England, the unit of all our social development, the germ of all that we have become, something almost too English to be true, certainly more English than London, Birmingham, Manchester or Liverpool, perhaps the mother of all cities, a memory lingering in the heart.

So, despite Morton's five books that had celebrated the vitality, the pageantry and the historic importance of London, he now spurned the city, along with his stupid gloves and black coat. The 'essence of England' just *has* to be a village. By saying that 'this village has no name', perhaps Morton was prudently realising that no actual, nameable English village would be capable of living up to the expectations that his preamble raised. But he was not temperamentally inclined to go very far in exploring the possibility that he was a trader in myths – in this case, one of the most powerful, irresistible cultural myths of all. And the convention of his column in the *Express* demanded not philosophical speculation, but simple traveller's tales. The spell must remain unbroken. So, after this rather portentous start, the column got down to the business of regular reports back from the byways, although the question of the village with no name arose again when Morton came to publish his series of *Express* articles as a book.

The car that Morton drove was a two-seater Morris Cowley 'Bullnose', a modest, 1500 cc vehicle, costing under £200 and with a top speed of about fifty miles an hour. (See plate 8.) Whimsy was one of his besetting sins, and it lured him into giving this car a name, 'Maud'. And as the instalments of his series in the *Express* rolled on, he gave his readers fragments of conversations he had had with Maud. As they leave London and motor off into Berkshire, they converse intimately:

> 'Hold me, hold me, h-h-h–h hold me!' cried 'Maud' as we shot ahead.
> 'In a little while', I whispered, 'we will go slow in a quiet place and get down to work, but let us put a few miles behind us . . .'

His first encounter, after leaving London behind him, was with 'the last bowl turner in England', William Lailey of Bucklebury. The narrator presents the encounter as if had happened purely by chance, the first, happy result of his trundling along the Berkshire lanes at random. Actually, the chances of his having accidentally stumbled, on his first day out, upon the workshop of the last maker of 'treen' – wooden bowls turned on an ancient pole-lathe – are pretty remote. It looks now as if there was a lot of stage management, the product of Morton's careful prior research. This is certainly the conclusion of Michael Wood, who has written his own account of William Lailey.

Wood argues that it would have been necessary, but easy, for Morton to have read about the bowl-turner beforehand.[1] For the purpose of Morton's narrative, William Lailey and his hand-turned wooden bowls are exactly what was needed. They gave him a motif for the newspaper series, and eventually for the book. They combine ancient, pre-industrial craftsmanship, extreme rusticity, and a rejection of the cash nexus. The narrator tells Mr Lailey that if he really wanted to, he could make a lot of money. But

'Money?' he said with a slow faun-like smile. 'Money's only storing up trouble, I think. I like making bowls better than I like making money.'

'Will you say that again?'

He leaned against the door of the hut, his homely brown face shaded by his floppy green hat, and said it again, slightly puzzled, and feeling, I think, that I was in some way 'getting at him'. But you will have guessed that I wished to hear for the second time the voice of a craftsman, the lover of his job, the proud creator of beautiful common things, a voice that is now smothered by the scream of machines.

I went on down the green hill feeling that my search for England had started well.[2]

And off Morton and 'Maud' went, driving down to the West Country as far as Land's End, then back to Gloucester, northward along the Welsh marches, and on into northern England, as far as Carlisle. Then, after a brief sally over the border to Gretna Green and back, the route turned eastward and crossed the Pennines to Newcastle, from where the southbound run started. At the Wash, the route turned eastward to Norwich and the Norfolk coast, and then, leaving East Anglia, it wound westward. The journey ended, not back in London, but somewhere deep in the Warwickshire countryside of his youth. As he travelled, Morton sent back regular dispatches to the *Express* in which the citizens of village, market town and cathedral city step forward obligingly, and generally deferentially, to utter, in formulaic dialect, gems of traditional legend, custom and wisdom. Between these encounters, the narrator keeps up the momentum by sketching in, very effectively, colourful romantic historical background – Morton always did his homework – and by pausing to reflect sonorously on the spirit of the places he visits: 'At night, especially under this witching moon, the streets of Shrewsbury take you back to Old England. Butcher Row at night is perfect.'[3]

The series of articles was meant to take the reader away from the mundane cares of modern life and into a more tranquil, essential England. Morton tended to shy away from intellectual questions, and he never formally considered the implications of his notion of having to *search* for England. One implication is that the country does not readily disclose itself to its native citizens. His whole project was predicated on a belief that the narrator and his readers live in an inauthentic, bogus version of England, and that the elusive, *real* England has to be searched for, and that the skilful, inspired narrator will find it, in some quiet corner of the shires, or in the corner of a cathedral close, or in the medieval alleys of a market town. This feeling that where we actually live is in some way inauthentic – that the real thing is somewhere else – is so deep in our culture that it is rarely examined. But it is not at all clear why we routinely concur with writers like Morton, and his modern equivalents, in consigning large tracts of countries – be they England or our holiday destinations – to the realm of the inauthentic, while we follow them in search of the essential, authentic England, or Ireland, or Provence, or Tuscany. Even a travel writer as fresh and unclichéd as Bill Bryson can write, in the opening chapter of *Down Under*, 'I was going to see the real Australia.'[4]

The potential clash between the essential England and the routine, everyday England erupted into the middle of Morton's *Express* series, although he cleverly smoothed it over. On the day that the paper announced his forthcoming series, 24 April 1926, the chief news story had been of a bid by coal-mine owners to reduce miners' wages. Within ten days, this attempted wage cut had led to the National Strike, which was announced by the *Express*, on 4 May: 'Momentous General Strike Begins'. The paper made no bones about where it stood on the issue: 'YOUR TASK', it told its readers, 'is clear. *Keep Calm: support the government: be true to your citizenship.*' Here was a version of England – an England of poor industrial workers whose claims were opposed by a Conservative newspaper – that jarred with Morton's light-hearted jaunt. Social and political conflict was conspicuously not a feature of his essential England. As a consequence of the strike, national newspapers were severely reduced in size, and Morton's articles were casualties of the shrinkage; the paper announced that his 'series is temporarily held over'. The strike lasted until 12 May. The newspaper soon grew back to its normal size, and on 24 May, it announced that Morton's series would shortly resume. 'Mr Morton, who returned to London during the strike . . . has now left again on his two-seater tour.' Morton himself, at his most whimsical and facetious, added:

I have had a frightful time with 'Maud'. I think the strike must have unnerved her. She indulged in two entirely temperamental punctures the first day and developed a hysterical engine yesterday, so that I could do nothing with her. An expert, however, has done things to her interior. I am back where I left off and will resume my daily story on Tuesday just as if nothing had happened. The country looks lovely . . .

In one effortless-looking sentence, he both trivialises the strike and feminises his car's breakdowns. Was that the end of the matter? Did the National Strike make absolutely no impact on his journey, beyond interrupting it for a few days? Certainly it was an aspect of the nation's life and character that would be difficult to incorporate into the England that Morton was half describing and half inventing. But he did incorporate it, subtly and obliquely. The narrator writes that when he reached Cornwall, he was put up for the night by an old farming couple. It is a Cornish Eden. But the culmination of this taste of paradise is his being invited up the lane to hear a neighbour's new battery radio set. (The BBC had started broadcasting in 1922.) After much tuning, the radio beams in a programme of dance music from the Savoy. The proud owner of the radio tells the narrator how closely it had kept them in touch with news of the General Strike: 'we liked that Mr. Baldwin, for he wor as plain as if he wor in this room.' (Baldwin was the Conservative Prime Minister, and although he was from a family of West Midland iron-masters, he subscribed enthusiastically to the English myth, publishing his own book, *On England*, with its evocation of the sounds of scythes against whetstones, and plough teams coming over the hill, in 1926.) Morton's own artful juxtaposition of the metropolitan sophistication of the Savoy's dance band, the world of abrasive political action, and the innocent lives of his Cornish hosts

is left to do its own work. No doubt the reader is meant to sigh at the
intrusion of vulgar, modern culture and brutal politics into Eden, but
the narrator does not step out of his narrative and draw a conclusion.
He leaves it at the elegiac but non-committal level of 'the new picture
of rural England: old heads bent over the wireless set in the light of a
paraffin lamp'.[5] And later in his journey, when he passes through
Lancashire pit villages, the narrator notes that miners 'sit on their
haunches against the wall, their hands between their knees . . . like
Arabs'. He does not point out that miners were still on strike.[6] (They
held out until August.)

The series of articles ran until 10 September, by which time the
narrator had reached Warwickshire. There is, however, no sense of
culmination in the final piece: the series trickles away with a sense of
anti-climax. Morton would attend to this defect when he came to turn
the series into what became his most famous book.

The success of his series gave him a very strong position on the
Express. He received a salary of £1,200 a year for his basic duties as a
reporter and for writing his articles, and, because of the shrewd
copyright deal he had struck with Baxter, royalties from the London
books were rolling in handsomely too. And yet more royalties would
flow his way when he had turned his *In Search of England* series into a
book. Furthermore, he was on very good terms with the paper's
proprietor, Beaverbrook. Not surprisingly, the editor of the paper,
Baxter, was not inclined to stand up and cheer his columnist's
new success. Near Christmas in 1926 they had a row, and even in
Morton's account, recollected in the tranquillity of old age, it seems
plain that Morton had taunted Baxter. Here is the passage from the
Memoir:

This row was really caused by a cheque for more than £4,000 which
Methuen had sent me for book royalties. It was the largest sum I had
ever earned or ever possessed. Baxter, with whom I was on 'dear old boy'
terms at that moment, asked me to stay on and have a talk with him
after the usual morning conference. We were chatting away, the best of
friends, when suddenly all discretion and all sense of self-preservation
deserted me, and, flipping my royalty cheque across the desk, I asked
'What do you think of that, Bax?' . . . Tossing back the cheque, he said,

'There comes a time in life when a man has got to decide whether his job is more important than his outside interests.' That of course led to a row in which I said 'I resign', and Baxter quickly responded with 'I accept your resignation.'*

Morton recalled that although this encounter was not as humiliating as his dismissal by Hulton from the *Evening Standard*, he felt, none the less, 'angry and injured'. It is hard to see what justification he had for feeling aggrieved, but in any case, his resignation never took effect, for Beaverbrook, who had been informed, presumably by Baxter, about the row, phoned Morton at home during the evening and proposed a way of patching matters up between his favoured columnist and his editor. His proposal was highly flattering to Morton, for it took the form of a fortnight's holiday with Beaverbrook and his entourage – which, pointedly, would not include Baxter – in the south of France.

Early in January 1927, then, Morton – there is no mention of Dorothy – was instructed to be at the Continental Boat Train departure platform of Victoria Station to meet Beaverbrook and his party. In his old age in South Africa, Morton recognised that such departures were part of an age that had vanished, and, as he wrote the episode up for his *Memoir*, he took a pace backward from his recollections of his feud with Baxter and delivered a small valediction on the unheedingly showy world of the Mayfair rich during the 1920s:

Beneath the grey light of a winter's day, filtered through the grimy glass dome above, moved porters wheeling trolleys piled high with Bond Street luggage. Beside them walked women wrapped in minks and sable, accompanied by men who conformed to an almost military pattern of dress and grooming, and would have been recognised anywhere in the world as English. They were the rich or the fortunately-born, sometimes both together, with their parasites, all of whom

---

*Whether the cheque was truly for £4,000, or whether Morton was dramatising his memoir for effect, is unclear. A few years later, in 1930, when he had more books in print, and was therefore earning more in royalties, he recorded in his diary – a more reliable source than his *Memoir* – a sum of 'about £2,700' as his likely half-year royalty cheque; 'the biggest sum I have ever made'. See chapter 5, p. 133.

revolved round a small area of London called Mayfair and formed a social group known, with a capital S, as Society.*

He went on to note that he was the only member of Beaverbrook's party at the suite at the Carlton Hotel in Cannes who did not bring a personal valet. Morton's instinct, as he had earlier written, was to be on the edge of the crowd, rather than a part of it. From the edge, he could take a detached, even mildly critical view, as he does here. But his criticism could hardly have been milder: he was really very pleased and flattered to have been invited to spend a couple of weeks in Cannes with the idle rich, away from the chill and grime of a London January. But he certainly wouldn't have seen himself as one of the 'parasites'. In the Riviera sunshine, thoughts of resignation faded, although Beaverbrook switched him briefly to the *Evening Standard* until his relations with Baxter had mended. He then resumed work on the *Express*.

Back in London, Morton worked on his England articles, preparing them for publication in book form. He did not simply join up, end to end, the articles that had appeared in the *Express* and submit them to Methuen. There was a fair bit of re-working and additional writing. 'I must give a word of advice to writers of newspaper series which they hope eventually to publish as books,' he scribbled in one of his notebooks for the *Memoir*. 'Don't. Rewrite. A book and a series of articles are two different things.' Morton did not often reflect on his craft, but in this notebook he opened up a little on the techniques that he had developed over a professional lifetime of travel writing.

I learnt a great deal about writing travel books on this journey [i.e. the journey for *In Search of England*]. I find it is unwise, as I did, indeed as I was obliged to do, to write impressions on the spot. The reason is that the real observer is one's self-consciousness, & one never knows what was important until a certain time has elapsed, which allows the subconscious to produce the really significant factors of any given moment.

---

*One of the titles for his memoir that Morton toyed with was *The Sound of Midnight Trains in Empty Stations*, a slightly misquoted line from the 1936 song 'These Foolish Things' (lyrics by Eric Maschwitz, under the *nom de plume* Holt Marvell). 'Sound' should have been 'sigh'. One of the pieces in *The Heart of London* is about the departure of the boat train from Victoria. See 'Sun or Snow', pp. 113–16.

The ideal way to write a travel book is to make all your notes & then to go as far away as you can from the country you are writing about & sit down to work. It is a method which I have, since I was able to, used with, I think, some success. [Morton was probably thinking here of his later travel books, which did not first appear as newspaper articles.] But I was unable to do so at first. I had to provide the D.E. [*Daily Express*] with a thousand words a day, often by telephone. This was not easy.

The book, which was published on 2 June 1927, is clearly recognisable as a collection of the thousand-word instalments that Morton had telephoned in to the *Express*. The numbered sections within the chapters, for example, correspond in length and sequence to the columns as they appeared in the newspaper. But there are significant differences, the chief perhaps being the simple fact of the hard covers binding together the otherwise ephemeral bits of writing. Reading Morton's book in a few hours is a quite different experience from reading, over a period of five months, his column in a newspaper: the very publication of the book automatically confers on the writing a new authority. It also gives greater definition to the shape of the narrative, which runs from springtime to harvest.

What changes did Morton make to the text as he modified it for publication? Some are fairly trivial. He abandoned, for example, both the whimsical name that he'd given his car, and the simpering conversations that the narrator had had with it, or her. I imagine that Morton's sense of literary decorum made him expunge such sentences as ' "Never mind dearest", I said as I comforted her with a spanner.'[7] Other changes, small in themselves, contribute to the book's *gravitas*. Even before readers reach the text itself, they encounter some potent symbols of what they are going to find. The dust jacket, painted by Alfred Taylor, bears on its front a picture of an archetypal English landscape, projected from above, with a lane winding through fields to a village church and onward to distant hills. (See plate 9.) Inside the front cover, the endpaper is printed with a romantic map of England, showing the route of the journey. In the ocean that surrounds the precious isle, galleons sail, and dolphins gambol. Then comes a frontispiece, a lovely, artful photograph entitled, emblematically, 'A lane in England'. Two trees in full leaf frame a half-timbered, thatched cottage that borders an untarred lane, down which, moving away from the viewer and towards the distant greenery, plods a team of unharnessed farm horses. (See plate 10.) Next, over the page, comes a strange poem of dedication. Although the text of the book rigorously maintains Morton's convention of presenting his narrator as a solitary traveller, the dedicatory poem describes not a solitary, but an intensely shared experience of standing, with a companion, in the early morning on Glastonbury Tor:

To
T.C.T.

You will remember, lady, how the morn
Came slow above the isle of Athelney,
And all the flat lands lying to the sky
Were shrouded sea-like in a veil of grey,
As, standing on a little rounded hill,
We placed our hands upon the Holy Thorn.

The 'lady' does not reappear when the text reaches the passage where the narrator describes Glastonbury: he is, as usual, alone.[8] T.C.T. was Theo – S.D.W., the 'semi-detached-wife' – of *The Heart of London*. Years later, in October 1940, Morton sadly recorded in his diary that he had just received a letter from a lawyer in the United States saying that Theo had died. She was, he recalled, 'one of the finest, most noble women I have ever known. We had a pact once that, if she died before me, she would send her ashes in an urn for me to cast out on the Tor hill at Glastonbury. How often she laughed about that.' So, Morton was not invariably a lonesome traveller, and one of the most intense moments recorded in *In Search of England* was shared with a lover.

Next comes an introduction, written by Morton expressly for the book. Here, Morton speaks not in the light-hearted, bantering tone of his narrator, but with a manifestly serious purpose. Readers, he says, must not interpret the book that they are about to read simply as a journal of a carefree jaunt through the byways. Morton wants his project to be taken seriously, for he is, he insists, addressing a momentous question. 'Never before,' he lectures, 'have so many people been searching for England.' His identification of the cause of this search is unremarkable; people are alienated from the lives and homes assigned to them in an urban, industrial society and feel an urge to go in search of a place that will be recognised and felt as the *real* England. He says that the search for the real England has lately been made easier, for cheap road transport now penetrates every part of the country, facilitating the search for the 'common racial heritage'. What will the searchers find though? Is the rural heartland in good shape? No, it is not. 'Behind the beauty of the English country is an economic and social cancer.' Ancient estates are being taxed out of existence and broken up. Cheap imported food is undermining farmers' livelihoods – 'the Roast Beef of England comes so cheaply from the Argentine.' What is the solution? It is idle to think that the 'intellectual solitude in which the rustic evolved his shrewd wisdom' can be re-attained; the radio, cheap transport, and newspapers are irreversibly bringing villages into a wider culture. But the nation as a whole will flourish only when attention is paid to the rebuilding of secure, prosperous and traditional agricultural communities, supporting 'a contented and flourishing peasantry', to which the town-bred searchers, suffering from 'racial anaemia', can go in search of spiritual and physical refreshment.[9]

Morton's is hardly a profound analysis. The 1920s and thirties were full of such jeremiads and they have a lineage that stretches back through the Edwardian and Victorian social critics, to the earliest commentators on the social effects of the Industrial Revolution. Indeed, the idea that the town is corrupt and that the country is pure has been a constant, universal cultural stereotype ever since the first towns were built. What makes Morton's introduction interesting, and a bit surprising, is that he reels off this rather clichéd analysis of the ills of England shortly after having published five books, each testifying to the vitality of city life. Some of the London lives he had described were cramped and hard, but he had never presented London as a degenerate place. Two possible explanations for Morton's change of approach come to mind. First, Morton was a pragmatic, working journalist. He always had an eye for a story that would sell, bringing him fame and fortune. The market for the myth of England that *In Search of England* exploits was (and remains) perpetually buoyant. It would have been quite out of character for Morton, who, it will be recalled, had freely chosen to spend a couple of years delving into the teeming life of London, not to have been able abruptly to change direction and feel his way into the persona of the champion of the countryside and provincial England. Back in April 1926, at the origin of his project, when he stood in the shadow of St Paul's, perhaps he sniffed not so much the spring, but a new publishing opportunity. He could turn his professional hand as readily to the countryside as to the city. But secondly, and less commercially, maybe the pull of the countryside, cathedral cities and sleepy little market towns was real: the vision he'd conjured in Palestine, when entwined with his childhood memories of the lanes and fields of Warwickshire, perhaps truly exerted a pull to which he was psychologically bound to respond, sooner or later. The book certainly reads as if it were heartfelt; there is no crack in its surface through which can be discerned a cynical journalist, scribbling away just for the money.

Indeed, the narrator's descriptions of the places he passes through are often brilliant. They are only rarely hackneyed. He is good on landscapes, evoking the intimacy of a peaceful sunset in a village in the New Forest and the loneliness and vast distances of the salt marshes of the Norfolk coast with equal attention and precision. Here, for example, is the conclusion to his description of the north Norfolk salt marshes:

> And it is lonely, with the water lapping and the birds crying and the wind pressing the blue thrift back from the sea, for this is a strange No-Man's Land: it is not land and it is not water, but a queer beautiful half land, half water; and it seems to you that the sea fights for it daily and the grass defends it. When you turn your back to the salt marshes you see, far away, flat meadows and green land and villages, clear-etched, and grey flint church towers rising above the trees. To the left and to the right a thin line of woodland is the colour of the bloom on a purple grape.[10]

Such landscapes, while not eternal, are subject to only very slow change. But other prospects that he describes are poised on the edge of extinction. Part of Morton's conscious programme was to record, and lament, the final passing of a horse-drawn rural society: his narrator is therefore drawn to weekly markets in self-contained provincial towns, places where all the rituals of agrarian life are unselfconsciously enacted. Here he is in Salisbury, lacing his account with a reference to Thomas Hardy, and a world-weary comment on the young farming women's desire for fashionable stockings:

> It was market day. The cattle market was loud with mooing and bleating. Country gigs stood in the square and over the pens leaned the burly, red-faced Wiltshire farmers. Many a Tess went off with a basket over her arm to buy – lisle-thread stockings, I suppose! I looked at the crowd and heard their bargaining, I met them in Ox Row and Blue Boar Row and Oatmeal Row, I watched them come from tap-rooms wiping their mouths with the backs of their big hands and – the railway might never have invaded Salisbury![11]

He is good at describing ancient buildings, often rolling out set-pieces in which he deftly supplies the historical background that will bring a building to life. His lifelong interest in archaeology served him well here. He could sketch in the Roman background to Bath, or Hadrian's Wall, colourfully, without getting too ponderous. Equally, he was alert to the history of Christianity in England and to the way it has been shaped by the invasions of the Vikings and the Normans. The narrator's meditation on Durham cathedral is a good example. It opens with him actually writing his piece: 'I am writing beside the River Wear, surrounded by flies, small winged dragons, and minute centipedes, which paddle drearily through the ink before route-marching all over the paper.' This typical, gently comical opening leads swiftly, as his gaze turns upward to the cathedral towering above him, to a conspectus that takes the reader, within the space of a couple of pages, from Lindisfarne and the early English Christians, through eleven centuries, to the building of the cathedral by the Normans as a mighty symbol of their new dominance over the region.[12] Morton's version of history was sweeping, anecdotal, full of colour, drama, and grand themes. As a child, he was always imagining that he stood where Romans had once stood; as a mature writer, he always physically placed his narrator, and thereby his reader, at a precisely delineated spot from which the present and past can be simultaneously contemplated – in the Durham case, at a spot on the bank of the Wear. Of course Morton did not invent the travel-guide-cum-history-book, but his mastery of the form was a major ingredient in his book's success.

In his grand set-pieces the narrator holds forth directly to the reader, as he does here in Durham, but often Morton interposes a bystander, whom the narrator regales with his learning and wisdom. Often this bystander will be an American. Morton has a whole stock of them – dense middle-aged men, loud, vulgar middle-aged women, beautiful long-legged young women – standing ready to be trotted out as ready-made stooges when he needs to show off the dignified splendour of some hallowed English site. Stock Americans had served him well in his books on London; they do equally valiant service in his book on England. Here is the male version, condescendingly dragged into the Lake District: 'One of England's great sights is that of a New York businessman, determined to get every cent's value from his tour, trying to work up enthusiasm for Wordsworth in the little churchyard at Grasmere.' And here is the female counterpart, deployed by the narrator in York Minster: 'There was only one fool in the party, an elderly and obviously too wealthy woman with a silver-headed cane, who asked more idiotic questions than I have ever heard in half an hour, culminating with: "Say, guide, do you have an Archbishop of York these days?" ' Only young women are deployed more gently, more protectively. A Southern Belle is on hand in Cornwall: ' "Tell me" she said, as we walked through the valley, "is it pronounced Tintagel, like that, or Tintadgel?" '[13] Young women of all nationalities get a special deal from the narrator, and they are not always introduced solely to bear the weight of some historical anecdote that he needs to unload. They appear simply because he likes the look of them and wants to show his readers how he can charm them. He is partial to 'silken knees' and to freckle-nosed young county girls in tweeds at a point-to-point. One section is given over entirely to a flickering-eyed damsel, in distress because her car has run out of petrol at a remote bridge across a stream somewhere in Dorset: 'She was distinctly charming, especially when she flickered. She was wearing a small brown hat into which a diamanté arrow had been shot by an unerring Bond Street jeweller. She was neat as a doe . . .' The narrator gallantly fills her car with petrol from his spare can and is rewarded: 'She flickered adorably three times.'[14]

Morton's deployment of stock figures is not limited to Americans and pretty young English women. He is equally ready to attribute distinctive regional character to the people he meets as he travels about. The people of Beaulieu, in Hampshire, for instance, are 'slow Saxons, well-mannered, deferential people, with their wits about them and their tongues padlocked'. A few days later, the moment he crosses the river Tamar into Cornwall, he observes that the people 'possess a fine Celtic fluency, so that their lies are more convincing than a Saxon truth'. And a month or so later, when he is driving around Norfolk, he briskly divides the people into two groups: 'In East Anglia, men are either neighbours or Vikings.' 'Neighbours' are suspicious folk whose character is inherited from those who, a thousand years ago, encountered the Danes as they came ashore on raids. 'Vikings' are the aggressive descendants of the invading Danes.[15] The historical background to Morton's books was often simplified, for the purpose of drama and colour. But sometimes, as here, in his unconsidered summaries of regional character, it was simplified to the point of parody.

The route through England that Morton's narrator followed looks somewhat haphazard, but it has a pattern of sorts, for its nodal points are cathedral cities – Winchester, Salisbury, Exeter as he sets off westward, and York, Norwich, Ely, Peterborough as he motors down from Durham. The book does not attempt to give equal coverage to equal areas of the country: that was never Morton's aim. What, then, governed his choice of route? In an early, pioneering article on the way in which myths of England are formulated, Alun Howkins argued that the essential England of the early decades of the twentieth century was always *southern* England: permutations of the hedgerows, ploughed fields, sunken lanes, downland and thatched cottages of the southern, arable landscape were typically presented as the defining features of the truly English landscape.[16] Morton's book starts by conforming to this pattern. When the narrator quits springtime London, he unquestioningly heads south and west, and well over half of the book has gone before his Morris has been steered decisively northward, at Gloucester. The vast area of the country left to be covered before harvest-time was traversed in leaps and bounds, but, brief as the narrator's acquaintance with northern and eastern England was, he incorporated their landscapes – be they the Pennines of Hadrian's Wall, or the Brecklands of Norfolk – into his vision of England. Morton was not parochial. His book gives no support to notions of a fundamental north–south divide. And even though his whole project was to search for an England away from the big cities and away from industry, his narrator expresses a sense of excitement when he crosses from Cheshire into Lancashire and starts to pass through industrial districts:

> With the beautiful Old England that I love so fresh in mind, I stood ready to be horrified by the Black Belt; yet strangely, I stood impressed and thrilled by the grim power of these ugly chimneys rising in groups, by the black huddle of factories, and the still, silent wheels at pit mouth [further oblique testament to the miners' strike] and the drifting haze of smoke.[17]

The narrator even, albeit rather dutifully, visits Wigan, a town that was already a byword in jokes about the grimy industrial north of England, and which later became legendary, when George Orwell visited it in 1937 and wrote a merciless account of his time there, in *The Road to Wigan Pier*. Morton's narrator's account was much more genial, though well short of ecstatic.

But it is of course the English countryside and its small market and cathedral towns that are the objects of his quest. This quest necessarily takes him to some of the most picturesque spots, but he tends to shy away from them, and he is saddened by their impending spoilation by charabanc-loads of trippers. He is well aware of what happens when a village becomes too conscious of its tourist appeal. He observes, for instance, that Clovelly, in Devon, with its immaculate cottages, its steep cobbled street running down to the harbour, where blue-jersied fishermen strike nautical poses, is in danger of sinking under the weight of its own quaintness.[18] Understandably, the narrator never confronts the dilemma of, on one hand, encouraging his readers to seek out the beautiful places that he has found for them, while recognising, on the other, that if they do, they will spoil them. But late in life, when he made trips back to Britain from South Africa, he was always aggrieved when he went to the beautiful places that he'd written about and found them full of what he saw as vulgar people. Many of them, he grumbled, didn't even wear hats.

The plot of *In Search of England* starts to build towards its climax when the narrator rolls out of East Anglia and drives westwards across the Midland Plain to Warwickshire. Not surprisingly, given the way Morton had spent his youth, he was drawn to Stratford-upon-Avon. The narrator acknowledges that he is on a pilgrimage, and that he will be on the most hallowed English ground, but, with a quite unexpected, almost sarcastic shift of tone, he recalls the Shakespeare Festivals that he had attended, and Frank Benson's proclaiming that

> Only through Stratford, the common meeting-place of the English-speaking world, could we heal the pains of Industrialism and make England happy again. We were to make the whole world happy, apparently, by teaching it to morris-dance and to sing folk-songs and to go to the Memorial Theatre. With the splendid faith of Youth we pilgrims believed that England could be made 'merrie' again by hand-looms and young women in Liberty gowns who played the harpsichord. Then, I seem to remember, shortly after that war was declared. However . . .

The adult Morton is a bit cruel to the youthful Morton.

When he reaches Stratford, he finds that it has changed. As he approaches, driving between 'well-loved Warwick hedges', he finds himself snarled up in 'a perfect death rattle of motor traffic'. And when he gets there, he finds that his 'quiet old Stratford was suffering from a rash of trippers'. But the trippers, and his embarrassment at his youthful enthusiasm for Benson's ideas, cannot obliterate the significance of the place for him. He is recaptivated, and returns to two of his old haunts. One is the wood by the river – presumably the wood in which he and Dorothy had courted so passionately. On this visit though, the wood is fancied by the narrator as Shakespeare's model for the wood near Athens in which he set *A Midsummer Night's Dream*: 'It seemed that Oberon and Titania had just hidden behind the great trees.' The other old haunt was the church of Shakespeare's burial, Holy Trinity. From a mossy seat on the wall, he gazes out across the river at what he considers to be 'one of the supremely English views'. It could not be more fitting, he muses, that Shakespeare's bones lie in such a quintessentially English place.

The book does not end, as it might well have done, at Stratford, symbol of Shakespeare's England. It ends a few days, and a few pages later, on a dying fall, when the narrator finds the England he's been searching for. His quest ends in a village, seemingly somewhere not far from Warwick. Significantly, though, the narrator does not disclose its name or exact location. The culminating, immaculately stage-managed final episode of the search opens with the narrator casually falling into conversation with the vicar, in the churchyard of the village. Standing among the mossy gravestones, the old vicar ruminates on the continuity of village life. He invites the narrator to stay overnight with him. They watch a hare on the vicar's lawn. They drink old port from Georgian glasses. The talk is of the ancient, naturally hierarchical traditions of the place, and of the mournful prospect of the break-up of the local estate when death duties are demanded. In the morning, the vicar conducts the harvest festival service in the church, before a contented, ruddy-faced congregation. And finally, with the narrator's prose at its most purple, the book ends:

> I went out into the churchyard where the green stones nodded together, and I took up a handful of earth and felt it crumble and run through my fingers, thinking that as long as one English field lies against another there is something left in the world for a man to love.
>
> 'Well,' smiled the vicar, as he walked towards me between the yew trees, 'that, I am afraid, is all we have.'
>
> 'You have England,' I said.[19]

Why does the narrator not tell his readers where this village is? It is because, I think, it does not exist. It is the unnamed village of the opening article in the *Daily Express* series. No actual place could bear the weight of Englishness that Morton's brilliantly conceived, imaginary village has to bear. The essential England, the object of his search, is to be found inside his head, not in the Warwickshire land-scape. The village is powerfully charged with features that make it a symbol of England itself. It is remote from industry and ugly urbanisation. Its fields, hedges and old buildings are achingly beautiful. The weather is sunny – though with just a hint of autumn in the air. The troubles of modernity have not yet reached it (although death duties are looming). It is quietly and benignly regulated by time-honoured church and land-owning authorities. And it is populated by a contented community of agricultural workers. It is, in short, a mythic place.

No matter whether *In Search of England* was the story of Morton's heart, or the product of his shrewd journalistic calculation, his book was a huge success. Thousands upon thousands of readers responded to his formulation of the myth of England. Twenty-nine editions were in circulation by 1943. A third of a million copies had been sold by Methuen by 1969.[20] There was an American edition, and many translations. The book made Morton's fortune.

It succeeded because Morton had a sharp eye and a sure commercial touch. His alter ego, the narrator of the book, is an engaging guide, who not only conducts his readers around the country, but flatters them by painlessly inducting them into a knowledge of the grand themes of English history that give particular locations their colour and significance. The book relies on a number of well-worn conventions about England, about English history, and about travel itself, but it was not entirely in thrall to them. The narrator's surprisingly positive response to industrial Lancashire, and his recognition of the absurdity of Frank Benson's vision of Merrie England, for example, stop the text from becoming bogged down in the cloying sentiment that awaits the celebrator of heritage, hedgerow and cottage. The narrator is solemn where solemnity is required – his voice is hushed when he is in a cathedral – but overall, the tone is witty and often winningly self-deprecating.

Morton had gone off on his quest at an opportune time. The generation that had survived the Great War was avid for news that the England that they'd been fighting for, or for which their sons or husbands had died, was still out there. And the England that they wanted to be reassured about was *rural* England. Morton himself had written, at the opening of his book, about 'a little London factory hand' whom he had met during the war, and who had confessed, 'when pressed, and after great mental difficulty, that he visualised the England he was fighting for – the England of the "England wants you" poster – as not London, not his own street, but as Epping forest, the green place where he had spent Bank Holidays'.[21] Modern, industrial, urban England could not supply satisfying images of the land that, it was hoped, victory would secure. In Wilfred Owen's poignant 'Anthem for Doomed Youth', for example, the bugles that faintly call for the slaughtered sound not from the industrial towns that were likely to have been the youths' homes, but from 'sad shires'. The 1920s and thirties were full of readers who were ready, in the company of writers like Morton, to will themselves back into the pre-industrial, pre-war, innocent rural world of those English shires. An audience for *In Search of England* was ready and waiting,[22] and even when memories of the Great War faded, the yearning for arcadia that an urban people never shake off kept Morton's royalties rolling in.

5

1928–1933

THE BRITISH ISLES

The book that immediately followed *In Search of England* was an oddity. Morton was on very good terms with Methuen, but his next book, *The Land of the Vikings*, a book about East Anglia, came out under the imprint of Richard Clay, in May 1928. It was never reprinted. It is a handsome little book, with pen-and-ink illustrations by Frank Mason. But its style is awkward. In Morton's usual fashion, the reader is addressed in the first person, but the narrator never properly establishes himself, even though some passages in the book are lifted straight out of *In Search of England*. The book is a blend of a personal record of travels around East Anglia and a conventional guide book to the region, complete with alphabetical gazetteers of places to visit in each county. The elegance of the book's production belies what, on closer inspection, looks like a rather hasty composition. Even so, there are some good passages, and, at a practical level, the gazetteer sections would still provide an itinerary for an interesting tour. As a record of Morton's life, the book offers scarcely anything, but two passages throw maybe a glimmer of light. The first is from his description of Colchester, the town in which he was stationed for much of his wartime service. Plainly, Morton knew the place much more intimately than he knew the rest of the region:

> The relics of Rome lie so thickly beneath the soil of Colchester that I have many times picked up coins and scraps of Samian pottery from the hedge-banks near Lexden after heavy rain. I remember laying bare a tessellated pavement only two feet below the level of a kitchen garden, and how well I recollect the thrill of seeing the sunlight fall upon those

red and blue cubes which had paved the room of a country house 1800 years ago.[1]

The purpose of this tantalising passage was not autobiography: it says nothing about why Morton, a keen serving officer in the army, should have been digging archaeological trenches in Colchester, while the more pressing task of digging battlefield trenches was being performed across the Channel in Flanders. (See plate 11.)

The other fragment from *The Land of the Vikings* that might be squeezed for a drop of biographical content is his description of Cambridge. As I have suggested,* Morton was ambivalent about his not having been to university. Although he travelled the length and breadth of England, he tended to keep away from Oxford and Cambridge. In a guide book to East Anglia, he could hardly ignore the city of Cambridge and its university, but he devotes just four stiff and stilted paragraphs to them, concluding with the banal 'The less said about Cambridge in a short space the better: it is a rich experience, an unforgettable town sacred to Knowledge, Beauty and Youth.'[2] For a writer who relished the chance to write about the cathedrals at Ely and Norwich, not to rise to the challenge of describing King's College Chapel is a strange lapse. His customary response to the cities he describes in his books is idiosyncratic, open-hearted and confident, but his response to Cambridge is inhibited and cursory. He seems to have been unable to come to terms with the place, and express what he felt about it.†

His next book was a more considered sequel to *In Search of England*. Methuen published *The Call of England*, another edited and revised collection of his newspaper pieces, in June 1928. In the introduction, he frankly confesses that he wants to make amends for the partiality of *In Search of England*. In that book, he says, 'I deliberately shirked realities. I made wide and inconvenient circles to avoid modern towns and cities. I went through Lancashire without one word about Manchester and Liverpool. I devoted myself entirely to ancient towns and cathedral cities, to green fields and pretty things.' His new book, he goes on,

*See above, p. 20.
†In his book on Wales, published four years later in 1932, he wrote, 'University towns always interest and depress me.' *In Search of Wales*, p. 199.

strives for a more comprehensive, more balanced view of the nation. In particular, he wants to challenge two conventional views.

The first is that the call of England cannot be heard from industrial cities. Morton's aim is to encourage searchers to visit the great industrial cities. If Morton could indeed integrate the industrial city into the essential England it would be quite a feat, for it would entail the drastic modification of the powerful myth of England that he had himself served, a year earlier, when he had located the essential England in the churchyard of a Warwickshire village. True to his promise, *The Call of England* contains sympathetic, vivid descriptions of the industrial Midlands and north. His description of the forging of steel wheels in Birmingham, for example, is as acute as his earlier description of the turning of wooden bowls in Berkshire. And his descriptions of the street life of Manchester and Liverpool show that he found more vitality there than he had found in Bath or Shrewsbury. But his fair-minded project is always being deflected by a vocabulary and a rhetorical tradition that takes for granted that the countryside is superior to the city, that agriculture is superior to industry and that the past is superior to the present. Even in his introduction, when he is at his most self-conscious in setting out his programme, he writes: 'It is only when we go there [the north of England] that we realize how very slightly the age of coal and steel has deformed the green beauty of England.' Why the word 'deformed'? The myth of England, which Morton cannot escape, demands it. He loved cities, including the industrial city in which he was brought up, but even in the face of his own lived experience, the myth that governed, or at least regulated his vision of England, obliged him to see the modern, industrial world as a deformation of an older, better world.[3]

The other conventional view that he says he wants to challenge is the view that the search for England is most promisingly conducted in the south and west of the country. He says that motorists leaving London 'instinctively' go south and west, as he had done for *In Search of England*. He now wants them to head north, for 'no man who wishes to understand the country in which he lives can neglect the north of England.' In *The Call of England*, Morton is certainly trying to present a more comprehensive vision of England, but its coherence is damaged somewhat by his blithe unawareness of the perspective from which the vision is projected. He does not notice that, despite his own Midland upbringing, he has made his narrator into a metropolitan investigator whose task is to bring reports of the provinces back to the metropolis. Furthermore, although his introductory comments challenge the view that England is to be sought only in the south, they do not challenge the whole notion of a fundamental north–south divide, even though both *In Search of England* and this sequel, by supplying sensitive delineations of the subtle changes in landscape and townscape as region shades into region, undermine this crude, disabling notion.

In practice, the twin aims of the book – to integrate the industrial city into the essential England, and to enlarge conceptions of the country, by describing a place called 'the north of England' – tend to get in each other's way, and it is the second of these aims that gets the better of the struggle: two-thirds of the book have gone before the narrator pays close attention to an industrial city. And even the exploration of the northern countryside has to wait until the narrator has detoured, from his starting point in London, to Colchester, in Essex, from where he addresses the reader with one of his historical set-pieces, this time of the Roman invasion of Britain. Then, four short paragraphs cover the narrator's speedy journey up to Hull, in the East Riding of Yorkshire.

His entry into Hull, by ferry from Lincolnshire across the Humber estuary, undermines, right from the start, the southern stereotype of 'the north', for here are no Pennine Hills, no black puddings, no textile mills, no clogs, no shawls, no coal mines. Rather, Hull's fishing fleet, and the city's flat surrounding landscape, merging imperceptibly with the North Sea, incline the narrator to associate it with Boston in Lincolnshire, and the Norfolk coast. A fancied – and fanciful – common east-coast Viking ancestry cements the association: the men of Hull 'are big, fair-haired pirates; the women are blue-eyed Danes'.[4]

The disruption of south–north stereotypes continues as the narrator leaves Hull and drives over the Wolds:

I topped the rise beyond Bishop Burton. Below me in green fields lay the ancient town of Beverley.

There come moments in England when travellers pause in their journey, brought to a full stop of mind and body by a beauty so sudden, so old, so right, and so English that there is nothing for a man to do but to look gratefully before him.[5]

So, just a few miles over the Yorkshire border, an England as familiar and reassuring as Stratford-upon-Avon or Winchester has been found. And Beverley is not a one-off. As the narrator meanders northward, from cathedral city to cathedral city, he regularly discovers the essential features of England. York, 'the loveliest city in all England' as he calls it, enchants him, and he stays for a few days. Ripon's Englishness is no less impressive than Beverley's: 'In a restless world that changes often for the sake of change you feel in little places such as Ripon that you touch the sturdy roots of England firmly locked in a distant and important past.'[6]

He pulls out all the stops when he reaches the ruined moorland abbeys:

> There are moments when the traveller stops and says to himself: 'My journey has ended before it has begun. There is no point in continuing it. I shall, if I follow the high-road for a hundred years, find nothing more lovely than this.'
>
> Three times have I said these words in one day's wandering as I stood before the ruined altars of Fountains, Jervaulx, and Rievaulx. These abbeys are the three glories of the North Riding. There should be some charitable fund for the transportation of all spiritually diseased and all unhappy people to these abbeys. Here, Peace and Beauty live hand in hand.[7]

But he does continue his journey, and winds his way northward, via Lindisfarne – which occasions a meditation on the coming of Christianity to England – to Berwick, where he turns west, tours through the Borders to Carlisle, and then turns south, running down through the Lake District and Lancashire. His Home Counties perspective sometimes throws places into weird juxtapositions, for he is inclined to use southern and western landscapes as a standard against which northern landscapes may usefully be measured. For instance, the narrator declares that 'every one in the south of England should visit Whitby if only to see how Yorkshire can imitate the best of Devon and Cornwall.'

How were readers who lived in, say Suffolk, or Northamptonshire, or Worcestershire – let alone Yorkshire, Devon and Cornwall – supposed to respond to that recommendation? Or again, a later passage is topographically so convoluted that it's difficult to imagine what would be made of it by readers who didn't happen to live in London and spend their holidays in Devon: he says: 'If a Londoner can imagine Dartmoor moved into Essex he will have some idea of the meaning of the Peak District to the crowded industrial cities of the north.'[8]

Eventually, he reaches Manchester. Industry has, until then, been virtually absent. It has put in brief appearances only when the narrator visited Rowntree's chocolate factory in York (a rather cosy, paternalistic enterprise), and in Newcastle, where he admires the view from the High-Level Bridge. Overwhelmingly, the search so far has been for the medieval, the sanctified, the enduring sites of England's heritage. Will there be a crash of gears as he changes into a mode suitable to record his impressions of the life of a hectic industrial city?

He sets up an expectation that Manchester will be a city of the sort that Charles Dickens created in *Hard Times*. The road over which the narrator drives into Manchester could have been designed by Mr Gradgrind: it is 'as hard as the heart of a rich relation', and runs on, 'in undeviating flintiness', dead straight, towards the city. But when he arrives, the narrator does not find himself in an oppressive city of dehumanising factories and sullen wage-slaves. On the contrary, he finds himself in an exciting, confident city, its pubs bursting with rowdy vitality, its shopping streets enlivened by 'the flash and twinkle of yellow silk stockings', and its commercial meeting places thronged with assured, droll merchants.[9] There is no sense at all that Manchester is some sort of affront to England. Even inside a cotton mill, often taken as a symbol of the way industrialisation subordinates humans to the ruthless demands of machines, the narrator finds the human spirit alive and well. As they hang up their hats and coats, the mill-girls sing fragments of *Madame Butterfly*. Usually, when Morton is setting his narrator up for a set-piece, he clears away bystanders, leaving him alone in the landscape, or standing by an ancient ruin, like the narrator of Gray's 'Elegy', ready to meditate on England's heritage. But in Manchester, the citizens are at centre stage, dealing in cotton at the Exchange, dancing at the weekend in their thousands at a gigantic ballroom at Belle Vue, singing in the pubs. In his introduction to the book, Morton said that the manufacturing districts, although they cover a surprisingly small area, have 'deformed the green beauty of England'. In an obvious sense, his narrator's report of Manchester endorses this view: he finds no green beauty there. But in another sense, the view that industry and urbanisation are deforming agencies is contradicted, for the narrator is positively exhilarated by them.

His sense of exhilaration persists as he visits Liverpool: 'how easy to fall in love with Liverpool, this elusive, moody city, so full of variety, beauty; so full of warm vitality.' The narrator is stirred by the volume and range of goods that come into the docks, to be hauled on horse-drays, along the Great Dock Road: 'This road is the spine of the north country. It is a magnificent epic of commerce.' But his elation is tempered by what he sees as 'the humiliating tragedy of casual labour' at the docks. He sensitively describes the way in which a crowd of hundreds of men stand hopefully at the dock gates in the early morning, in the sure knowledge that only a favoured few will be picked by the foreman for a day's work. Morton's description is a good example of the way in which he calls forth the reader's sense of pity, or injustice, without pointing the way to a change in the system of labour relations in the docks. Morton rocks the boat a bit, but never threatens to capsize it. At the dock gates, the rejected workers 'melt away in slow groups . . . drifting off up side streets. I suppose it ends for most of them before a woman's eyes. No need for a woman to ask questions as the rejected body hunches home, head down, hands in pockets . . .'[10] Lest this be interpreted by readers as a practice peculiar to Liverpool, the narrator points out that he has seen the same degrading selections taking place outside the London docks.*

His journey resumes, and he heads across the Pennines to Sheffield, whose 'hard ugliness' he finds 'queerly grand', [11] and then southward. The continuity of the book goes a bit awry when the narrator reaches Birmingham. He is supposed to be on a car journey from Sheffield, but he arrives by train from Euston. This disjunction is a consequence of an uncharacteristically slack transition from newspaper column to

---

*Later, Morton wrote a piece about casual workers in the London docks who were hired for the dangerous and filthy job of scraping out the sludge from oil-fired ships' fuel pumps. See *Our Fellow Men* (2nd edn., Methuen, London, 1936), pp. 246–67.

book. The Birmingham section started life as a short series called 'The Heart of Birmingham' in November 1925, in the *Daily Express*.

But however he arrived, Morton is on his home territory in Birmingham, although he never allows his narrator to disclose to the reader that the author was brought up there. Birmingham is the city 'which clasps metal rings on the arms of African chiefs and turns out tropical gods by the gross; the city whose buttons hold up the trousers of the world; whose pins assist civilization in a million ways; whose nails go into cradle and coffin'. Morton gives his narrator free rein to write exuberantly and knowledgeably about the place. He establishes the unique character of the city with such comments as 'if Birmingham is not a city in the sense that squares are wide and streets majestic, it is, as a series of industrial encampments held together by the tramways department, the greatest workshop the world has ever known'. And, in a wonderful description that exhibits Morton at his imaginative best, he writes, 'For me the great thrill in Birmingham is the Town Hall. It stands there as if attempting to make up its massive mind to walk down Hill Street and catch the last train back to Rome. Its solemn, classic grandeur kills every building in the locality stone dead.'

The chief civic building in a city as uncompromisingly dedicated to manufacturing as Birmingham, can offer a 'great thrill'. What higher testimony could there be for the pleasures of the industrial city? He concedes that the 'industrial encampments', as he calls them, sprawling ever outward into the countryside, are ugly, but they are redeemed by the restless energy of the people working there: 'you realise with almost a shock that beneath the ceaseless effort is the play of the human comedy, desire, failure and success, but well in hand, well-controlled, most marvellously disciplined. Here work is life.' [12]

The book might well have ended on this exultant, celebration of Birmingham, but powerful conventions re-assert themselves at the last minute. Industry has to be shown in its role as deformer, both of the countryside and of a noble past, and the essential England has to be moved to where it truly belongs – in the country. The narrator pays a melancholy visit to Sandwell Hall, a decaying eighteenth-century mansion that is waiting for the demolition crew: industrial West Bromwich will soon engulf it. Industry, he says, has swept away many lovely things, it has planted its pit shafts in deer parks, it has driven its railway lines through the place where hounds once met on cold winter mornings; and before it the Old England has retreated rather mournfully, understanding it as little as old Sandwell Hall understands the coal mine.[13]

This elegiac note persists, through to the final pages of the book, which record the narrator's return to Holy Trinity Church, Stratford-upon-Avon. Sitting on his old seat in the churchyard, gazing out at one of his favourite English scenes, he reflects on the significance of the journey he has just completed. Save for the briefest of references to 'the energy of the city', his peroration activates the standard tropes of Englishness:

I can conceive no greater happiness than that of going out into England and finding it almost too English to be true: the little cottages, which vary from county to county, the churches with their naves in Norman England, the great houses, the castles, the incredible cathedrals, the strange little places which will, let us hope, never quite emerge from an earlier, and, I believe, happier world . . . There will come a time in any tour of England when most men from a city will feel that no matter how life disappoints them there can be always one thing worthwhile at the end of the journey: the sight of the wind moving over their own wheat field; the moon rising behind their own home; the knowledge that they have fought their way back to the country and have planted their feet in the splendid sanity of English soil.[14]

So, the book's earlier affirmation of the industrial city is not powerful enough to withstand the myth of England. Manchester, Liverpool, Sheffield and Birmingham are no match for little cottages, or for the wind moving over a wheat field.

Morton opened his 1929 diary with a retrospect on the year that had passed. 'The year 1928 has been a remarkably good one for me . . . My books have astonished me. They are selling in a way difficult to explain. D. [Dorothy] and I have got used to our big house . . . I have made a name for myself in my profession; and I am 36.' He also reflects on his emotional life. 1928, he writes, has been a turning point: 'At the age of

35 I changed completely, mentally and physically. I have only now got into calm waters.' This reflection was premature. On the next page of the diary he is in rough seas again. On New Year's Eve, he spends the day drinking. He winds up, after drinks at the Café Royal and the Cecil, in bed with one of the women with whom he was to have affairs in 1929. He arrives home 'just in time to let in the New Year. It was a horrible business. D. had been waiting up for me and was quite rightly fed up and miserable.' This set the pattern for the year. There are entries that record the pleasures of family life – children's parties, evenings out with Dorothy – but they are outnumbered by entries that record his sexual adventures and his guilty homecomings. For example, a *Daily Express* assignment in February to cover the enthronement of the new Pope gave him the chance, on the way back, for a 'hectic night in Paris' during which, according to the system of symbols he used in his diaries, he scored three times. The list of sexual encounters he kept registers his three Parisian partners as 'wh' – whores. In a separate notebook, he wrote descriptions of brothels and of numbers of casual liaisons.

He was working very hard on his books, knocking into publishable shape the articles he was writing for the *Express*. But he was irritated by his routine reporting duties. In May 1929 he was sent off to cover Ramsay MacDonald's general election campaign. This commission led to another tense meeting with the editor. Baxter complained that Morton was spending too much time on his books and not enough on his newspaper work. Grudgingly, Morton acknowledged, in his diary entry for 29 May, that there might be substance to this complaint: 'I've promised to pull up my socks like a good little boy. I hate being corrected.' However, the entry for the next day – polling day – has only the words 'Bloody Gen. Election'. The day following has the bare entry 'Socialists sweeping the country. Ramsay MacDonald certain to be Prime Minister.'* He says nothing about the political issues involved. As usual, he made no attempt to examine the rather thoughtless prejudices that constituted his own politics, and give them some sort of coherence.

---

*They didn't exactly sweep the country. MacDonald's Labour Party gained office, but only as a minority government. They won 287 seats. The conservatives won 261 and the Liberals 59.

He was, as Baxter had rightly discerned, fully engaged only when he was working on his travel column for the paper, and on the books that the column could be turned into. The success of *In Search of England* prompted him to make equivalent journeys around Scotland, Ireland and Wales. Fortunately, he was genuinely free from the English vice of conflating 'England' and 'Britain'. His having had a Scottish mother – to whose memory he dedicated *In Search of Scotland* – may have had something to do with it. He recognised that Scotland, Ireland and Wales each had a unique history, culture and landscape, and that each country demanded its own, respectful search: they were not to be tacked on to England as mere Celtic appendages. This lack of English chauvinism happened also to make sound commercial sense, for it opened up opportunities for three more books. In the event, he was able to stretch the three obvious new 'search' books – on Scotland, Ireland and Wales – to four. Scotland generated two books. He published these four books, plus another, unrelated book of essays, in just over four years, between August 1929 and October 1933, thereby keeping up the strike rate of over a book a year that he maintained for nearly twenty years.*

In Search of Scotland came first. It was published on 1 August 1929. Morton was in Scotland for the launch, spending '3 drunken weeks' there and scoring with women three times, according to his diary. 'My book,' he noted on his return to London on 31 August, 'is a best seller.' Like his previous books, *In Search of Scotland* was based on articles in the *Daily Express,* but the process of revision and expansion had been more thorough than it had been for his earlier books. For whom was he writing? In the books on England the narrator is tacitly addressing an English, Home Counties readership. This did not, it seems, put off readers in the rest of Britain. The books sold well in America, too. And there were translations of the book. Clearly, plenty of readers were happy to overhear, so to speak, the narrator talking to his southern English compatriots. And what they heard him saying was something like, 'Go out and search for your country – and if you can't, no matter,

---

*During the eighteen years between 1925, the year in which he had made his breakthrough with the London books, and 1943, during the Second World War, when his productivity started to taper off, he published twenty-six books. Thereafter, he issued new books at the rate of about one every three years, until 1969, when his output of completely new work ceased.

for I've found it on your behalf and can testify that it's there (although I'm not going to disclose the precise location of its quintessence).' This mode could not be maintained, unaltered, when the narrator left his own country, in search of another. The narrator of *In Search of Scotland* frankly presents himself as an Englishman, driving over the border, eager to discover a country he says he does not know. But behind this guileless persona hovered a writer who'd done a very great deal of homework, and who had stacked piles of books on Scottish history and literature into the boot of the Bullnose Morris. The narrator does not bowl along, turning down any lane that entices him, and gazing through the windscreen with innocent eyes. He comes well-informed, equipped with the shaping myths of Scotland – from Sir Walter Scott, to John Knox, to Highland Cattle, to Bonnie Prince Charlie, to tartan, haggis and Clydeside shipbuilding (although not of the Act of Union, which the book ignores).

These myths, unlike the myths of England, tend not to direct the search for the nation's soul to a village, deep in the countryside. The trajectory of the narrator's quest, therefore, does not end in the Scottish equivalent of the anonymous Warwickshire village. Nor do the myths of Scotland inhibit its cities from playing pivotal roles in conceptions of the nation's culture. In searching for Scotland, it would be unthinkable for the narrator to have avoided industrial cities, and when he rolls into Dundee, Aberdeen and Glasgow, he conveys no sense of having to make some sort of special plea for them, as he had felt obliged to when he had rolled into Manchester, Liverpool and Birmingham. In searching for Scotland, Morton was deploying a richer, more complex set of myths. And his deployment was very successful: the number of editions that were called for kept pace evenly with *In Search of England*. Although he writes frankly as a visiting Englishman, his book on Scotland found favour with plenty of Scots, judging by the quantities of copies that sit dustily on the shelves of Scottish second-hand bookshops.

Indeed, for three modern commentators, Morton's nationality seems not to have been an obstacle to his presentation of Scotland. J. R. and M. M. Gold, in a book that examines the ways in which Scotland has been imagined and represented, show some of the ways in which Morton's account was regulated by myths, but they do not conclude that his account was in some way doubly regulated – by his also being English. And in a review of the re-issue in paperback of *In Search of Scotland*, Alan Taylor concludes that Morton's account is more compelling than that of his contemporary, the Scot Edwin Muir, who published an account of his own *Scottish Journey* in the early 1930s.[15] Of course it is not unusual for visitors' accounts of a country to be recognised by the natives as particularly insightful. The best-selling recent travel book on Britain, *Notes from a Small Island*, was written by an American, Bill Bryson. But whereas Bryson makes great play with the comic possibilities inherent in the encounter between a native of Des Moines, Iowa and the natives of Britain, Morton, in his books on Scotland, does not trade heavily on his being English. He succeeds in presenting Scotland in its own right, rather than in its relationship with the narrator and his own country.

In Search of Scotland opens, on an early autumn morning, with the narrator motoring up across the Northumberland moors to the Scottish border at Carter Bar. What determined his route, which took him up through Edinburgh to Inverness, then west to Skye, and south to Glasgow? He does not make his plans explicit, but it becomes plain fairly soon that the narrator is not travelling at random: he is guided by some recognisable conventions of the travel writer. His conception of the country, and therefore of what he wants to see, is threefold. It is drawn from literature, from a version of the nation's history that gives pride of place to the acts of great men and women, and from an underlying notion of the nation's deep, racial characteristics. This threefold conception means that he will be attracted to landscapes that he encountered first in the pages of Burns or Scott, it means that he will search out the exact spots at which decisive incidents in Scottish history took place, and it means that he will interpret the behaviour of the people he encounters along the way by reference to their supposed 'Celtic' character.

The literary influence on Morton's conception of Scotland is clear from the start. And in this respect, he was not at all unusual. There is no innocent eye through which a landscape may be viewed. The viewer's sensory impressions are elaborated by his or her precon-ceptions, and chief among them are those implanted by art. Examples of our readiness to yield to the characterisations of landscapes given by artists are manifold: Hardy's Wessex, Constable's Essex–Suffolk border, Wordsworth's Lake District, Mark Twain's Mississippi . . . the list is endless. Landscapes are not intrinsically enchanting. Artists enchant them. And as visitors to these landscapes, we readily fall under the spell of these enchantments. In Morton's case, it is the Border ballads, and, in particular, the collection made by Scott for his *Minstrelsy of the Scottish Border* (1802), that govern his response to the landscapes he passes through as he crosses the border. The Border ballads, the narrator asserts, 'come down to us with the wind and the rain in them, and between their lines the thin echo of a harp. We cannot fail to recognise in them the authentic gateway to another world.' So convinced is he that these ballads are reliable testimony to an ancient, violent, magical world that he is impatient with scholars who try to separate the genuinely ancient from Scott's own, late-eighteenth-century imitations. 'It is enough for me that these songs recreate the spirit of their time so deftly that, as I read them, I can feel a horse under me and a spear beside me at the saddle-bow.' The feedback between the landscape and literary representations of it gives rise to some colourful, if fanciful descriptions. The spell of the borders, he writes, is

the spell of a country wild and untameable, whose every nook and corner is marked down on the map of romance. There can be no wild place in the world which men have embroidered more richly with daring deeds. It shares with all places in which generations of men have loved or hated an arresting importance, almost as if some part of their passion had soaked itself into the grass and into the hard surface of the rocks, making them different from other grass and rocks. [16]

Morton readily yielded to Scott's enchantments: he read the *Minstrelsy* as straight history and topography. Somewhat contradictorily, though, he could break the spell and shrewdly recognise that Scott 'created the modern conception of Scotland' by writing books that glamorised the Highlands, the clans and the kilt. Morton also noted that it was Scott's astute choreography of the visit by a tartan-clad George IV to Edinburgh in 1822 – the first visit from across the border by a Hanoverian monarch – that habituated Scots to the alien dynasty. Morton acknowledges that Scott prepared the way for Queen

Victoria's Balmoral love affair with the Highlands. Jacobitism had been transformed from a persistent threat of civil war to a romantic, noble memory.[17] Morton makes all this plain, and by so doing, he knocks much of the stuffing out of one of the key Scottish myths – one to which he had himself been susceptible.

The second source of Morton's conception of Scotland is the nation's history, especially the dramatic episodes. Royal intrigues, especially tragic ones, and battles that involve claymores, bagpipes and heather are his staples. How does Morton incorporate into his text the lengthy passages of complicated historical background that are essential if his narrator is to bring to life the sites he visits? His account of Melrose Abbey and the story of the heart of Robert the Bruce is a good example: 'I was sitting on a stone in the grass beside the broken north aisle of Melrose Abbey. Birds were singing . . .' (A handsome sepia plate of the abbey is inserted in the text at this point.) Then comes a pretty young woman, entering vampishly, as if on to a stage from the wings:

> I became aware of a strange scratch and rustle on the other side of the wall. Some one was trying to walk along the narrow ledge and turn the corner without falling off. Then – such things do occasionally happen to the traveller – a remarkably long, thin leg in a brown silk stocking appeared round the corner of the wall and felt blindly for a foothold. Lower and lower it felt, revealing itself with the generosity of authentic beauty. My intention, which was to spring forward helpfully and guide the foot to stone, was arrested by the sight of a narrow garter.

Flustered by having been observed by the narrator, the young woman expresses her embarrassment. Her accent instantly identifies her to the narrator as an American college girl, from Boston. She requires instruction, for she wants to know the story of the heart of Robert the Bruce. The scene is set. It needs only the final touch, the once common, almost automatic bonding ritual between two people. He asks:

> 'Shall I tell you?'
>> 'Why, certainly, if you know the story.'
>> 'Have a cigarette?'
>> 'Well, yes, I guess I will.'

And he's off. While she 'sits with her superb legs crossed, flicking cigarette ash on the daisies', he entrances her with the story of the Bruce's heart, carried off on a pilgrimage to the Holy Land, before being brought back to Scotland to be buried at Melrose. He concludes this romantic story by dutifully pointing out that the office of work's excavations have failed to substantiate it.[18]

In this episode, Morton's stage-management is pretty obvious, but elsewhere in the book, especially when he makes the narrator speak straight to the reader, free from the contrivances of chance meetings with suitable interlocutors, he writes superb passages of popular history. Among the best is his evocation of the year 1566, which his narrator conducts from the ramparts of Stirling Castle. The focus of his evocation is the baptism, in December of that year, at the castle, of the future James VI of Scotland and I of England, son of the Catholic Mary Queen of Scots. Without appearing breathless, and within the space of seven pages, written in the vivid present tense – 'Stirling is full of foreign fashions and loud with the tongues of France and Italy' – Morton sets James's baptism against the backgrounds of the Reformation, the voyages of exploration to the New World, the infancy of Shakespeare, the claims of the French on the Scottish Court, the strains in Mary's marriage to Darnley, the charms of his rival Bothwell, and the diplomatic manoeuvres of her Protestant second cousin, Elizabeth I of England. It is a tour de force, combining panoramic sweep, vivid detail and extreme compression. Of course some of the detail is imagined – 'Every house in Stirling lodges members of the courtly suites. Foreign swords lean against homely Scottish firesides; barns are full of foreign horses' – but this is romantic history in the grand style, a perfect example of what made Morton's books so deservedly popular.[19]

When Morton uses the device of drawing history from the mouth of one of the characters that the narrator meets on his travels, the result is not as panoramic and stylish as the Stirling Castle passage, but it can still be very effective. For example, the narrator stays at a hotel in Perth, on his way north. There he meets a commercial traveller whose job takes him regularly to every corner of the Highlands, and who is scornful of tourists who go there 'to drivel about Bonnie Prince Charlie and the clans'. His own, unromantic analysis of the decline of the ancient Highland way of life is based on demographic and economic considerations. The clan system, he argues, was doomed as soon 'as the Highlands made definite contact with the modern world'. When brought into sharp juxtaposition with a modernising Lowland Scotland, the Highlands' archaic, anachronistic condition became plain.[20] The commercial traveller's analysis is couched in more coherent terms than might be expected from a chance encounter in the lounge of a hotel: no doubt Morton either tidied it up and elaborated it, or simply invented the commercial traveller, for the purpose of incorporating a necessary counterweight to the romantic version of Scottish history.

Underlying his literary and historical conceptions of Scotland is a third, racial conception. When touring England, Morton had breezily characterised the people of the regions through which he travelled as 'Saxon', or 'Viking'. He is no less confident when he is in Scotland. Scots, he asserts, are different from the English, and within the Scottish nation, Highlanders express a particularly exalted version of the national character, for their aristocratic souls, unlike those of the Saxons, have never been imprinted with the cultural memory of feudal serfdom. The Highlander is 'an almost dangerous sentimentalist. His pride is nearly always greater than his poverty. Appeal to him and you find the aristocrat; offend him and you find the eternal warrior.'[21]

The racial conceptions that underlie the book are at their most insistent when the narrator is describing the National War Memorial, in Edinburgh. Today, war memorials have tended to merge with the routine street furniture of towns and villages: they tend to be noticed no more than pillar boxes or telephone kiosks. But for Morton's generation, they were new and poignant civic expressions of each locality's recent grief. Morton's narrator regularly comments on the quality of the memorials he sees as he travels around. Galashiels's memorial, for example, wins high praise from him, whereas Sir Edwin Lutyens's memorial to the dead of the LNER railway, in York, is dismissed as 'third class'.[22] The Scottish national shrine, to which he devotes a sepia full-page plate, draws forth homage from him, for it embodies, he argues, the Scottish national temperament. He compares the florid shrine with Lutyens's severe Cenotaph in Whitehall, asserting that they 'are the most remarkable symbols in existence of the temperamental difference between the two nations'.

> One is Saxon and inarticulate; the other is Celtic and articulate. Grief locks up the English heart, but it opens the Scottish. The Celt has a genius for the glorification of sorrow. All his sweetest songs are sad; all his finest music is sad; all his greatest poetry springs from tragedy.
>
> That is why Scotland has built the greatest war memorial in the world.[23]

At the close of the book, the narrator drives down through Galloway, from the cottage in Alloway where Robert Burns was born, to Dumfries, where he died. This climax to the Scottish journey is the equivalent of the narrator's decision to end his England books in Shakespeare's Stratford-upon-Avon. But Burns and Shakespeare, he insists, do not have an exact equivalence in their respective nation's lives: 'Burns means more to Scotland than Shakespeare means to England. Shakespeare is reverenced in England; in Scotland Burns is loved.' There is no English poet, he says, whose songs, like Burns's, 'have curled up like an old dog on the hearthstone'. To demonstrate the Scots' deep affection for Burns, the narrator engineers a boozy evening in a Dumfries pub that the poet was supposed to have frequented. The narrator respectfully insinuates himself into the company of a group of drinkers, most of them ex-soldiers, and one of them blinded at Ypres. Drink flows, Burns's songs are sung, his poems are recited from memory, and, just before closing time, one of the company, a road-mender with 'great hard hands', is moved to proclaim the sense of common humanity that runs through Burns's verse. The narrator is touched by what he calls this 'expression of a great truth'. And so the book ends, with the drinkers going their ways into the moonlit Dumfries night, and the narrator preparing to drive back home, the following morning, to England. The culmination of Morton's search for England had been a hierarchical, deferential village. The culmination of his search for Scotland, by contrast, is a pub, where the common people sing the democratic songs of their finest poet.

*

In Search of Scotland gave Morton another success, and, with the formula now well established, he pressed on with books on Ireland and Wales. A few years later, in 1933, and building on the success of his Scottish book, he published its successor, *In Scotland Again*. Although the books on Ireland and Wales intervened, it makes sense to break with chronology and look at the second Scottish book here.

When Morton had gone off on his second English journey, he had declared his purpose, which was to make redress both to northern England and to the industrial cities. He had no such clear purpose for his second Scottish journey, and it shows. The book is rather aimless. It is, from time to time, lit up by brilliant bits of description. Eyemouth, for example, 'stands facing the sea like someone warding off a blow'. Equally, there are brilliant encapsulations of bits of Scottish history. In the Cairngorms, for example, he stays overnight with a Catholic deerstalker in his bothy high in the mountains, and comments: 'Little Catholic communities exist in the hills like unmelted snow, for the fires of Calvinism never reached so far.'[24] But overall, the book is uncharacteristically plodding. The pace of the first Scottish book is kept up by the excitement the narrator communicates as he drives through a country unknown to him, and the historical episodes, chosen judiciously and told with great verve, never slow the narrative's wheels to a stop. But the successor volume is weighed down with lengthy summaries of, and quotations from, the books that Morton was reading as he made his tour. If, along his way, the narrator picks up an old book of local custom and legend at a second-hand bookstall, undigested slabs of that book quickly appear in his own text. And the route of the journey is shapeless and unbalanced. He starts in Galloway, and a quarter of the book is over before he leaves for the rest of the country.

There are, though, some interesting sections. In two of them, the narrator leaves his car and sets serious foot on the Highlands. The first is his account of a walk of about twenty-five miles, across the Corrieyairack Pass, from Laggan to Fort Augustus. This is a formidable day's walk, but the narrator seems to manage it fairly easily, interpolating into his account lengthy asides about General Wade, the eighteenth-century builder of the now derelict road,* and

---

*Following the defeat of the Jacobite rebellion of 1745, Wade was commissioned by the British government to build roads to open up the Highlands.

extracts from a book about the failure of Sir John Cope, the Hanoverian commander, to engage Bonnie Prince Charlie's Jacobite army on the pass in 1745. The second is the narrator's account of a yet more formidable walk, the two-day, forty-mile trudge from Aviemore, through the Larig Ghru Pass, and down Glen Tilt to Blair Atholl. Oddly, when he is contemplating the walk ahead of him, he writes: 'it was a rash and impetuous adventure for one who had done no walking since the War.' Either he has forgotten that, a week or two (and eighty pages) earlier, he had walked the Corrieyairack – not a walk that would readily fade from the memory of someone who'd actually done it – or there was a bit of poor continuity in Morton's editing together of the various bits and pieces, written over several years, from which the book was constructed. His account of the walk through the Larig Ghru, with its details of the terrain and the weather, and its details of the aching limbs, sodden feet and stabbing knee pains that attend walks of this severity, is entirely plausible, save for one small incident. He stays overnight, half-way through his trek, at the lonely bothy of a deer stalker (the Catholic mentioned above). In order to intensify the feeling of remoteness of his lodging, he uses a device that he had used before – at the cottage in Roseland, Cornwall – and would use again, the device of the crackling, distant sound of a London West End dance band coming intermittently through on the owner's radio earphones. [25]

Did Morton actually undertake these walks? And if he did, did he go alone? The painlessness of the crossing of the Corrieyairack Pass, together with the speed with which the walk was forgotten by the narrator, makes the account a bit dubious. But the account of the Larig Ghru walk seems more authentic, and there is diary evidence to support it, although it is from the diary for 1929 – four years before the publication of the book in which the walk is described. The entry for 12 September in the 1929 diary reads: 'Night train to Edinburgh', and the entry for the following day reads: 'Motored up to Aviemore with Freddie and Neil Maclaren from Edinburgh.' On 13 September, he wrote, 'Set off to walk the Larig-ghru. 20 miles in one day. Slept in Lamont's cottage – a stalker.' The next day he records 'Another 20 miles through Glen Tilt to Blair Atholl. Dead beat.' He makes no mention of companions – or indeed of anything else – in these brief entries, so it is unclear whether the Maclarens accompanied him on the actual walk or not, although an aside from a later book hints that he did not walk alone.[26] If Morton did undertake the walk alone, he was intrepid. What is clear from the diary entry, though, is that he did the walk as part of a special trip from London, by train and then with friends in a car, in 1929, and not as part of a single, continuous, solo journey in his Bullnose Morris. The 1929 diary shows that Morton patched together *In Scotland Again* from a number of trips that he had made, often with friends, over the years.[27] The narrative spine of the book – the lone traveller chugging through the glens, on his own, in a little car – is a clever literary device, not a plain transcript of the events in Morton's life. For example, the passage in the book where the narrator records his impressions of Inverary, home of the Duke of Argyll,[28] does not break the convention of the narrator's always being a lone, amused spectator, on the edge of the crowd. But the diary for September 1929 records that Morton was travelling with a friend and that they 'lunched with the Duke of Argyll at Inverary Castle'.

When the narrator is in the far north, motoring from glen to glen, try as he might, he cannot hold back the tendency of his descriptions of breathtaking landscapes to slither together into one composite picture: there is only so much that can be done with mist, lochs and heather. Moreover, the book is weighed down by an incorrigibly tragic version of Scottish history. The Highland glens, in the narrator's account, are still suffering from post-Jacobite gloom, and even Galloway, in the south west, is haunted by the viciousness of the Reformation. But there is a marked shift in the tone of the book when the narrator reaches Aberdeen and goes to sea with a trawler crew for a few days.[29] He is at once intimately cooped up with ten crewmen who are, initially, none too pleased to have a landsman sharing their cabin and getting in the way of their dangerous work. The narrator gives a brilliant description of an incredibly hard life. He cannot resist trotting out the device of the crackly radio, tuned in for herring prices, but picking up a foxtrot coming faintly over the airwaves from the dance band at the Dorchester, but on the whole he stays close to the job of describing the trawler crew's pattern of bursts of wet, cold labour, interspersed with brief periods of sleep in a reeking cabin. The twenty pages describing his experience on the trawler are among the most vivid in the book, and, strangely, this is because when the trawler puts out to sea, it breaks free from the sometimes suffocating constraints of Morton's version of Scottish history. The crew is a collection of unique individuals, which the narrator respectfully describes. Interestingly, their nationality isn't remarked on: the trawler could equally have put out from Hull, or Yarmouth, or Ostend. Maybe Morton was liberated by his few days' respite from the enterprise of having to interpret every person he met as the embodiment of some aspect of the ponderous legacy of Scottish history.

Taking the two books on Scotland together, there is no doubt that Morton felt and communicated a real bond with the country. When he crossed the border, his spirits rose, and he looked and listened avidly. His attempts to transcribe Scottish accent and dialect, for instance, differentiate carefully between Highland and Lowland speech. He did his historical homework assiduously, and at his best he makes the past live again. Of the two books, *In Search of Scotland* is the finer. It is fresher and more shapely. Morton's love of Scotland, and his commercial instincts, made him follow through with the sequel, *In Scotland Again*, but in comparison, it is rather heavy-handed: it is clogged, rather than invigorated by its freight of historical anecdote, and it lacks the vitality of the narrator's first encounter with the country.

Morton spent much of 1930 working on *In Search of Ireland*. It was published in December. His regular assignments for the *Daily Express* included coverage of the R101 airship disaster in October, and earlier, in January, a trip to Rome to cover the wedding of Prince Umberto and Princess Marie of Belgium. On his way to the wedding, when the Rome Express stopped in Paris, he had just enough time to dash off to a brothel and get back to the station in time to catch the train for its onward journey. In a notebook of random recollections and ideas for books, he sketched a plan for a piece about a Paris brothel called 'The House of All Nations'. He planned to include the story of a man – though not, he punctiliously noted, himself – who was

> due to leave St. Lazare at 8.45 who at 8 p.m. dashed here, demanded a
> girl, 'tout press', took her, paid for her, and was out in 10 minutes with

his shoes untied, looking for a taxi. Departing, he pressed a chestnut into the hands of Madame & the girl & was seen off with broad smiles and cries of 'Bon voyage'.

In the same notebook he wrote: 'the thing a successful man does is to indulge his instinctive polygamy. Poverty is the great moralist. Most rich men have harems; all men who have made money satisfy their sexual hunger.' This is written as a detached, neutral observation, but it describes his own practice as he became richer – although he had not been exactly celibate when he'd been young and short of money.

In his diaries, he records, with a touch of incredulity, the gratifying way in which the royalty cheques were flowing in from Methuen. In January 1930, he wrote: 'I am delighted – I can hardly believe – that Scotland has sold over 30,000 since August. My half year's royalty cheque will be about £2,700. This is, of course, the biggest sum I have ever made!' The entry goes on to record a bid by Hodder and Stoughton to lure him away from Methuen with £1,000 advances on his forthcoming books. He reckons that he can write two books a year, and muses that the extra £2,000 that a switch to Hodder would bring is 'not to be winked at'. But in the event, he stayed with Methuen, for the time being.

The groundwork for his book on Ireland was laid carefully. He had been making trips there at least since 1928. Among his correspondence are two letters from his children, Michael, then aged nine, and Barbara, aged seven, sent to him at the Shelbourne Hotel, Dublin. (Michael makes the very practical request to his father that, 'If you can not catch a lepricorn, get me an Irish motor car,' and supplies a drawing of the model he wants.) In June/July 1929, Morton went to Ireland again, for a fortnight, and this time, unusually, he took Dorothy. 'Lovely time. Enjoyed Ireland thoroughly.' Their trip, however, was blemished by an incident in a hotel that indicates how touchy Morton was about his appearance and ancestry. On their return to London, he wrote in his diary:

Was terribly annoyed and hurt at Valentia [Valencia, in the south-west?] when some commercial traveller wrote 'mongrel' against my nationality in the hotel register. It was a filthy dirty trick & I can't see

his motive. Possibly he was one of the many enemies of the "D.E."
[*Daily Express*].*

Early in the following year, 1930, he got down to work in earnest. On
Sunday 9 February, he 'stayed in bed all day reading up books on
Ireland'.

In mid-June, after a long gap, he made an entry in his diary that
summarises the preceding months. His half-yearly royalty cheque, for
£2,700, has come in, the children have measles, he's won £200 on the
Derby in a sweepstake, he's writing his book on Ireland, two recent
mistresses have departed from his life, and he and Dorothy are 'very
happy'. Five months later, in mid-November, he made another
reflective entry in his diary. This one, however, expressed frustration:

> *16 November.* Am having a thin time at home. Doll nervy and hysterical.
> Says I criticise her, wants to leave me etc. It is a fact that she at times
> drags behind & doesn't understand social life or opportunities; but I
> don't care. Her other qualities balance this inevitable provincialism.
>
> Now when I am making good I need enthusiasm and support for all
> my schemes. If I live for 20 years I would like to see my family set in
> English soil with an old house & a few trees, a stream & a field or two.
> But what can I do with a wife who has no real interest and no real
> ambition?

His marriage was now in a bad way. But his career as a writer was
flourishing: his income would soon be large enough for him to buy his
way into the myth of England, by purchasing an old house, set in
English soil.

In December 1930, just a couple of weeks after he made this gloomy
assessment of his marriage, his ambitions, and Dorothy's alleged lack
of them, *In Search of Ireland* was published. Morton was generally very
cautious about making his political views public. His narrator's
studious avoidance of overt reference to the National Strike, while on
his journey around England in 1926, is typical. But Ireland was a

---

*Later, when travelling in Palestine, he did not like it when, because he was wearing a hat, an Arab woman
thought that he was a Jew. He immediately bought himself a Bedouin headscarf. See *In the Steps of the
Master*, pp. 278–80.

different matter. Would it be possible to travel around an island that had such a bitter history of relations with England, without indicating where he stood? In Scotland, the final Jacobite Rising, about which Morton sensitively, but uncontentiously, wrote, was nearly two hundred years safely into the past, but in Ireland, the Easter Rising of 1916, the Anglo Irish Treaty of 1921, whereby the Irish Free State and a partitioned Northern Ireland were established, and the Civil War of 1922–3 were all far too recent, too painful, too raw to have been moulded into manageable, uncontested myths. The easy way out for Morton would have been for him to have tiptoed around all these problems, and to have resorted to older, hoarier Irish myths. St Patrick, Celtic Christianity, leprechauns, poteen, blarney, fair colleens, Americans seeking their roots . . . there is plenty for him to have worked on. But surprisingly, he did not avoid the recent politics of Ireland. Indeed, he took them head on, in an openly partisan fashion, declaring both his conviction that Ireland's claim to sovereignty was just, and his belief that Partition would be only temporary. 'Every man,' he wrote, 'no matter of what nationality, must be glad that this generation has seen the end of the fight and the victory of the Gael.'[30] If this seems sanguine, it has to be remembered that Morton was writing forty years before the unresolved troubles associated with Partition erupted, in 1969, into a seemingly interminable period of sickening violence. To Morton, writing in 1930, the treaty of 1921 satisfactorily answered the ancient 'Irish Question': 'the most unhappy and regrettable chapter in the history of Great Britain has ended, and the two nations are at last free to make friends.'[31] As he travelled around post-treaty Ireland, he had no way of knowing that Partition would heap up intractable problems: he wrote as someone relieved and glad to be in a country that had finally achieved a measure of justice. When he crossed the border from the Free State into Northern Ireland and saw the new parliament buildings going up, at great expense, he was slightly exasperated, believing that unification of the entire island would quickly make them obsolete. The narrator says that he is aware of the view that Northern Ireland will remain outside the Free State for ever, and he presents an encounter with a Belfast Protestant hard-liner who responds to his mild suggestions about the advantages of unification with the south by blazing up with ' "how could we be ruled by a lot of Catholics?" ' But his optimism is not seriously dented: 'I cannot help feeling that if the right moment came the Churches could bring the north and south together in six months.'[32]

In Search of Ireland is by no means all about the island's recent political past. It is a record of a tour that celebrates Irish landscape and culture. The book does not always manage to keep out of the Celtic Twilight; it gives way from time to time to such characterisations of the landscape as 'buried beneath the grass and hidden in the trees, is something that is half magic and half music'.[33] But overall, the leprechaun-ridden version of Ireland is kept in check. The narrator's response to the country is fresh and vivid. For instance, when he is in a Connemara village he observes that 'sometimes a hen, making busy ruminating noises, will walk out of a cabin and stand a moment in the sunlight on the threshold, looking round with one foot lifted rather like a man-about-town putting on his gloves on the steps of his club.'[34] Even the ritual tourist visit to the Guinness brewery in Dublin – an occasion unlikely, it seems, to produce any original prose – delivers this brilliant little sentence: 'Yeast is added to assist fermentation, and as you look through a door you see this khaki-coloured scum moving in a slow, repulsive manner, opening and closing a bubbly eye here and there with a kind of obscene intelligence.'[35]

The narrator's encounter with Ireland, as with England and Scotland, is mediated by historical and cultural myths, but in one respect, as the narrator himself notes, Ireland is different. It has had no Sir Walter Scott.[36] There is of course no shortage of great Irish writers, and, just as important, and as Morton discovered, the country has a living oral tradition of story-telling, but there is no Irish writer who stands in relation to his or her country as Sir Walter stands to his – that is, as a popular author who has helped shape and codify the nation's conception of itself by writing sweeping historical novels, in English, that dramatise the key episodes in the nation's history. The myths of Ireland are more diffuse and are often encoded in a language, Gaelic, and an oral tradition that is frustratingly impenetrable to the narrator.

The great national myths, then, are incompletely formulated and many of them are, in any case, inaccessible to the visitor. The myths that are accessible – the leprechauns, the blarney – are a bit threadbare and limited. But Morton's book could not do without some sort of commanding conception of the nation. What did he come up with? A notion that he elaborates as the book develops is that Ireland has somehow managed to reach the twentieth century without having had to sever its links with its medieval, horse-drawn, anti-mechanistic, spiritual past. Ireland has had no Reformation and no Industrial Revolution. Thus, it has escaped the Protestant work ethic and the curse of the machine. 'Ireland may be poor, but at least her flesh and blood are not humiliated by that tyranny of mechanical things which is inseparable from the production of modern wealth.'[37] Spiritually Ireland is still in intimate touch with the Celtic saints, and materially it lives in the eighteenth century. This is not a startlingly original notion, and it depends on some questionable assumptions, especially about Belfast, which is a thoroughly industrialised city, but it is serviceable and it helps Morton to equip his narrator with a perspective from which he can make his observations as he travels round the country. And what he observes are, first, the handsome Georgian streets of Dublin, and then a placid green countryside in which horses are venerated and machines are merely tolerated. To take some examples: race-meetings, the narrator says, have a 'Hogarthian robustness', for 'Ireland is a country of vivid personalities, as England was in the eighteenth and nineteenth centuries before life was influenced by standardization.' His summary of the view from his hotel window of market day in a neat little country town is: 'it is all so peaceful and so drenched in the sanity of the eighteenth century.' And his conclusion, as he walks away from a grand house where he had been very civilly entertained to lunch, is this: 'I looked back at the walled house. That wall protected a few acres of the eighteenth century.'[38]

The image of a benign, sane, paternally-regulated Georgian land-scape is powerful. It is as if Morton had found in Ireland what, in England, could now be only imagined: the essential England is maybe alive and well in Ireland. Morton is certainly tempted by this conception of Ireland, but there were too many glaring objections to it for him to have been entirely captivated. Chief among the objections is the brute fact that far from there having been a natural, benign harmony between Irish landowners and their tenants, as there would have been in the landscape of his dreams, there was a history of oppression. The narrator fully recognises this and acknowledges the injustice of it. In Kerry, for instance, he stands in the ruins of a grand house and explains how it was burned down, in 1922, in a long-awaited act of retribution by the descendants of the ancient Irish owners of the property, who had been dispossessed by Cromwell during the seventeenth century.[39] And in another passage he honestly demolishes the picture of a stable social order that he was, in some ways, tempted to paint:

> It seems to me that the pictures of Irish life are desperately incomplete. Behind all the laughter, the horse-coping, the steeplechasing, the drinking, the intrigue is a character who never appears, but one who has proved himself the most important in modern Irish history: the sullen countryman with a pitchfork. He stands behind a stone wall watching the hunt go by, a member of an inferior race but, in his own imagination, the descendant of saints and kings.[40]

Another objection to the otherwise attractive idea of a peaceful, agricultural country, making its way without resorting to industrialisation, is the extent and depth of rural poverty, especially in the west. The narrator spends time in Connemara, in a region of thin soil and barefooted people who live in earth-floored cabins, close to their animals, and who are kept alive by remittance money coming across the Atlantic from sons who have been forced to emigrate. The narrator makes no bones about the harshness of their conditions, but leaning heavily on the guide books he was using as he travelled around, he invests the people with a dignity that derives from their possession (he assumes) of an unbroken Gaelic tradition of song and legend. He yearns to be able to understand the songs that he hears being sung in the fields, and even though his yearning remains unappeased, he concludes that 'the manner in which these Irish peasants have kept alive the traditional literature of the Gael is one of the wonders of the world.'[41]

Although the narrator finds the idea of a non-industrial Ireland appealing, he is not a Luddite. He visits a vast hydro-electric scheme on the river Shannon, and canvasses the arguments for and against it. Will it draw in industrial development and thus disastrously transform the character of the country? Or will it dispel some of the useless darkness

The frontispiece of *In Search of England*, a fine sepia photograph by B. C. Clayton, entitled, with studied topographical imprecision, 'A lane in England'.

Morton, in uniform, in a trench during an archaeological dig, in search of Roman remains, in a back garden in Colchester, where he was stationed during the First World War. This peaceful trench – the only sort that he experienced during the war – contrasts savagely with the battlefield trenches across the Channel in France.

One of Mary Morton's photographs from *In the Steps of the Master* (1934). This is 'The old road from Jerusalem to Jericho'. Mary, Morton's second wife, accompanied her husband on many of his journeys.

Morton's house, 'South Hay', in Binsted, Hampshire, photographed for an article in *Country Life* in 1942. This is the sort of house Morton dreamed of when he said that he wanted to see his family settled 'in English soil with an old house & a few trees, a stream & a field or two.' The *Country Life* article described the house as 'a picturesque medieval farmhouse, altered in the sixteenth or seventeenth century, with a glorious southward view.' (Photograph by courtesy of *Country Life*.)

The frontispiece to *Through Lands of the Bible* (1938). The photograph, of the Coptic monastery at Dêr es Surian, was taken by either Mary or H. V. Morton; they shared the credits in this book.

Morton in an unusually informal, rather bohemian, corduroy jacket – although with his customary hat. This was probably taken some time in the nineteen-thirties or forties.

The Binsted Local Defence Volunteers (later the Home Guard) parade on 28 June 1940. Morton commands the volunteers – 'ungrateful yokels' as he once privately referred to them. He looks somewhat ill-at-ease in his badly-fitting uniform: as a cavalry officer during the Great War he was used to rather smarter tailoring.

PARACHUTE LANDINGS SIX RULES

1. RING CHURCH BELL TO AWAKEN VILLAGE.

2. RUSH TO VICARAGE AND TELEPHONE BORDON 48 EXTENSION 37 : SAY WHERE ENEMY HAS LANDED : TIME : HOW MANY.

3. THEN PHONE. H.V.M. (BORDON 239.)

4. IF PHONES CUT, RUSH CYCLIST TO H.V.M AT SOUTH HAY.

5. RUSH CYCLIST TO D. SECTION, KINGS FARM.

6. WATCH CAREFULLY FOR ENEMY MOVES.

THE CORPORAL OF THE GUARD IS RESPONSIBLE FOR CARRYING OUT THESE SIX VITAL ORDERS, HE MUST TAKE COMMAND IN ACTION. HE MUST THINK AND MOVE QUICKLY.

Signed W.M.
Platoon Commander

L.D.V.

Schapenberg, the house at Somerset West, near Capetown, that the Mortons built when they moved there. This view is from the garden. Mary stands at the top of the steps with one of the family's dogs.

Opposite Morton's hand-written draft of the six rules he drew up, in June 1940, for his Home Guard unit to observe in the event of enemy parachute landings. It is signed by the platoon commander, Morton, who refers to himself as 'H. V. M.' in rules 3 and 4. The official 'L.D.V.' stamped over his signature stands for 'Local Defence Volunteers' – the forerunner of the Home Guard.

The elderly Morton at his desk in Schapenberg, with one of the pets of which he was extremely fond.

of the rural areas? His unsentimental conclusion is that the scheme is vital for the future of the new country and that it should be welcomed.[42] And when he reaches Belfast, the only substantial existing industrial area in the island, he looks forward to a happy union of the industrial energy of the north and the agricultural virtues of the south.

'In Ireland,' he writes, 'there is no ancient history: all history is contemporary.'[43] There are no safe, neutral versions. For a writer who liked to enliven his text with historical set-pieces, this was a problem. But he does not shirk, and he tacitly accepts that he cannot be disinterested. His most vivid passage recounts the story of the two sieges of Limerick by the Protestant forces of William III, in 1690. The narrator makes plain his view that the hero of Limerick was the Irish patriot, Patrick Sarsfield. By contrast, the narrator's account of the siege of Derry of 1689, in which the Protestants held out against the Catholic army of James II, is merely dutiful; it does not have the passion of his account of Sarsfield's heroism.[44] Morton was not a Catholic. Any sympathy he had for the old Jacobite cause was purely romantic. And his handling of the sieges and battles in seventeenth-century Ireland shows that he was well aware that the unfortunate country was the site for proxy wars, fought between Louis XIV and his continental rivals, in which the Irish, both Catholic and Protestant, were caught up. But his real sympathy for Irish nationalism is undisguised.

Finally, given the way in which he airily used racial stereotypes when he was characterising the Scots, or the supposedly various peoples of the English regions, what did he make of the Irish? His characterisation is unsurprising. He says that they are anti-materialist dreamers who love talk. The Irishman is 'like a child in parts'. The subject of the narrator's most sustained search for the national soul is a young woman gathering seaweed on the Connemara shore. Casually lighting his pipe, he sits on a rock, watching her closely. He makes her out to be a primitive, and imputes to her the virtues of the noble savage: 'there was a fineness about her, characteristic of all the Connemara peasants, and a queer smothered nobility. This is also typical of the men and women here.' But there is more than anthropological fieldwork going on here. The narrator is a voyeur. 'Those fine legs had never known, or wished to know, the feel of silk.' And there is more than a touch of wishful thinking when he ponders what might happen if, instead of being traded in marriage as part of a deal involving cattle and potato patches, the young woman were to be swept up by a man who 'took her to a city and tried to fit her into his way of life? From Connemara to Curzon Street.' The narrator's erotic interest in the woman comes through disturbingly plainly, but beneath it is an attempt to identify what he sees as essential elements in the Irish character – wild beauty (in the young women, at least), stoicism in the face of an unfruitful, stony land from which a living must be wrested, and a nobility of soul that derives from a magical Celtic past.[45] No surprises there: an Irish myth is in firm control.

In Search of England, and its successor *In Search of Scotland*, had established for Morton a format that could safely and successfully be reproduced whenever he chose to write about a new country. But *In Search of Ireland* is notably not just another commodity rolling off Morton's production line. As the passage describing the young Connemara woman indicates, he fell back from time to time on stereotypes and on self-indulgent writing, but overall he made a serious and quite brave attempt to represent a country in which the recent past was still raw. He could have satisfied his readers with nothing more than tales of Irish saints, and of trips in jaunting cars around the lakes of Killarney, but he faced up to the reality of a country emerging from centuries of what he recognised as English and Scottish injustice, and he responded imaginatively. Fifty years after the book was published, in a letter to Methuen concerning a reprint of the book, Morton's widow wrote, 'It was the book that my late husband preferred in the *Search* series.'[46] It is not difficult to see why.

1931 opened well for Morton. He was a star writer on the *Express*, and the royalties from the nine books he had in print were rolling in. On 9 February he noted in his diary that his next six-monthly royalty cheque would be £5,000. This was almost twice as much as for the equivalent period in the preceding year. 'This is amazing. I have got my public. I ought to leave the "D.E." & cultivate it.' The editor, Baxter, evidently felt the same about his future on the paper, although for different reasons. Ten days later, on 19 February, Morton's diary entry reads: 'The blow has fallen. Baxter tells me I am not pulling my weight. He suggests a pay cut & putting me on a retainer. Upset of course, but it's probably the best thing.' Baxter had upstaged him. The next day's diary entry records the atmosphere at the *Express*: 'I feel rather like Cardinal Wolsey. Everyone in the office knows that my number is up. No-one says anything. All are secretly glad. There is joy in the sight of a favourite fallen from power.' It was not even worth appealing to the proprietor, Lord Beaverbrook. Morton's days at the *Express* were over.

By mid-March he had swiftly moved across to the left-wing *Daily Herald*, at a salary of £5,000 a year. The *Herald* was a Labour, trades-union-oriented paper, whereas the *Express* had been staunchly Conservative. Morton's move, however, signalled no change in his own political outlook; professional journalists move with surprising ease back and forth between left and right-wing papers, and in any case, Morton rarely covered the day-to-day world of politics.

The upheaval in his professional life was mirrored by domestic upheaval. In early 1931, he had started an affair with Mary Grieg, E. V. Lucas's secretary at Methuen. Mary had been divorced in November 1930 and was keen to make a go of her new relationship with Morton. But he could not make up his mind, and at one point he took Dorothy to America for a trip that, he half hoped, might make him forget Mary and inspire him to revive his flagging marriage. But it didn't work. On 1 December he reviewed the preceding eight months:

> I have scoffed as a young man when people have employed such clichés as 'the bitterness of success.' My God – I am tasting it now. I have £10,000 a year & am drinking myself to death. I am unhappy. Since I last wrote in this diary my whole life has been taken up with Mary. We have lived together since March. D. knows & wants a separation. I don't. M. & I are totally unsuited – two violent excitable people. She wants marriage & I <u>must must</u> give her up.

Far from giving her up, his relationship with Mary intensified.

Meanwhile, he was establishing himself on the *Herald*. His *Express* travel column could be transferred without a hitch, and on 25 May 1931, the first article in a series on Wales appeared. And in the by now customary fashion, the series was turned into a book, which was dedicated to Mary and published in June 1932.

The narrator of *In Search of Wales* tours right round the country, recording experiences as diverse as climbing Snowdon and going down a coal mine. He describes castles and cathedrals. He attends an Eisteddfod. He visits a slate quarry and a steel-works. He goes out in a coracle with salmon fishermen. He listens to choirs. He goes to chapel. He writes historical set-pieces on the pivotal moments in Welsh history. He even meets Lloyd George. In short, the book is a comprehensive response to the features of the country that outsiders – and maybe many natives too – are likely to regard as characteristically Welsh. But the book rarely takes wing. Morton was by now a thoroughly accomplished, professional writer, producing prose that is always readable, but the book has a dutiful feel to it. It's as if he was a bit weary as he came to the end of his programme of producing books on each of the countries of the British Isles.

The narrator is badly handicapped by his ignorance of the Welsh language. In the opening paragraph of the introduction to the book he writes, 'I cannot pretend that it was an easy book to write, because the Welsh people possess that surest of retreats from the outsider, their own language.'[47] In Ireland he had been just as ignorant of Gaelic, but his ignorance seems to have been less of a handicap. Why was this? Ireland, and especially the far west, is a long way from England, and when Morton was there, it was not a major tourist destination. To the English, the far west of Ireland was a foreign country, with a foreign language. Morton no more expected to be able to converse with the people of Connemara than, later, he expected to converse with the people of Syria or Turkey. But Wales is contiguous with England along the length of its 150-mile border, and it has long been a regular holiday destination for the English, from well-to-do tourists in the nineteenth century – Ruskin is a famous example – to the working-class holiday-makers that Morton's narrator rather disapprovingly observed arriving by charabanc from the factory towns of the English Midlands and the north. The geographical accessibility of Wales to the English sets up an expectation of an equivalent cultural accessibility, but Morton's narrator finds that this expectation is confounded: Welsh-speakers will not invariably yield to his friendly overtures, and he can see their point, for he acknowledges that, over the centuries, Wales has been treated badly by the English, and that memories are long. He is on the side of the Welsh.

Even the ease with which the motorist can traverse the country brings its disappointments. Driving out along the Lleyn peninsular, the narrator hopes to find a remote and isolated landscape, but finds instead a hotel in which two young Englishmen in golfing outfits are ordering gin-and-its.[48] He does not pause to reflect that by publishing his own rhapsodies about remote places – when he can find them – he is likely to make them less remote. Nor does he note the incongruity of his complaint, when he is visiting a waterfall at Bettws-y-Coed, that 'this waterfall has been sanctified by centuries of sightseeing. I went on to it with the faint feeling that I was being bullied by Ruskin.'[49] He seems never to have considered the possibility that a future reader, on visiting a precious site, would feel that he or she was being bullied by Morton. Perhaps, though, he was wise not to analyse the conventions of the travel book: it might have made his pen stumble.

There are, however, plenty of engaging passages in the book. Little touches, rather than the set-pieces, are the best. In a dreary hotel room, 'a hateful dressing-table mirror reflects the disillusion of a weary double-bed'. Later, on a wet day, he writes: 'Welsh rain . . . It descends with the enthusiasm of someone breaking bad news.' And his comment on a Welsh chapel that he visits is that it 'is a fairly large and hideous building that stands in open country. Welsh chapels belong to the Woolworth Georgian period of architecture; stern buildings that, unlike the English parish church, have never made friends with the landscape.'[50] The historical set-pieces, by contrast, lack sparkle. They are as painstakingly researched as ever, but his accounts of Owen Glendower and of Henry Tudor lack the excitement of his accounts of Patrick Sarsfield in Limerick, or of Mary Queen of Scots in Stirling.

Perhaps the boldest feature of the book is its determination not to confine itself to the picturesque vales, mountains and shorelines. The narrator gives over his final two chapters to his impressions of the industrial areas of south Wales, and he succeeds in integrating industry into his overall conception of the country's character – an achievement he had never been able to manage when he was writing about England. He presents the Welsh coal-miners and steel-workers not as aberrations but as authentic expressions of the national character. They are as essentially Welsh as the farming families of Snowdonia. Near the beginning of his tour, when he was in Caernarvon, in the rural north of the country, he had stopped to hear a choir in a girls' school singing Welsh songs. When he reaches the industrial south, he goes to hear a choir of miners practising in their local village hall. The two choirs are expressions of a single culture, a culture that stands in contrast to its English counterpart:

> This miners' choir was as interesting and in a way as typical of Wales as a cricket match on an English meadow is of England. These men were expressing the Welshness in them. I sensed again that foreignness which I felt in Caernarvon, where most people talk Welsh.[51]

Welsh choirs are not in the realm of politics. They can thus be discussed without inhibition. But depressed industrial areas are fraught with politics, and Morton's narrator treads very carefully when he enters, for he was always cautious about making his political views explicit. He makes no mention at all of the National Strike that had brought the mines and steel-works to a halt five years earlier. There is no doubt that he was humanly sympathetic to the plight of workers and their families: he describes their grim living and working conditions uncompromisingly. But he establishes for himself no political stand-point from which he can attempt to make sense of the ugliness and poverty he describes. His conclusion, for example, to a section in which he describes the desolate life and prospects of a young sixteen-year-old collier is the limp 'It is, of course, all wrong.'[52] Morton was surprisingly fearless in attributing blame to the English for their treatment, throughout the centuries, of Ireland and Wales, but in matters of economic justice between masters and men he had nothing much to say. He is always tugged on the sleeve by a tendency to try to escape, taking his readers with him, into an imagined past where social conflict never arises. But he didn't shirk the task of describing the depressed industrial and mining areas of Wales, and in the peroration with which the book concludes, and in which he looks back at the people he has met, and who collectively symbolise the nation, one of the people is the coal-miner, 'standing silently among the crowd of white-faced men who smelt of coal dust as he waited for the wet cage to spring up out of the earth's dark bowels'.[53]

*

Morton's next book was a selection of essays entitled *Blue Days at Sea*, published in October 1932. Despite its title, and its dedication, 'To all who serve on the high seas', few of the essays are about the sea. The book is a ragbag of pieces left over from other projects. Many of the essays are interesting, but they are so disparate – ranging from an account of a naval burial at sea, to a piece on amateur theatricals, to a piece on a guide to the antiquities of Cairo – that the book fails to add up to anything very coherent. What it indicates is that Methuen could now profitably issue virtually anything that their star author submitted.

But Methuen did not issue the book that followed *Blue Days at Sea*. Improbably, the new book was published, in 1933, by the Labour Party, as *What I Saw in the Slums*, with a foreword by the leader of the party, George Lansbury. This little book, or large pamphlet, priced 2d, is a collection of pieces that Morton had written for the *Daily Herald*. As a working journalist, Morton could turn his hand to any assignment if he had to, no matter how disagreeable he might have found it. An assignment from the editor of the *Herald* to tour the slums may not have been as congenial as a commission to bowl off through the countryside in a little two-seater, but it was entirely within Morton's professional capabilities, and may have been, as a challenge, just as congenial as writing about thatched cottages. And in any case, as the books that record his own, self-selected journeys around Britain show, he was by no means averse to scrutinising and recording the drab, inhumane aspects of urban life. So, although the avowedly political frame that surrounds Morton's text is a real departure for him, the text itself is of a piece with his own regular practice as a writer.

The pamphlet is illustrated with photographs taken by James Jarché, the photographer with whom Morton had first worked back in 1920, when they were both on the *Evening Standard*.* In his introduction, Morton declares that he is not a member of any political party, and that the pieces were not written for propaganda purposes. (Maybe he had little control over what the *Herald* chose to do with his articles.) He insists that his aim was simply to write 'a perfectly frank account of a short journey through the slums of six great industrial cities of England'. This assumed attitude of political detachment did not mean

---

*See above, chapter 3, pp 56–8.

that Morton's human sympathies were disengaged: on the contrary, his text, as it moves from slum to stinking slum, expresses outrage at the conditions he encountered and contempt for slum landlords. They should be 'flung straight into jail'; they should be 'stripped to the waist and whipped squealing through their own kennels'.[54] His sympathies are entirely with slum tenants, especially with the old, with war veterans, and with women, whose dispiriting job it is to maintain the family's respectability in such discouraging circumstances. Of these heroic women he writes:

> What a ghastly life they lead in mean streets. Always washing. Always cooking minute quantities of food. Always cleaning something that cannot be cleaned. Always enriching the earth. Always worried about something. This waste of energy is awful. [55]

The pamphlet is impressive. Morton and Jarché looked closely and talked at length with the victims of slum conditions. They were not just casual passers-by. And the pamphlet is more than a burst of outrage. Morton fortified his text with grim public health and housing statistics gathered from the civic authorities in the cities he described, and he developed an argument about what should be the aim of slum clearance programmes. He is sure that private enterprise is incompetent to solve the problem that it has created. Slums are a problem for the state. Furthermore, he argued, it is not simply a matter of knocking down slums and building housing estates on the edges of cities. Slum tenants cannot afford the rents that would have to be charged in the new estates, and the bus and tram fares that would have to be paid to bring them back into the city for the sort of casual, low-paid work that they depend on would be prohibitive. Slum dwellers need decent, new public housing, built in the very areas occupied by the reeking slums in which they presently have to exist. And despite his avowed political non-partisanship, he singles out Sheffield's Labour City Council for its imaginative and vigorous slum clearance programme.[56]

The book that is taken to be the definitive account of conditions in the north of England during the depressed 1930s is George Orwell's *The Road to Wigan Pier*, published in 1937. Unlike Morton, Orwell chose to stay in cheap, squalid lodgings. He thus gave himself a vantage point denied to Morton. And although Morton's pamphlet drew him, against his habitual impulses, into the world of politics, Orwell's book, right from the start, grew out of, and expresses, a confident, powerful political analysis of a sort that Morton would never have attempted. *What I Saw in the Slums* is not likely to dislodge *The Road to Wigan Pier* from its premier position in the canon of writings about the thirties. But Morton and Jarché's pamphlet deserves a place. It was produced four years before Orwell made his celebrated journey north from London, the photographs are superb, and Morton's text hits home. It is entirely possible – probable even – that Orwell read Morton's pamphlet or the articles in the *Daily Herald* from which it was composed. In Orwell's own book, the description of a kneeling woman, seen from the train, poking a stick up a blocked drain-pipe, has become an emblem of the wretchedness of slum life. When he sees the desolate, hopeless expression on the woman's face, it strikes Orwell that it is a mistake to believe that slum-dwellers are so ignorant that they can imagine nothing better than their slums. Morton was no egalitarian, but he would never have made this insensitive assumption in the first place. Morton's own descriptions of women are just as powerful, and are less patronising. He writes, for example, of women who strive to put a symbolic barrier between their home and the even more squalid street beyond, by whitening the doorstep: 'Thousands of horrid doorsteps, worn as thin as wafers in the centre, are whitened or raddled. Every time a door opens you see a woman cleaning something.'[57] *What I Saw in the Slums* is an impressive little book.

6

1934–1939

THE MIDDLE EAST

In December 1933, Dorothy divorced Morton, and on 4 January in the
following year, he and Mary were married. They lived in what he called
'a rather sumptuous flat' (now demolished) on the corner of Wilton
Street and Grosvenor Place, overlooking the grounds of Buckingham
Palace. Morton's new marriage elicited unusual fidelity from him. His
list of sexual conquests records only a single encounter during its first
two years.

His energies as a writer during the next six years were directed chiefly
toward the Middle East. He produced a trilogy of substantial books on
the region and a couple of lighter-weight books. The first of the trilogy
was *In the Steps of the Master*, based, as usual, on a series of newspaper
articles, but greatly expanded when it reached book form. It was
published not by Methuen, but by Rich and Cowan. According to
Maureen Duffy, the historian of the Methuen publishing house, the
firm's managing director, C. W. Chamberlain, had left after a row. He
moved to Rich and Cowan, and took Morton with him. He and
Morton had always been friendly, but the lure of a thirty-three per cent
royalty, as against the top rate of twenty per cent paid by Methuen,
surely also had something to do with it. Rich and Cowan published
two of Morton's trilogy. Then they went bankrupt. Both Chamberlain
and Morton then moved back to Methuen, with, it seems, no hard
feelings.[1]

At first sight, *In the Steps of the Master* looks like the result of a
shrewd calculation. There was a steady market for guide books to
the Holy Land, aimed at pious tourists, and Morton was never
averse to supplying a promising market. The job of a simple gazetteer

for Christian tourists would have been to take the reader first to Bethlehem, the site of Jesus' birth, then on to Nazareth and Galilee and finally to Jerusalem, the site of his crucifixion. But Morton wrote a hefty book, running to 380 pages, and its pious title turns out to be somewhat misleading. The narrator follows a route substantially different from, and far lengthier than the one trodden by Jesus.

The route that the book records zigzags around the region. It starts with the narrator arriving in Jerusalem, after a train ride from the Egyptian border. This was probably a re-working of Morton's recollections of his first journey to Palestine, back in 1923, when he had finished covering the Tutankhamun story in Egypt. From the point of view of the reader trying to trace Jesus' footsteps, Jerusalem is at the wrong end of his life. But the narrator feels no need to justify his strategy. He assumes that his readers will be so intimately familiar with the Gospel account of Jesus' life that he can himself dip in and out of any part of it, at will. It does not matter that on his first foray into the streets of Jerusalem the narrator immediately loses his way in the maze of the city's alleys, and blunders accidentally into the climax of the story, by turning a corner and finding himself on the *Via Dolorosa* – the road supposed to have been taken by Jesus, carrying his cross, from his trial to his crucifixion on Calvary.

From Jerusalem, the narrator travels south to Jericho and Beersheba, and then north to Nazareth and Galilee, visiting the New Testament sites. At each of them he imaginatively recreates the incident in the life of Jesus that gives the place its significance. A good example is the narrator's description of the few days he spent by the Sea of Galilee, getting to know the fishermen who worked there, exploring the sites associated with Jesus, and filling in the historical background to the Jewish and Roman administration of the area in Biblical times. But as a whole, the book is much more than a New Testament gazetteer. It is a record of an ambitious, extensive Middle Eastern journey. The narrator is interested in not just the sites associated with the life of Jesus, but in the history of the Romans, the Greeks, the Jews, the Bedouin, the Crusaders, the Phoenicians, and any other group that has left its mark on the region – including the British soldiers administering Palestine under the League of Nations mandate.* The journey also gave him the chance to indulge the passion for archaeology and antiquities that he had felt since he was a boy. He is delighted, for example, when he is rooting around in a Jerusalem antique shop, to find a fragment of a Roman Tenth Legion tile.[2] And he is always ready to leave the footsteps of the master, and make detours that follow the footsteps of completely unrelated, unbiblical characters. When he visits what is now Lebanon, for instance, he makes a special trip to the hills above Sidon to visit the ruins of the house built in the early nineteenth century by the eccentric Lady Hester Stanhope, from where she held court as the self-styled 'Queen of Jerusalem'. He tells her strange story as carefully as he tells the stories associated with Jesus.[3] And from Lebanon the narrator takes off on a route that has no documented associations with Jesus, and which he is highly unlikely ever to have travelled. The narrator crosses into Syria and goes to Baalbek and Damascus. Later, on another expedition from Jerusalem, he goes into what is now Jordan, but was then known as 'Trans-Jordan', to visit Amman, El Kerek and Petra.

Why did Morton devise this project? Nothing, either in his early diaries or in his mature *Memoir*, suggests that he was driven by a Christian impulse to go on a pilgrimage to the holy places. But he had always been interested in ancient history and archaeology, and he was powerfully attracted to Middle Eastern landscapes and cultures. His trip to cover the Tutankhamun story had thrilled him, and had left him wanting to return. The impulse for *In the Steps of the Master*, and for his later travels to Mesopotamia, Turkey and Greece, came, I think, from this fascination with both the ancient past and the Middle Eastern present, rather than with anything devoutly Christian.

How did he travel? The book maintains the convention of the lone traveller, although the convenient device of the Bullnose Morris, chugging along the lanes, obviously had to be dropped. The narrator

---

*Until 1917, Palestine was part of the Ottoman Empire. Following Turkey's defeat in the Great War, the League of Nations gave Britain, in 1920, a mandate to administer the region. The 'Balfour Declaration' of 1917 had committed Britain, in principle, to support the establishment of a Jewish homeland, provided that the interests of the non-Jewish communities in Palestine could be secured. The prodigious difficulties of reconciling these two aims led to riots and open warfare between Jews and Arabs, as well as attacks on the British, throughout the twenty-seven years of the mandate. The state of Israel was established in 1947.

concedes, from time to time, that he is being ferried about by local drivers,* and he lets drop information that shows that he was being assisted by officials in high places. But the chief impression that Morton makes the narrator convey is that he travelled alone, on a single, uninterrupted journey. There are no diaries with which the book can be compared, but it is clear that for much of the journey, and maybe for all of it, Morton was accompanied by Mary. Save for a fortnight in Ireland, Morton had not taken Dorothy with him when he was writing his books, but he changed his practice when he met Mary. She was already well-travelled – she was born, on the last day of the nineteenth century, in China – and for the first three years of her marriage with Morton there were no children to be considered. So she was keen to take to the road with her new husband. She is mentioned nowhere in the text of *In the Steps of the Master*, but her presence is tacitly acknowledged, for she is credited with having taken some of the photographs that illustrate the book. (See plate 12.) Morton had complained that Dorothy lacked ambition and wouldn't enthusiastically back his schemes. Mary, by contrast, despite his fears that they were temperamentally unsuited to each other, filled the bill as a travelling companion and willing secretary. Her presence at Morton's side during the journey (or journeys) that resulted in the book is additionally confirmed by something she herself wrote. In the book, the narrator relates an incident concerning a starving stray dog that he encountered in a Syrian village. He is disgusted by the villagers' indifference to the dog's plight, even though he acknowledges that their resources scarcely enable them to feed themselves, let alone a stray dog. He pays a man to look after the sick creature and nurse it back to health, and returns a week or so later, after visiting Damascus, to see that his instructions have been followed.[4] Forty or so years later, when the Mortons were living in South Africa, Mary gave a talk to a group of children about animal welfare. The notes for her talk survive, and contain her own detailed account of the finding of this Syrian dog. She told the children that she had travelled with her husband and that she

---

*In his second book of Middle Eastern travels, *In the Steps of St Paul*, published in 1936, he makes a back reference to the mode of travel he had adopted in *In the Steps of the Master*. For the journey recorded in his second book, he re-engaged Stephan, 'the Armenian who had once driven me through Palestine'. See *In the Steps of St Paul*, p. 3.

had taken a particular interest in the welfare of animals in the countries that they visited.

Even if the primary impulse for the writing of *In the Steps of the Master* was not religious, it would have been difficult for Morton, in a book nominally about the life of Jesus, not to have revealed at least the outlines of his own beliefs about the significance of the Gospel narratives. As a man not given to self-revelation, how did he handle this challenge? Without seeming deliberately evasive, he manages never fully to declare himself. His narrator is neither a sceptic, out to demystify the divine and the miraculous in order to present a completely secular account of the life of a historical person called Jesus, nor a pious, orthodox Christian, intent on exhibiting the literal truth of every word of the Gospel stories. He is an elusive presence, somewhere in between. He never preaches, even though he often has a Bible in his hands as he sits musing at some hallowed place. Indeed he never goes very far in reaching conclusions about the significance for Christians of the sites that he painstakingly describes, and which he compares with the Gospel accounts.

The characteristic note is struck early in the book. In Jerusalem, he catches his first glimpse of David's Tower:

> I saw it with the emotion which any relic of the time of Christ must inspire, whether the observer be a devout Christian or merely a devout historian. Those huge yellow stones at the base of the tower existed in the Jerusalem of the Crucifixion. Perhaps His eyes saw them.[5]

This is cautious, although the Christian convention of capitalising 'His' is observed. The narrator doesn't say whether he's the Christian or merely the historian. This studied ambiguity in the narrator's standpoint continues. A few pages later, reflecting on the historical episodes that have been enacted in Jerusalem, he remarks that 'the greatest event in the history of Mankind' – he seems to mean the Crucifixion – 'occurred on this bare plateau.'[6] He does not enlarge. Any historian might acknowledge the significance for world history of the foundation of Christianity, but it would take a Christian to declare a belief in the resurrection of the crucified Jesus and his eventual ascent into heaven. Again, the narrator does not say which of the two he is.

Does he come any closer to declaring himself in the following passage, describing a possible site of the synagogue in Capernaum?

> Some experts say that it is the very building in which Jesus preached and performed his miracles; others say that it is not actually the building, but one erected much later on the same spot. But does it matter? It was here that Jesus Christ lived during the two or three most important years in the world's history.[7]

Again, there is a reasonable – though not incontestable – claim about the importance of the life of Jesus for the history of the world, mixed together with a statement of Christian faith. The whereabouts of Morton's own beliefs in this passage remain elusive, but both here, and in the book as a whole, one aspect of Morton's handling of the life of Jesus is quite clear. He accepts wholeheartedly that the New Testament narratives supply reliable evidence of the life and times of a real historical figure called Jesus. The book is founded on this proposition. Whether he concluded that the evidence is as persuasive when it is describing miracles as it is when it is describing Jesus' travels is not quite so clear. There is no doubt that the writers of the Gospels believed that miracles were performed: whether Morton believed that they really were, is not so plain. Probably he did, but he never confronts the issue head-on. The careful ambiguity of the narrator's position is maintained right up to the closing passage of the book, which paraphrases St John's account of Mary Magdalene's discovery of the empty tomb. St John says that a figure that Mary at first took to be a gardener, but which she quickly recognised as Jesus, spoke to her, convincing her of his resurrection. Morton ends his book with 'In the greyness of the morning the woman ran back with the message that Christ had Risen.'

Morton's handling of the religious issues that lay at the heart of any book calling itself *In the Steps of the Master* was skilful. Was he as skilful in his handling of the political issues that were bound to intrude themselves on any traveller in Palestine under the British mandate in 1933? He was, after all, travelling through a region that was (then as now) fraught with animosities that erupted regularly into violence. He could hardly present Palestine as if it were simply a timeless region, peopled by shepherds, carpenters and fishermen, who go about their activities in picturesquely Biblical fashion – although there are plenty of passages where he does drop into this mode. As might be expected, he never commits himself to any particular view on the way to resolve the intractable problems of Palestine, but he does, informally, present a range of characters and incidents that illuminate the problems quite extensively. He sees a Muslim festival procession in Jerusalem in which some of the participants are chanting 'O Zionists what right have you in this country?' He meets the objects of their scorn, eager young Zionists who, in turn, are slightly embarrassed at the devotions of Orthodox Jews at the Wailing Wall, and are themselves much more interested in tractors and electricity schemes. He observes a British policeman keeping an eye on a Jerusalem flashpoint. He tenderly describes a Bulgarian Christian pilgrim worshipping at the Holy Sepulchre ('The old man sank down on his knees and turned again to the Tomb, unwilling to leave, incoherent with faith and devotion, his big, scarred hands touching the marble as if stroking the hair of a child'). He gets to know a group of Lake Galilee fishermen making a meagre living. He joins a Jewish family for their Passover meal. And he is moved by the Abyssinian priests, whose claim to their own patch of space in the Church of the Holy Sepulchre, in the great rivalries among the various Christian denominations for pride of place there, has secured them nothing more than a group of huts, built on the roof. ('There was something impressive in the sight of these black men worshipping Jesus Christ with a ritual so old that it has borrowed something from the ceremonies of ancient Israel and ancient Egypt.')[8] The narrator, then, is comprehensive and mostly non-partisan in his accounts of the competing communities in the region. But he does repeatedly express one dislike: he finds the atmosphere of Jerusalem unpleasant:

> . . . never had I seen a more intolerant looking city. All the hardness of the rock and the smouldering fires within the rock seemed to have boiled up out of the bowels of the earth and cooled into the city of Jerusalem. It was a perfect expression, so it seemed to me, of the cruelty and the fierceness of the Judaean highlands. This high city, perched above ravines and lying among the débris of centuries, might, it seemed, be the abode not of men and women and children, but the dwelling place of ruthless emotions such as Pride and Arrogance and Hate.

In Holy Week, when three antagonistic religions each celebrate a festival, British troops – Seaforth Highlanders, he notes – have to be stationed on the rooftops to watch out for riots as the city gives itself over to a 'strange agglomeration of ignorance, cynicism, simple piety, sophistication, scholarship and stupidity'.[9]

On the other hand, he is equally candid about his likes. The Abyssinians who perform their rites on the roof of the Holy Sepulchre particularly impressed him. He went out of his way to visit a little church that they had built on the banks of the Jordan, not far from Jericho. He is touched by the monks' welcome and by their piety: 'I have never encountered any people who seem so gentle and so meek.'[10] Morton here, and elsewhere, was resisting the stereotypes of the Orient that lie in wait for European travellers, and was responding with remarkable freshness. But he does not escape the waiting stereotypes altogether. One of them puts in an appearance when he visits a Bedouin encampment in the Jordanian desert. Regretting that his lack of Arabic kept him from fully understanding the bond that had developed between desert tribes and men such as Doughty and T. E. Lawrence, he wrote,

> I can perceive, in a dim way, the bond of sympathy and mutual respect that could exist between Bedouin and Englishmen. The desert, I think, is an excellent school, and the Englishman instinctively comprehends its code of conduct. Aristocracy, and all the fine things that come with conscious pride of race, are slowly and surely dying from the world. But they are still alive in the desert.[11]

This world-weary, aristocratic note, which corresponds perfectly with his weakly-formulated views of British politics, is sounded only once. By and large, the narrator of *In the Steps of the Master* is an unstuffy, open-minded traveller who produces, beneath a remarkably unpromising title, a remarkably informative text.

Rather in the way that the success of Morton's first book on England had fired him to go in search of the rest of the British Isles, the success of *In the Steps of the Master* fired him to travel further into the Middle East and the eastern Mediterranean to write more books based on the wanderings of characters from the Bible. A few months after the launch of *In the Steps of the Master*, he noted in his diary, in early January 1935, 'Collecting books on Asia Minor in preparation for the cruise to Greece and Turkey.' The subject of the book that resulted from his next journeys was the travels of St Paul. But this second book in Morton's Middle Eastern trilogy did not appear for another two years. The intervening years – 1935 and 1936 – are rather thinly documented, but there is enough to establish the outlines of his life at this period.

The entries that survive from his 1935 diary show that it was taking him a long time to fully reconcile himself to the finality of his divorce from Dorothy and of his marriage to Mary. The Christmas and New Year holidays had been difficult. Dorothy, he wrote, 'is up against me for a number of things' – money, and his access to the three children. 'This business hurts me terribly sometimes,' he wrote on 3 January. The following day was the first anniversary of his wedding with Mary. They celebrated by going to a London show – 'a rotten musical comedy' – and on to supper at the Savoy, among a 'vulgar crowd' that Mary didn't care for. 'So we left, not too cheerful, at about one A.M.' A few days later, their cook, a German woman, upped and left, upsetting Mary: 'M. is fed up. I am very glad. I never did like Gertrude & never thought her such a marvellous cook.' Morton's domestic life, it seems, was not exactly blooming. He found himself drawn back to the scenes of his life with Dorothy. In late January he even recorded, sadly, 'I go often, as I went today, to Victoria Station to stand before the "Stations to Orpington" [platform] that I know so well. What do I expect? Why do I do it?' This was the platform for the train that used to take him home to Dulwich, to Dorothy and the children. A few days after this gloomy visit to Victoria Station, he recorded a day of hitting the bottle: 'Had a frightful break out today. Boiling up for months.' Mary was away, visiting her parents, and Morton spent the day going from bar to bar. He spent the following day in bed 'full of remorse'. 'Drink is my demon.' Respite came in the form of the cruise that he had been preparing for. He and Mary went off in February to the eastern Mediterranean.

Morton's father had re-married, some time after the death of his first wife (Morton's mother), and was now living in Carshalton with a new wife and family. In May he wrote to his son, delicately asking for financial support. Morton senior had never been able to re-establish the prosperity that he had enjoyed back in Birmingham, and his health was now beginning to fail. Morton, who had never been very close to him, none the less bailed him out financially and took him out for a meal from time to time.

In July, he and Mary went north to Orkney and Shetland. In his books on Scotland, Morton had never crossed the Pentland Firth to the northern isles, but the sight of Orkney, a few miles across the firth from John O'Groats, had intrigued him and he had always wanted to go back for a visit. Morton's paper, the *Daily Herald*, published the series of articles he wrote. The series reads well and succeeds in capturing the distinctive character of these isles – a character quite different from the Hebridean islands and from the Highlands of mainland Scotland. Morton, who, as usual, had done his homework, weaves into his account the Norse history of the isles. Sections of the book make the narrator's journey seem intrepid. He takes his first aeroplane flight, in what he considers to be a terrifying machine, from Kirkwall to North Ronaldsay, and he goes with a local fisherman, in a small motor boat, through huge Atlantic swells, to visit a jagged set of offshore rocks called the Vee (or Ve) Skerries, ten miles off Papa Stour, Shetland.

In Morton's customary fashion, the narrative was written in the first person, by a lone traveller. It is certain though, that Mary travelled with him, for postcards that she sent from Orkney and Shetland to her mother in Eastbourne have survived. The narrator's account of the boat trip to the Vee Skerries, which is written as if it were just him and the boatman aboard, makes the most of the wild sea: 'As our small motor-boat left the shelter of Papa Stour, we sank into the valley of an Atlantic roller, and the next moment rose wave-high on the crest of the one behind. The sky-line was always being hidden from us as we wallowed in the sweep of the sea.' Mary's postcard to her mother, dated 20 July, says simply 'Went to the island of Papa Stour yesterday, & out to the Vee Skerries! Very rarely is it calm enough to go there.' Morton's account makes the better story, but Mary's may be closer to the truth.

His practice of turning his newspaper series speedily into books was by now a well-established routine, and he went to work on a book that was to be entitled, unsurprisingly, *In Search of the Northern Isles*. He prepared the manuscript by editing together the articles, and Methuen set up a specimen page in type. But for some reason the project stalled. Five years later, he noted in his 1940 diary entry for 14 May that he was trying to revise and finish it, but, with the war on, 'how can one create anything?' The book was never completed and published.

Morton had a habit, at the turn of each year, of making entries in his diary that reviewed his life. There is a sequence of entries in December 1935 that show that he had still not come to terms with his divorce and re-marriage. On 5 December he succumbed to the lure of the train to Dulwich and went down to his old haunts, starting at the pub near the station, where 'I have had so many gins and whiskies before catching a taxi to the Avenue' – the street in which he and Dorothy lived. He goes on, in somewhat maudlin fashion, about what he's thrown away, conceding that he 'was always deceiving her' by 'going to bed with various women'. He concludes: 'That was not right. Something was wrong,' and ruefully says that Dorothy's maintenance is costing him £3,000 a year. He writes 'I am happier now, I think,' but it looks less than wholehearted, even though, in this casting up of emotional accounts, he says that now, for the first time, he has 'a real partner, interested in the things that interest me. I rely tremendously on her help & criticism.' As Christmas approached, he wrote 'Thinking far too much this Xmas of the children and D,' and on Christmas Day itself, he confessed to Mary that he'd recently been to see Dorothy. This put a damper on the festivities: 'neither of us could eat a thing', and after a walk, they returned to 'dreary, miserable solitude'. On 29 December, after a wretched few days, he wrote 'Still in depths. M. wounded. Self full of remorse . . . This sentimental turning back to Dulwich has been going on all year . . . This is more serious than I realise. I must stamp it out or see my second marriage crash.' The next day, he cheered up a bit: over lunch with his editor, Dunbar, a plan for a new series, on the depressed areas of Scotland and England, was hatched.

In January 1936 Morton covered the story of the death of George V. In old age he wrote his recollections of the event for his *Memoir*. He recalled that, from the study window of his flat, he had often caught sight of the old King, taking a stroll in the grounds of Buckingham Palace. The *Herald* sent him up to Sandringham, where the King had died, to cover the transportation of the body back to London, and then to cover the lying in state and the funeral.

In February and March, he and Mary travelled again through the eastern Mediterranean, collecting material for his book on the travels of St Paul. Morton probably had some of his travels subsidised by a cruise ship company that gave him a cabin, in return for lectures to the passengers. A couple of letters sent to him, a few years later, from another cruise ship lecturer, the archaeologist Leonard Wooley, suggest ways in which their two lecture programmes might complement each other.[12] On 5 April Morton noted in his diary. 'Arrived back after a tremendously successful journey. Went right across Asia Minor. Mary was a wonderful help to me.' He spent the next few months turning their travels in the footsteps of St Paul into a series for the *Herald* and then into a book. (*27 May.* 'Am on chapt. 1 of St Paul. Difficult.') He notes, with some amazement, that Rich and Cowan have had advance orders for 100,000 copies.

The book on St Paul took up most of his time, but he also managed to issue a pot-boiler of assorted essays called *Our Fellow Men*, a collection that resembled his very first books on the lives of Londoners. This new collection included vignettes of the lives of cab-drivers, typists, dustmen, and other stalwarts of the city. But Morton was getting less interested in the type of journalism that gave rise to books of this sort. In November, he was working on a successor series and wrote in his diary: 'Went down a sewer to-day – the Fleet – for a series of articles . . . I am too old & too big for my boots now. I hate such things.' And an article on coach-drivers brought him a letter from a member of the Transport and General Workers Union, saying that he'd got his facts wrong about the wages paid to drivers. Morton was now more interested in his foreign travels. But even in that area of his life, he was much more the hard-headed author than the romantic traveller. He compared notes with the writer A. J. Cronin about making money from what he called, in his diary entry for 24 November, 'the book racket'. 'I have no illusions either about the book trade or public. I know the days will come when the sales frost will set in. It's inevitable.'

His life with Mary during 1936 settled down a bit. According to his diaries, she was still fearful that his children would always push her into second place in his affections, and that he might even return to Dorothy. However, the prospect of a reconciliation with Dorothy slowly faded, as did his attachment to his children. Morton kept in touch with them at Christmas and birthdays, and he stuck into his diaries polite little letters that they sent to him. But as time went by, he grew apart from them. On 23 April, he wrote in his diary:

> I rang up Mike today [his oldest son, then at Lancing College] & told him I couldn't see him these holidays. I also spoke to Barbara [his daughter]. Why don't I feel more emotion? I suppose I ought to. To be called 'Daddy' doesn't give me the faintest thrill. I suppose I ought never to have had children.

This feeling was unfortunate, for Mary was desperately anxious to have a child of her own, hoping to stabilise the marriage. Morton was privately dreading the prospect of her becoming pregnant, and was, again privately, angry when she conceived. On November 11, with her pregnancy now certain, and with the prospect of a very difficult nine months, for Mary was in danger of miscarrying, he wrote 'I detest the whole business & the great danger is for me to have a couple of drinks & speak the truth. <u>Blast and damn it all</u>.'

In the Steps of St Paul was published on 30 October 1936. Morton's loyal readers would not have been disappointed by the opening of the book, which brilliantly conveys the excitement the narrator feels as he approaches the coast of Palestine from the sea, at sunrise:

> St Paul must have known this moment: the grey light, the last star, the cold wind, the fusty cargo, the smell of beasts and tar, the movement of the mast against the sky, the smooth pressing forward and the rhythmic hiss of water running back along the sides of the ship . . . I looked down to the fo'c'sle head, where, grey in a grey light, mules tied to the rails were unaware that the worst was over. These creatures, so strange at sea, so firmly linked in association with hill-paths and olive trees, now stood heads down before grey hills of water that launched themselves monstrously in a dim light. It was a sight as old as travel in the Mediterranean.[13]

However, the impetus of this opening, with its vivid sense of the continuity of past and present, is not powerful enough to carry the reader right through the lengthy book. The narrative drive fades. The book has no single, clear trajectory. First, St Paul did not make a single journey that Morton could follow, towing the reader along behind him. The New Testament records a number of journeys made by Paul, and supplies a very limited chronology and itinerary of his life. Morton had to make some speculative leaps to fill in the gaps. Secondly, Morton's own narrative is patched together from the various journeys he had himself made to Palestine, Turkey, Greece and Italy. The result is that the narrator follows a rather incoherent route, criss-crossing the eastern Mediterranean and the lands bordering it, trying to follow the sometimes vanishingly faint traces of Paul's footsteps, and recording his impressions of the sites associated with the saint. At the same time, the narrator is recording his impressions of the present-day state of the countries he was travelling through, even when these impressions are irrelevant to his exposition of the story of Paul.

A further feature of the book gives it, here and there, a poignant feel. In his diary entry for 16 April 1936, Morton wrote:

> We have returned to talk of war [Hitler's Nazi party had come to power in Germany three years earlier, in 1933]. Oh Lord, oh Lord. Are we to end like this? Sometimes it seems to me that civilisation hangs on a hair-thread . . . War wouldn't be so bad if it was just death, as it used to be. But now it's disease & air raids & the destruction of books, pictures, antiques – everything that one cares about.

This sense of foreboding finds expression in the text of his book. The narrator visits Tarsus, the Hellenistic city where Paul was born, but which, when the narrator visited it, was 'a shabby little town where rows of wooden shacks faced each other across roadways of hard mud'. The decline of Tarsus provokes this gloomy outburst:

> Politicians of Western nations ought not to be eligible for election until they have travelled the ancient world. They should be made to see how easy it is for the constant sea of savagery, which flows for ever round the small island of civilisation, to break in and destroy. Asia Minor was once as highly organised as Europe is to-day . . . I cannot understand how any

traveller can stand unmoved at the graveside of the civilisation from which our own world springs, or can see a Corinthian capital lying in the mud without feeling that such things hold a lesson and a warning and, perhaps, a prophecy.[14]

However, not everything on his travels spoke of decline. He was impressed by the way in which Turkey was secularising and modernising itself after the revolution led by Kemel Ataturk in 1921–3. The narrator liked the way that children were being sent to new, mixed schools. He liked the way that women could now go unveiled in public. He applauded the government's attempts to stamp out corruption, and its decision to abolish the Caliphate. There were other signs, especially in the decline of traditional Turkish costume and in the disbanding of dervish and other religious orders, that he found regrettable. The picturesque fez had been outlawed, to be replaced by that 'most hideous of Western head-coverings', the flat cap. But on balance, he approved of the way things were going in Turkey. [15]

The narrator's views, explicit and implicit, on the contemporary political world occupy only a tiny portion of the book. The chief purpose is of course to celebrate the life of Paul, by dramatically placing the narrator in the sites where Paul can be presumed – sometimes with the addition of hefty doses of guessing – to have once stood, and by giving him set-piece speeches that imaginatively reconstruct Paul's attempt to found and encourage the infant Christian churches. Whether or not readers were beguiled by these passages depends, I imagine, on whether or not they were enthusiastic Christians. Plenty of Morton's readers were, and many of them wrote to him saying how their faith had been enriched by his books. They also tried to coax him into being more explicit about his own beliefs. Morton always declined. Readers who were not quite so devout, and who read his books as conventional travel books, may have found his lengthy commentaries on Paul's doctrines a bit tiresome, although the title *In the Steps of St Paul* should have alerted them to the nature of Morton's project. But either way, sales did not suffer. The initial printing twice covered the 100,000 advance order that had so amazed Morton. Two hundred thousand copies were printed, and they sold out. This printing alone would have brought Morton over £20,000 in royalties. Morton was in the big time. The book reached a fifth edition by 1949.

Back in 1930, when he was having his 'thin time' with Dorothy, he had written in his diary that he wanted to see his family 'set in English soil with an old house & a few trees, a stream & a field or two'.* With the success of two Middle Eastern books secure (in November 1936 he noted that nearly half a million copies had been sold), with a back catalogue of his *Search* series ticking over nicely, and with a job on a national newspaper as a star features writer, he could now see about that dream house. The family to be planted there – Mary and the baby she was carrying – was not the one originally envisaged, but the move could now be encompassed. On 5 November 1936, he wrote in his diary, 'Have decided to buy South Hay for £5,550. Fancy that. It is a lovely old house & I hope we shall be happy there.' A couple of months later, on 12 January 1937, the deal was complete: 'Became the owner of South Hay today & of seven acres of English soil – a thing I have always longed for.' The house that satisfied his longing was a half-timbered brick, stone and tile medieval farmhouse, with sixteenth or seventeenth-century additions, in the archetypally picturesque village of Binsted, just on the Hampshire side of the Surrey–Hampshire border. (See plate 13.) The views southward, across the Wealden landscape of field and wood, stretched as far as Selborne Hangar, the site of Gilbert White's distillation of the English countryside, *The Natural History and Antiquities of Selborne*. Morton now had his handsome patch of English soil. Straightaway, he commissioned an architect to build a passage that would connect the old house to an adjacent barn which, in turn, would be converted into a library.[16]

Throughout 1936 Morton was absorbed by the Abdication Crisis. George V had died in January, but there was a serious problem with the smooth accession of his son. There was a widespread view, shared by the Prime Minister, Baldwin, that the uncrowned Edward VIII could accede to the throne only if he would give up his girlfriend, the American divorcée Mrs Wallis Simpson. Edward decided that he could not bring himself to renounce Mrs Simpson: he therefore had to

*See chapter 5, p. 134.

renounce the throne. Morton, as a journalist living in a flat that overlooked the garden of Buckingham Palace, and often dining in the expensive restaurants favoured by Edward and Mrs Simpson, took a keen interest in the story. He also intimated, in his diary entries, that Edward's dilemma as to whether he should choose the path of duty or the path of passion was akin to the dilemma he had himself faced when he had had to choose between Dorothy and Mary. He made regular entries in his diary as the crisis developed. On 7 December, just four days before Edward abdicated, Morton made an entry that expressed interests in both English usage and Restoration court poetry: 'Someone told me that on the Stock Exchange Board someone wrote "Cunt or Crown?", which must surely be the first public use of the word in connection with the Monarchy since Rochester wrote his obscene ballads about Charles II.' A day or so later, he wrote up the abdication story for the *Herald*, and mused sadly in his diary about 'Poor Edward VIII, going out of his own free will to join the seedy army of ex-kings who drift unhappily from hotel to casino.' And, on 13 December, with Edward gone, he reflected on the whole dismal episode. Alcohol and jazz, he thought, had a lot to answer for:

> Edward was a man with unerring eye for the wrong friends. He loved the cocktails & the trap drums [i.e. the drum kits used in jazz and dance bands] & he loved them with the sincerity of a brainless stockbroker. One evening many months ago in the summer, Mary & I, taking our summer evening walk from 35 Grosvenor Place . . . saw three buck niggers going into Buckingham Palace with band instruments.

The Mortons' new baby, a boy, was born in May 1937 and christened Timothy at Binsted parish church. Despite the reservations Morton had felt when Mary had become pregnant, he was delighted with the child. The family divided its time between South Hay and the flat in Grosvenor Place, and Morton wrestled with the staff problems that his new wealth and property entailed. Cooks came and went. Nannies fell out with chambermaids. The gardener at South Hay was acrimoni-ously fired. Soon after Timothy's birth, it was decided that the London flat, which had been kept on when he bought South Hay, was too small to accommodate the expanding family when they were in town. Larger premises were sought. In August, Morton bought a house in Markham Square, Chelsea, just off the King's Road.

When the family was at South Hay, Morton's work sometimes kept him in London, an arrangement that facilitated the resumption of his infidelities. He was soon back into his stride, and his list of sexual encounters steadily lengthened. Mary seems to have had her suspicions about what he got up to, for he noted in his diary on 1 October,

> M. & I not having too good a time. At S. Hay her ghastly surveillance caused a row & I said that unless she altered I would leave her. Most unpleasant. I really meant it, too. I am too old, & am making too much money, to be treated like a slave.

Later in October he left for a long trip to Egypt to gather material for a series for the *Herald* which, in his customary fashion, would be turned into a new book of Middle Eastern travels, the final volume in his trilogy. He and Mary made a further trip to research the book, this time to Baghdad, in February and March of 1938, covering the sea voyage to Alexandretta (present-day Iskenderun, in eastern Turkey, close to the Syrian border), by courtesy of Hellenic Cruises.

Meanwhile, his father's health was failing. Early in 1938 Morton settled a pension on him so that he could give up work, but by the spring he was on his deathbed. During the final month of his life, Morton ruminated on the unsatisfactory relationship he had had with him. 'It is heartrending to me because I have never really loved him,' he wrote in his diary. His father's death made him reflect, too, on his own life: 'I remember Mother once saying to me: "If you treat Dorothy as your father treated me, I'll haunt you." And I did that.' It is possible only to speculate on the basis of Morton's mother's complaints about her husband. Was it infidelity? If so, Morton's frosty, uneasy relations with his father are partially explained. Like father, like son. Perhaps Morton was duplicating, in his own life, the behaviour that, at the hands of his father, had made his mother wretched.

The final volume of his Middle Eastern trilogy came out in the autumn. Back with Methuen again after his profitable flirtation with Rich and Cowan, he entitled the new book *Through Lands of the Bible*, and he illustrated it with a series of sepia plates derived from superb photographs taken by himself and Mary. (See plate 14.) As in the earlier books, the narrator presents himself as essentially a lone traveller, although he acknowledges the presence and assistance of drivers and officials and even, on one trip into the desert, a military escort. Morton was now sufficiently famous and well-connected for him to have counted on the support of the authorities. But the essence of his style was the encounter between a lone traveller and the people he meets along his way. To sustain this mode the narrator has to pretend that he can communicate freely with the people he comes across, even though Morton could not speak the languages of the countries through which he was travelling. The narrator's dramatisation of fragments of conversation with Greek sponge divers in an Egyptian harbour, the local guards of the excavations at Ur (in present-day Iraq), an old woman in the back streets of Cairo, a sheikh in a desert oasis, a Bedouin guide on Mount Sinai – all are given as if the narrator's communication with his subject was direct, unmediated by the translators who, it must be supposed, were actually on hand. Whether every one of the encounters recorded in the Middle Eastern books actually took place is another question. It is likely, given Morton's general practice, that at least some were imaginatively elaborated, or invented from scratch.

The narrative of the book is slightly disjointed, for it was assembled from at least three trips, one across Syria to Mesopotamia (present-day Iran and Iraq), one to Egypt and one to Italy. The title suggests a strongly biblical theme, but in practice, the Bible only loosely governs the contents of the book. The Valley of the Kings near the Nile at Luxor, visited and described by the narrator, is not mentioned in the Bible, but it earns a place as a land of the Bible because the Israelites were supposed to have been once held captive in Egypt. Italy appears because Rome was a key city in the early life of the Christian church. The book's biblical remit is so loose that it scarcely serves as an organising principle at all. The narrator seems to be a Christian and he evidently sees his book as an aid to the faith of fellow Christians, but, as in the first two volumes of the trilogy, his attention is as fully engaged when he is describing some pagan site as when he is describing a biblical site. The narrative is carried along not so much by Christianity as by Morton's all-embracing interest in the history and antiquities of the Near East and the Mediterranean regions, no matter whether the sites he visits are associated with Alexander the Great, the Copts, the Pharaohs, or Abraham.

The narrative is also carried along, as it is in all his books, by the zest the narrator feels for the terrain he's covering and for the people he meets. He is delighted, for example, by the enterprise of three New Zealanders who had established a long-distance bus service, using specially-built American vehicles, across the desert between Damascus and Baghdad. He is delighted too, as he travels on their bus, to find that one of the rest stops, in the middle of nowhere, is run by an English ex-serviceman from the Palestine Police Force who, in an immaculate dining room that reminds the narrator of a country hotel in Hampshire, serves roast beef and Yorkshire pudding.[17]

The book tends to get bogged down, from time to time, when the narrator launches into exposition after exposition of the various bits of historical background that are necessary if the reader is to grasp the significance of the Roman, or Mesopotamian, or Coptic or Hellenic sites that are being described. The number of different cultures that have left their marks on the territories through which the narrator travels, and the absence of a chronological thread to the book, leaves the reader sometimes a bit disoriented. The best passages in the book are those in which the narrator has been captivated by a particular place and hasn't been squashed flat by the weight of history that the place bears. A good example is his account of a visit to a service at a Coptic church in Old Cairo. The Copts fascinated him: 'having seen them, it is impossible not to feel respect for these Christians who, heresy or no heresy, have kept faith with Christ through twelve difficult centuries [including the centuries of Islam in Egypt], and who have preserved in the secrecy of their churches much that is beautiful from the bright morning of Christianity.' Another aspect of their fascination is the survival in Coptic language and liturgy of remnants of ancient Egyptian, pre-Christian religion. The narrator describes the service, which combined the mass with the baptism of an infant, minutely and tenderly. He is charmed by the informal manner in which very small children sit around the steps near the altar, sometimes getting in the way of the celebrant, who good-naturedly steps over them, as he prepares the holy mysteries. The narrator is touched by the baptism, which brings another soul into a community that has survived in a Muslim country by maintaining a blend of dogged faith and judicious anonymity. The culmination of the service surprises him:

> The priest came to the door of the screen attended by the deacon, who held a *gulla* of water. He poured a stream of water on the priest's hands and the priest instantly tossed it up towards the roof. There was a wild scramble as men and women pressed forward to receive a drop on face or body. Three times the priest tossed water into the air, and three times the congregation rushed for it. When they looked up from their last scramble, the priest had vanished, the haikal door was closed, and the sanctuary curtain had fallen back into place.

As he leaves the church, he, as a stranger, is given one of the little loaves baked freshly during the service but not used in the actual consecration. Throughout the narrator's account of his visit to the service there is no irony, no condescension: he is enthralled and he is respectful. [18]

The same tone colours his accounts of his visits to monasteries, one Coptic and one Greek Orthodox, deep in the desert, and each a day's difficult drive, in different directions, from Suez. Perhaps it was the profound sense of otherness of these places that impressed him. The landscape of the deserts bordering the Gulf of Suez is about as different from the landscapes of Hampshire and Chelsea as it's possible to imagine, and no greater difference could be conceived than that between the worldly Morton's proclivities and those of the grimy, ascetic monks who dedicated themselves entirely to Christian observance in these remote monasteries. The starkness of the contrasts seems to have burnt away any feelings in Morton of superiority, or of lofty, patrician detachment. He seems to have been genuinely humbled. Even when he is describing, elsewhere in the book, the practice of early saints, such as St Simeon Stylites, who lived in the deserts of what are now Libya and Syria, subjecting themselves to the utmost privations (St Simeon spent thirty years living at the top of a pole), he never suggests that the practice of these filthy old hermits was ludicrous. No. They were adhering to regimes of self-subjugation that were oddly heroic. It is significant that in the bibliographies that Morton appended to his Middle Eastern trilogy, Gibbon's *Decline and Fall of the Roman Empire* is absent. Morton had no time for the ironic, sceptical, Enlightenment tone of Gibbon's rubbishing of the desert fathers. Later, in 1944, Morton took part in a couple of editions of the BBC's 'Brains Trust'. His contributions to the debate were rather diffident and unimpressive, but in the 25 April 1944 edition, devoted to the subject of St George, he burst out with a denunciation of Gibbon's handling of St George. Gibbon's anti-Christian purpose, Morton said, caused him, for the sake of amusement, deliberately and maliciously to confuse two potential Georges.[19] Although Morton never crossed the border into the frank realm of open Christian apologetics, he invariably treated Christian belief and practice, whether of the sort he found on his travels – in the Mount Sinai Monastery, or the Cairo Coptic church, for instance – or of the sort he found in the scriptures or in records of the early church, with respect, and even reverence.

Through Lands of the Bible completed Morton's trilogy of Middle Eastern books. A few years later, in 1940, he issued a sort of coda, a collection of pieces entitled *Women of the Bible*. It is an odd little book, for although Morton's ideas about gender were pretty much those that would be expected of a man born in 1892, he does not systematically use the Bible stories to reinforce the usual stereotypes, even though his aim in the book was to show that the women in the Bible are archetypes of women down the ages. ('One must know very little of human nature if one has not met Ruth.')[20] He resists, for example, the opportunity to present Eve as the archetypal female temptress: her sin, he argues, 'was shared in an equal degree by Adam'.[21] In this book Morton comes no closer to making a plain profession of his own faith, although the sections on the women associated with Jesus are written with particular piety. And he comes no closer to making plain his beliefs about the status of the scripture stories. Was Lot's wife, for example, *really* turned into a pillar of salt, or is the story symbolic of some greater truth? Morton does not permit his narrator to decide, although he does make him say that the writers of the Bible are master story-tellers. As a professional writer himself, Morton knew a good, concise narrative when he saw one, and he therefore admired the scriptures. But by never allowing his narrator to plainly say what he believes to be fact, and what he believes to be fancy, Morton left

Women of the Bible, like the much more substantial trilogy of books that it followed, a somewhat enigmatic book.

Taking Morton's Middle Eastern project as a whole, it is clear that he certainly wanted to enlarge his Christian readers' understanding of their faith, and he seems to have wanted to imply, though never directly state, that he shared that faith. His narrator never delivers sermons, but he is frequently on the verge of doing so. But putting to one side the question of belief, Morton wanted to communicate his undoubted passion for the region and the extent of his knowledge of its manifold histories. He also wanted – let it never be forgotten – to enlarge his income. The books the project produced are sometimes a bit tangled and indigestible, and the gravity of the subject matter makes them more solemn and portentous than his earlier travel books, but the comic touches that enliven his pages when he was writing on less exalted topics do break through from time to time. Few sites can be more awe-inspiring for believers than the summit of Mount Sinai, where God delivered the Law to Moses. Morton's narrator is suitably, genuinely awed as he ascends, but he cannot resist telling his readers that, as he sat eating his sandwiches, crouched between the little mosque and the little Christian chapel on the summit, a plump mouse came out of the mosque to hunt for a few crumbs, followed by a family of Christian mice emerging from the chapel. Morton, the brilliant recorder of the wayside incident, devotes as much attention to the mice as to Moses.

7

1939–1945

THE SECOND WORLD WAR

Reviewing his financial accounts for 1939, the forty-seven-year-old Morton wrote, 'This is without doubt the last of the Golden Years.' The shiniest of his golden years had been 1937–8: 'an incredibly prosperous year & I am never likely to have another one like it'. Royalties had brought him in nearly £31,000, and his salary from the *Daily Herald* had added a further £5,000. Taxes took £5,700 of this, and maintenance payments to Dorothy took a further £3,000. Staff wages were not much of a drain: the half-dozen servants the Mortons employed, including gardener, cook and Timothy's nurse, cost £460. In this most prosperous year, Morton's income was 250 times greater than his gardener's, 500 times greater than the nurse's. In January 1939 he made a summary of his assets. He had £30,500 in the bank, houses in Hampshire and Chelsea that were together worth nearly £10,000, and investments and insurance policies worth a further £10,000. In sum, his previous year's income had been £36,000 and he commanded assets of £50,500. He was doing very well. (See plate 15.)

He seems, however, to have been not entirely contented. He and Mary were having rows, and even the prospect of a cruise with her to the West Indies, away from the English winter, didn't lift his spirits. On 11 January 1939 he wrote in his diary, 'I don't want to go but it costs us nothing & it is an experience.' As a famous travel writer, he could now take for granted free travel, in exchange for a series of articles for the *Daily Herald* and publicity for the country he was visiting. Not only did he find the prospect of the West Indian cruise irksome, but he also wasn't happy to be working for the *Herald*, even though the paper was preparing to renew his £5,000-a-year contract. In his diary entry for 16 January 1939 he wrote, 'I detest the paper & its idiotic Labour policy, its commonness & its dreariness.' However, in February, he managed to drag himself and Mary – but not young Timothy, who stayed behind – off on the cruise to the Caribbean, and he dutifully wrote it up for the paper.

On his return from the cruise, in March, he started to muse in his diary about the prospect of war. On 1 April he wrote:

> More war talk. Will this tension never end? We are to support Poland. The Jews who rule the world are determined to force us into war with Germany. I am convinced that the only policy for this country is friendship with Germany. I also think we're nearer Fascism in this country than most of us know. But who would be the leader? I can't see him yet.

A few days later, on 4 April, he continued: 'I wish the Fascist movement was stronger. Our only solution & that of the world is Fascism & a linking up of England, Germany & Italy.'

It's hard to know why Morton valued democracy so cheaply, and why he espoused fascism. He never set out the reasons for his conclusion that people are incapable of governing themselves and that, rather, they need to be subordinated to the will of a leader. Perhaps he was still in thrall to the dominant vision of Britain that was embodied in his travel books from the 1920s. Maybe he really believed that there was a fundamental rightness in the ancient hierarchical, deferential social order of rural England, and in its counterpart in Scotland, the loyalty and mutual obligations of clans and chiefs, and that the appropriate modern expression of these old systems was fascism. Morton, along with plenty of others who had initially welcomed Hitler and fascism, of course had no way of knowing, in advance, the full, monstrous consequences of Nazism. Even so, Morton's understanding of the crisis that led up to Britain's declaration of war, on 3 September 1939, was particularly weak. Political acumen and democratic principles were not Morton's strong points. For him to have persisted with a rosy view of fascism, long after others had seen the light, indicates more than naivety. The Nazis' oppressive, vicious treatment of Jews in Germany during the preceding five years was plain enough to those who had cared to look, and in Britain, the anti-Semitic sentiments of Oswald Mosley's British Union of Fascists were plain too.

The BUF – the 'Blackshirts' – had been formed by Mosley in 1932, and had its headquarters in the King's Road, Chelsea, just round the corner from Morton's Markham Square town house. The marches and rallies that the Blackshirts organised initially attracted a measure of public support. The *Daily Mail*, for example, was sympathetic for a couple of years. BUF membership grew to about 20,000. But Blackshirt meetings steadily became more violent and anti-Semitic, and Parliament eventually stepped in to give the police wider powers to prohibit meetings that threatened public order. By 1937, the anti-democratic, vicious nature of British fascism – like that of its German and Italian inspirations – became clear, and public support withered. But Morton's private support for its general principles did not wither. As his 1939 diaries show, he was still attached to the idea that fascism, and a British alliance with Hitler's Germany and Mussolini's Italy was the way forward. Why?

As we have seen, Morton never, either publicly or privately, set out his political views at length. Indeed, it's unlikely that he ever had anything approaching a mature, coherent political creed, although he did steadily maintain some powerful prejudices. He probably never publicly supported the fascist movement in Britain, although it is inconceivable that he knew nothing about them and their activities. In matters of politics, I think that he tended to scribble in his diary the first thing that came into his head. He was impulsively blown this way and that, though never towards a defence of liberal democracy. In his pamphlet *What I Saw in the Slums*, he had championed the cause of slum-dwellers and had praised Labour councils' slum clearance programmes, but in his diaries he regularly expressed hatred of democracy, affection for monarchism and resentment at having to pay taxes to support those he saw as the idle and feckless. There is also, running right through his writing, an uncritical deployment of the stereotype of the Jew as a grasping, scheming alien. And in his 1939 diary he was ready to trot out, uncritically, nonsense about 'Jews who rule the world'. His anti-Semitism may have an obscure origin in family rumours about the possible Jewishness of his paternal grandmother.* Dislike of a particular group is sometimes the result of a secret recognition that one may be a member of that group.

Because of the Holocaust, the stereotype of the Jew has acquired a special place in the dismal world of racial stereotyping. In Morton's pre-war, pre-Holocaust battery of prejudices and preconceptions, it is just possible that his characterisation of Jews was no more sinister than his characterisations of Celts as mournful dreamers, Bedouins as aristocrats of the desert, Greeks as wily merchants, or Vikings as rapists and pillagers. Just possible – but not at all likely. It is clear that when Morton drew attention to someone's Jewishness, he usually, but not invariably, meant to be disparaging. For example, in a brief section of *In Scotland Again* (1933), describing the auction of 'the property of a gentleman', near Carlisle, he wrote:

> A little Jew stood regarding the vast and intricate stone coat of arms over the fireplace in the ballroom: 'Now, what's the use of that?' he said petulantly in a whining voice. 'You can't sell it – even to an American. I wouldn't give five bob for it.'[1]

The Jew whiningly fails to comprehend the tragedy of an ancient English family going under. Another example: in his *Memoir* – written in old age, and therefore in the knowledge of the outcome of fascist anti-Semitism – Morton drew attention to the Jewishness of the proprietor of the *Daily Herald*, Julias Elias, Lord Southwood. Compared with Lord Beaverbrook, with whom Morton had been on good terms during his time on the *Express*, Elias was a remote figure who rarely summoned staff to his presence. Morton recalled:

> One day while we were having lunch he suddenly did something that only a Jew could do. He bent forward and, crinkling his face into that Tiny Tim smile, pinched the sleeve of my jacket as if he were testing the quality of the cloth. 'What nice clothes you wear, Morton', he said winningly. 'Who's your tailor?'

And as a final, somewhat chilling example, when he paid his first visit,

---

*See chapter 1, p. 2.

in May 1937, to the hospital to see his newborn son, he went home and recorded his observation that the infant's 'nose is extremely large. It was the largest nose in the creche.'

In May 1939, on behalf of the *Herald*, he went off on a tour of England, in a hired car, with Mary. The project was to write a series of forty articles on the state of the country. The *Herald* published them throughout the summer. As usual, the series was to be turned into a book, but the declaration of war in September made him suspend his plans for publication.

On 8 June he took Mary up to London from Binsted for her to 'have her hair waved', and for him 'to do nothing in particular'. This 'nothing' involved lunch with a friend at the Waldorf, and then, as his diary's symbolic code records it, a spot of sexual adventuring. Two days later he wrote, 'Am feeling low, depressed and worried. Full of self criticism & self contempt. I have everything that I want & love & yet must go & spoil it all.' In sexual matters, he seems to have been a hopeless recidivist.

Later in June he was approached by the BBC to prepare a radio script. Morton had made his debut as a broadcaster two years earlier, in 1937, when he had given a couple of talks on London as background to the capital's preparations for the coronation of George VI. These two talks went out on 27 April 1937 and 4 May 1937. An internal BBC memo reporting on Morton's performance says that he took a long time to get the hang of what was required, and that his first broadcast was only 'mediocre to good'. The second was much better, although 'very far from first rate'.[2] Since then he had done the odd broadcast on Palestine for the schools service, at about ten guineas a time. Broadcasting was another useful string to his bow, and although he never became a star performer, he received modest commissions from the BBC, especially for its overseas service, throughout the war. His commission in June 1939 was to prepare a script describing the countryside of southern England for a programme on 'The South Coast'. The script would then be translated, inter-cut with recordings of English folk songs, and broadcast to Germany. With the prospect of war looming, Morton was keen to work on the programme. He wrote to F. N. Lloyd-Williams of the BBC: 'I am very keen on <u>anything</u> that makes for better relations between this country and Germany.'[3] It was broadcast on 2 July.

But by August he was gloomily reconciled to the certainty of war. On 26 August he wrote, 'The temper of the country is very different now. It wants Hitler put down once and for all.' With Mary and Timothy away visiting her parents in Eastbourne, Morton spent the week preceding the declaration of war disconsolately mooning about at South Hay, feeling old, feeling desolate about the coming crash in his fortunes, pondering why the sacrifices of the Great War had led only to the prospect of another conflict, wondering whether to seduce the nurse 'to relieve her obvious sex repressions', and lamenting that he was himself 'sexually starved & can't say anything to M. because of pride'. On 1 September Mary returned and they bought twenty yards of oilcloth to make blackout curtains. On 3 September, the awful tension was relieved: '11 – 15 AM. <u>WAR</u>. Chamberlain announced it over the wireless. M & I listened to it & then went up to church. Everyone shattered & bewildered & miserable.'

The *Herald* at once went on to a war footing. Morton noted that Dunbar, the editor, 'put my name down as a war correspondent but have declined to go off in the dark at my age. [He was forty-seven.] There is a better looking job going at the Ministry of Information. I shall wait and see.' Dunbar then encouraged Morton to make a tour of England to report on its response to the war, but Morton would not be rushed: 'I will not go out on this story until the govt. is ready to offer all assistance & until the country has got into its war stride.' A couple of weeks into the war, Morton was still as gloomy as ever:

Are we going to lose the war? The English apathy is creeping in, the spoilt lower classes are wandering back to London [having temporarily left in order to avoid air-raids] & the censor must not let out any news. God, how we need a leader. We need publicity. We need patriotism.

The only bright note in the diary is one of his symbols of sexual success, unexpectedly linked with 'M' for Mary. Perhaps his time of domestic sexual starvation was over.

In October, the Mortons shut up their Chelsea house for the duration and established themselves full-time at South Hay, Binsted.

In October too he secured the support of the Ministry of Information for a trip around England and went off, with an official car, an unlimited supply of petrol, and introductions to war-sensitive locations. He wrote up his journey for the *Herald* in a series called 'England is ready'. In the pre-war world of publishing, he would have quickly turned this series into a book, but not now.

Meanwhile, he sullenly tried to reconcile himself to the world of blackouts, ration books and sandbags. In December, he was peeved when about seventy troops were billeted in the grounds and outhouses at South Hay. Mary insisted that four of the officers be put up in the house, and his grousing at having to share his bathroom and lavatory annoyed her: 'She is angry and talks about patriotism.' He seems eventually to have come round to the inevitable, and a week or so later, just before Christmas, he noted that he'd presented a well-received lantern show of his pictures of Egypt to an audience of thirty troops in his library. His and Mary's hospitality to these troops, who were unable to get back to their homes for Christmas leave, was rounded off with a barrel of beer and plates of sausage rolls.

His regular New Year's Eve entry in his diary summed up his feelings as he came to terms with the prospect of a lengthy war. He resented the invasion of his property and privacy, he knew that his income would plummet as the book trade contracted, he was not at all sure that the war would be won, and he believed that even if the war miraculously ended, national bankruptcy and revolution would ensue. 'I wish I could see one gleam of hope somewhere, but I can't.'

In the early months of 1940 he was still struggling to come to terms with the war. He disliked going up to London from Hampshire. Train services were disrupted by air-raid warnings, piles of sandbags disfigured his beloved London streets, everybody carried gas masks, museums and galleries were being emptied of their treasures, there was a distressing decline in the quality of the food at the Savoy and the Waldorf, his editor was giving him disagreeable commissions, at sunset there was a blackout, and there was the constant fear of being killed by a bomb. One of the few compensations for a trip to London was the prospect of a sexual liaison. On 7 February he scored, but the following day he decided that he really ought to shape up: 'this is the day I turn over a new leaf, pull myself together & try to live a decent life. I am getting slack, lazy, fat, & am drinking too much. I will now stop.'

The new leaf, however, turned out to be pretty much the same as the old one. He still resented having to work harder at the *Herald* in order to make up for the loss of his book royalty income. On 14 February he wrote:

> I am suffering agonies. For 3 weeks have been sitting here trying to get a start for [a series of articles on] London in War Time. All thought & all ability to write has deserted me. I am in utter despair. Oh God in heaven how I wish I had some other way of making £5000 a year.

Raising his eyes from his personal financial predicament to the nation's prospects of victory, he was no more optimistic. In April, he accepted a commission from the Ministry of Information to write a little book that would alert the public to what would happen if the Germans invaded and conquered Britain. He seems not to have doubted whether he was quite the right author for such a project: he kept his partiality for fascism to himself and presented a patriotic face to the world. The little book came out in the form of a novella called *I, James Blunt*, but, like much wartime writing, it had to wait a couple of years before it reached print. Meanwhile, as summer 1940 approached and as the German army relentlessly advanced through Europe, he privately concluded that Britain would not win the war – indeed that in many ways it did not deserve to. Defeat, though undesirable, would be a fitting reward for '20 odd years of flabby socialism, pacifism, financial exploitation, softness and general slackness'. He concluded this wretched diary entry for 14 June by writing: 'How I wish I did not despise & hate so much in modern England. The old England I adore: this flabby England, mouthing about Democracy, I deplore. Well; if the Nazis come here they will release me from my blood-sucking Jew – Reubens.' 'Reubens', or Rubens, seems to have been somebody involved in one of the companies that Morton had set up. The purpose of the companies, into which his royalties were paid, was to limit his taxes.

At the end of June, he went up to London to see Dunbar, the editor of the *Herald*, and at the same time managed to fit in two sexual encounters. So far, Morton's war effort was, unlike his sex effort, somewhat underwhelming. But during the summer, the Local Defence Volunteers – soon renamed the Home Guard – were formed, and Morton at once offered his services. He was appointed as the commander of the platoon guarding his village, Binsted, and he put a great deal of energy, throughout the war, into turning it into an efficient unit. (See plate 16.) He drilled and trained the volunteers, badgered the higher command for better equipment for his platoon, and set up rosters for patrols and watches from the church tower, from where a field telephone line was run to his house. He was probably reviving the skills he'd been taught during his time with the signals unit at Colchester during the 1914–18 war. On 19 June he drew up a notice setting out six rules that his unit should observe in the event of an enemy parachute landing. The rules stipulate that the church bells should be rung and that he should be alerted at once. (See plate 17.) As the summer wore on into autumn, it became distinctly possible that soon these rules might need to be put into practice. Binsted suffered numerous air-raid warnings that sent the Morton household, along with every other household, out into its garden and into a shelter. And when the Blitz finally started, in early September, the log-book of Binsted Home Guard platoon records nights when, from the church tower, the glow of burning London could be seen. Invasion scares were frequent. Stray bombs fell, and shot-down aircraft ploughed into the surrounding fields. In September, Morton attempted to resign, in protest against the calling-in by the War Office of nearly all his platoon's rifles to meet more pressing needs for them elsewhere, leaving Binsted's defenders with only a vestigial armoury. His resignation never took effect: he was soon back on duty, working hard and conscientiously. Occasionally, though, he would flare up angrily. In his diary for 8 October, he reports having had to settle a feud between two of the men in his platoon: 'This sickened me. I can't bear this sort of thing. Why should I mix myself up with village feud and gossip; why should I waste my time with these ungrateful yokels?'

His domestic staff exasperated him just as much. According to his diary entry for 30 September, 'servants are the last of the pampered and leisured class. The war has not touched them. They are perpetual, reluctant guests in the home,' and while Mary valiantly turned herself into a keeper of hens, manager of ration books, eker-out of meagre petrol allowances, servants continued to

> demand their weekly or bi-weekly visit to the cinema and what they call 'gaiety' . . . These people make me savage. I loathe the very word Democracy, which merely cloaks self-indulgence, slackness, softness and snobbism. Yet that is what we are supposed to be fighting for. I prefer to think we are fighting for England, not for a political catch-word.

The preferable, undemocratic England for which Morton was fighting – although 'fighting' is maybe too active a word – had vanished almost entirely into the realm of literature, a realm that had always tended to be its natural home. By and large, he loathed the wartime England that he actually lived in. The alternative, seductive, untroubled version of England made appearances – often extraordinarily powerful appearances – in Morton's books of this time, but it appeared in his diaries and letters only rarely.

The most powerful evocation of the imagined England came in *I Saw Two Englands*. The book takes its title from Morton's juxtaposing of the two series that he had written in 1939 for the *Herald* – the first, on Britain's last summer of peace, and the second, on Britain's immediate response to the outbreak of war. It was intended as a highly topical book, but wartime printing delays meant that Methuen, working to the new authorised economy standards, did not manage to issue it until 1942, by which time it was a bit dated. But a comparison between the dogged, Britain-can-take-it tone of the narrator of the book and the disgruntled, defeatist life recorded in Morton's 1940 diary is instructive. Never was the gap between Morton and his alter ego wider.

I Saw Two Englands opens, as *In Search of England* had opened fifteen years earlier, with the narrator bowling along in his car away from London and into springtime England. This time, he headed into Kent to cover a corner of England that he had hitherto neglected, and then swung west through Sussex and then northward, up through Oxfordshire and finally to Peterborough. The narrative is enlivened, as before, both with wayside encounters with timeless rural characters – a hedger, a hurdle maker – and with little lectures on historical incidents associated with the sites he visits. The story of the execution of Mary

Queen of Scots at Fotheringhay Castle in Northamptonshire, for example, is touchingly related. Broadly, the narrator is reassured by the England he finds. But two clouds threaten. The obvious one is the coming war. Everywhere there are ominous preparations. Fotheringhay church has a notice in its porch advising parishioners what to do if there is an air raid. In Peterborough, people are queuing up for the issue of gas masks.

The other cloud is what would now be termed suburbanisation. The essential tranquil, remote England was becoming harder to find. To the narrator's dismay, the fifteen years that had passed since his first journey had produced miles of monotonous arterial roads, petrol stations built in a 'peculiar and horrible style of architecture', ribbon developments of mock-Tudor houses, and, along the Sussex coast, new housing developments that are 'among the most hideous objects in modern England'. The narrator does not consider the possibility that he has been an agent, albeit a minor one, in the promotion of a vision of England that sent its citizens out in their cars to search for it themselves and to build the cottages of their dreams in its midst. He frankly dislikes 'the bright, vulgar, crowded England of the main roads', but he does pause, after chatting to a man who was nailing up fake beams across the façade of a small new house on a bypass, to reflect that

> no doubt in the eyes of the proud depositors of fifty pounds down and the rest over Eternity, those little houses with their absurd beams were a revulsion against a factory or heartless chain store, or some horrible soul-stifling job in which no human being could possibly take the slightest pride or interest. Foul and regrettable as these monstrosities are to me, the product of some cheap speculative builder's dream to get rich quickly, they must be to someone that ideal cottage in the country which haunts the heart of Englishmen.[4]

Patronisingly and grudgingly, Morton was tacitly acknowledging that his own impulse to buy South Hay – the genuine Tudor article – had its counterpart among the vulgar.

The second part of *I Saw Two Englands* is his record of the wartime tour he made, with full official support and backing, in October 1939. In his diaries, he had been going on and on about how inconvenient the war was to him personally, about how he loathed democracy, about the attractions of fascism, and about the prospects that would be opened up by Britain's defeat. His narrator, of course, expresses none of this. His patriotic job is to visit a representative sequence of locations where the war effort was at its most impressive – a factory that rolls out a steady stream of Wellington bombers, an army unit on tank exercises on Salisbury Plain, an agricultural college where land girls are being trained, a shipyard hammering out new warships. And Morton, the professional journalist, does his stuff, making his narrator deliver an upbeat, inspiring report. His conclusion is that England (his tour had not reached Scotland, Ireland or Wales) is 'sound as a bell, loyal and determined, war-like but not military'.[5] This section of the book is not, though, wholly a propaganda exercise, even though the route of the journey had been laid down by the authorities. Along his way, the narrator makes his customary sidelong, illuminating asides. For example, he stops at a pub in Somerset for a sandwich, and gets talking to the locals. They tell him about the evacuees who have come down to their village from the cities. The locals are appalled at the raggedness of the newcomers.

> There was some ill-feeling, too, that strange women from the cities were in the habit of coming into the tap room in the evening and drinking half a pint, or even a gin, like a man. Such a thing had never happened before in the village, and no one liked it.[6]

The book concludes with a 'Postscript', written in the autumn of 1940, during the Blitz. On the beaches of Dunkirk, in late May and early June, the last British troops in France had been driven by the Germans into the sea. The Battle of Britain had begun in August. How was Morton to end his book? Was it possible to leave his readers with a bit of hope? His solution was to evoke, deftly and powerfully, the mythic England of the rural parish. Fifteen years earlier, he had ended *In Search of England* by sending his narrator to the harvest festival celebrations of an organic, harmonious village community. He ends *I Saw Two Englands* by sending his narrator to an equivalent community, but this time, the community is facing up to the prospect of a German invasion.

The 'Postscript' describes two nights in the life of a village Home Guard unit. (Morton, it will be recalled, had privately called his own unit 'ungrateful yokels'.) On the first night, the narrator leads his men, some of them veterans of the trenches of the Great War, and all intimately familiar from youth with every hedge and tree in the locality, in a sweep across moonlit stubble fields in search of reported German parachutists. 'The combined local knowledge of farmer, poacher, and sportsman had been pooled for a moment in order to hunt the invader from our corner of England.' On the second night, the narrator stands watch on the tower of his village church and spends the quiet night gazing out over the sleeping village and musing on what the war is doing to England. (Scotland, Wales and Ireland have slipped out of the picture altogether.) The slums, the industrial towns, the arterial roads, the mock-Tudor bypass houses do not disturb his musings. The threat posed by a German invasion has pushed all the troubling aspects of England aside and has revealed the underlying, enduring England:

> Should the rest of England fall, our own parish would hold out to the last man. The responsibility of defending our own village has given that village a gigantic significance in our eyes . . . If all villages throughout England think as we do, what a hedge of opposition they present to anyone who dares to set an invader's foot upon this island . . . Brooding on these parish matters, it comes to me that one of the most remarkable things about this war is the quiet way England has ceased to be a country or even a county for many of us, and has become a parish . . . My parish has become England.[7]

It is a testimony to the power of the myth of England that Morton could, in the conclusion of a book that describes the gearing up of a huge industrial and military war machine, make a tiny Home Guard unit, defending a tiny village, symbolise the nation's response to the German threat.*

*

---

*It is perhaps no coincidence that one of the most enduring post-war television comedies is *Dad's Army*, a series in which the nation's resistance to Hitler and a German invasion is symbolised by a bungling, ineffectual, but ultimately heroic Home Guard unit.

Morton's showing in the 1914–18 war had been rather enigmatic, but if he had been conscripted into the forces in 1939 he would, like nearly all conscripts, probably have done his duty. But his circumstances did not give him the inescapable duties enjoined by King's Regulations. Instead, he had to make the difficult choices of the civilian family man, and, perhaps understandably enough, he did not invariably choose the bravest course of action. With the Blitz at its most ferocious, going up to London was for him a fearsome prospect. On 8 October 1940 he wrote, 'I am going up to London tomorrow. I am terrified, but I must go, coward that I am, to prove that I can go. I would give anything not to go, but there it is.' He did go, and, as a by-product of his courage, was rewarded with a sexual encounter. In November he was asked by the *Herald* if he would join a collier sailing from Southend to Newcastle on Tyne and write up the story for the paper.

> I was horrified. Why risk mines, torpedoes & dive bombers for a D.H.
> story? I told him I had a wife and family. If there was any need to run
> into danger these days – and we all live under a nightly shadow of death
> – I would do it if it helped to win the war. But I really cannot see why
> I should run into danger at the age of 50 to give the *Herald* a front page
> story.

On the other hand, he resolutely declined an opportunity to get away from the whole ghastly war altogether. On 30 November, at a time of an almost 'constant procession of death chugging overhead' that sent stray bombs falling randomly on the Hampshire countryside, he wrote:

> Dunbar rang me up the other day and asked me to go to America for
> the *Daily Herald.* He said I could take Mary and Tim. Here, if ever a
> coward was given an open door. But of course one couldn't dream of it.
> There is no one locally to take command of my [*sic*] Home Guard.
> Everything I have is here. How terrible to go away and to learn that
> one's house had been destroyed with all one's books; how awful if this
> country were invaded and one wasn't there to do one's little futile bit.
> No; it's a prospect, pleasant as it is, that one just can't contemplate.

And then he gives a glimpse of the England that makes him stay: 'In

the early morning after a sharp frost when I go up to the field to feed
Mary's poultry, it seems hardly possible that this lovely world, with
each blade of grass a miracle in white, and the cold winter sun rising in
red clouds, can be at war.'

He spent the first seven months of the next year, 1941, chiefly at
South Hay, commanding the Binsted Home Guard unit, writing
patriotic articles for the *Herald*, and making contrary, subversive
entries in his diary. In February, for instance, he wrote an article for the
paper on the Home Guard and the threat of invasion, while in his diary
he wrote, 'I don't for a moment regard the H.G. as more than a good
publicity stunt.' Privately too he was continuing his diatribes against
democracy and Jews, and was expressing his sympathies for fascism. 'I
must say that Nazi-ism has some fine qualities,' he wrote on 17
February. Despite this admiration, he did not desire a German victory.
On the contrary, and somewhat inconsistently, he was certain that
every effort had to be made to defeat Germany: 'Above everything
stands out the clean cut choice of independence under our own rulers,
or conquest. Rather than be conquered, even by a creed we can admire,
we would gladly die.' He mused too on the possibility of America's
entry into the war. He considered that the British talk of 'that utterly
meaningless word "Democracy" ' was a sop to America – 'that craven
nation of Jews and foreigners' – for the Americans could scarcely be
expected to come into the war to fight for the principles that Morton
himself admired, namely, King and Country and the British Empire.

The contrast between the disagreeable version of England that he
was enduring and the enchanted version that he felt was worth fighting
for comes out plainly in an entry he made on 27 April:

> I often ask myself why I love England so much. There is so much I
> detest about her: our Labour leaders, the crude, uneducated, spoilt
> lower classes, the Jews. And yet how small a thing this is compared with
> the grand sweep of history which is England, the green fields, the quiet
> rivers, the dark woods and the chalk downs, a lovely country inhabited
> by a race that is true and good at heart, brave and resolute, and, as
> human beings go, honest.

The 'race' that inhabits Morton's mythic England certainly does not include the Jews, and it seems not to include the 'lower classes' either. He seems never to have stopped to ponder whether, by and large, Jews and the lower classes might have been doing more to win the war than he was. A few weeks later, he contemplated his own death. 'The odds are that I shall die at Binsted cross-roads', in action with his Home Guard platoon, in defence of the village.

> I suppose when the time comes it will be as well if one dies on duty, for if we lost this war the enemy would show no mercy to people like myself or my family. It's very grim for I have never felt much aversion to fascism or Nazism as political creeds.

His life at South Hay was further disrupted by the call-up for military service of his gardener. 'This is the last straw and I don't see how we can possibly go on living here without him.' He did though, and he and Mary kept chickens, goats and rabbits: like thousands of other middle-class people unfamiliar with domestic chores, they learned to grow their own vegetables, cook their own food, and do their own washing up.

In mid-July, however, his routine changed sharply. He was asked by the *Herald* to become a parliamentary correspondent. This was the sort of journalism that had never appealed to Morton, but he made the best of it and started going up to London every day. One small perk, he noted, was that Parliament still managed to serve a decent sherry. His new career did not last long though, for on 2 August, at very short notice and with very great secrecy, he was called upon by Brendan Bracken, the newly appointed Minister for Information, to be ready for an official assignment that would take him overseas.

Morton packed luggage that, he hoped, would meet any eventuality (it included a dinner jacket and his Home Guard uniform) and presented himself the following day at Marylebone Station. As the special train headed north, he joined the second of the two journalists covering the mission, the writer Howard Spring. Their speculations about the destination and purpose of their assignment became more informed when the train stopped and a party headed by Winston Churchill boarded. It emerged that the train was bound for Thurso in the far north of Scotland. From there the entire party was to be transferred by ship to Scapa Flow in Orkney. And from there, it was to be transferred finally to the battleship *Prince of Wales*, which would then steam out across the North Atlantic to Placentia Bay, Newfoundland, where the British party was to rendezvous with President Roosevelt of the United States for top-secret discussions between the two leaders.

The voyage gave Morton the opportunity to observe Churchill at close quarters, but the secrecy attending the mission meant that neither he nor Spring could file reports back to their newspapers. With the war leader and his staff at sea in an area patrolled by German submarines and aircraft, obviously the tightest possible security was demanded. Morton was closer to a scoop than he had ever been, yet was bound by government regulations that prevented him from making the most of it. It was not until 1943, two years after the voyage, that he was able to publish his full account, in a little book entitled *Atlantic Meeting*. From the British side, the purpose of the meeting at Placentia Bay was to draw America directly into the war against Germany. Roosevelt, however, would not be drawn, although economic and military support to Russia and Britain was stepped up. The formal product of the meeting was the Atlantic Charter, a noble-sounding declaration of Britain's and America's shared aims for the post-war world. By the time Morton was able to publish *Atlantic Meeting*, the Atlantic Charter was stale news. Events had dramatically moved on. The Japanese had attacked Pearl Harbor, on 6 December 1941, and, a few days later, Hitler had declared war on America. By the end of 1941, Roosevelt's caution at Placentia Bay had been replaced by full military commitment to the defeat of the Axis powers. America was in the war.

Naturally, Morton's private sympathies with Nazism make no open appearance in *Atlantic Meeting*. It is as patriotic as could be, and presents an entirely laudatory picture of Churchill, and the officers and men both of the British battleship and of the American ships that brought Roosevelt to Placentia Bay. The most interesting bit of the book is Morton's analysis of what it is that makes Churchill such an outstanding leader, for it perhaps reveals something of Morton's own, obscure politics. During the voyage, evenings ended with showings of commercial films that Churchill had brought with him. He would sit in the front row, relishing every moment, no matter whether it was a

Laurel and Hardy comedy or a cowboy film. His judgement on Laurel and Hardy's *Saps at Sea*, delivered as he went off to bed, was that it was 'a gay but inconsequent entertainment'.[8] Churchill also enjoyed popular music: he demonstrated, to the accompaniment of an officer's gramophone, that he was word perfect on Noël Coward's 'Mad Dogs and Englishmen'. But it was a showing of a film about Nelson and Lady Hamilton that gave Morton his decisive insight into what he took to be the essence of Churchill's character and his appeal. In the final moments of the film, as Nelson lay dying on the *Victory*, Churchill unaffectedly wept.

> Looking at Winston Churchill at that revealing moment, I thought that in some extraordinary way he belongs definitely to an older England, to the England of the Tudors, a violent swashbuckling England perhaps, but a warm and emotional England too, an England as yet untouched by the hardness of the age of steel. I have sometimes studied the effect of Churchill's voice and words upon an ordinary gathering of men in a public-house. Why, I have wondered, should they have been so firmly held, so silent until the last word? And I have wondered if it may not be that he speaks with the voice of an older England, that we recognise the voice, not of an industrialist, but of one who has, so to speak, missed the Industrial Revolution and speaks to us as if from the deck of the *Golden Hind*. Churchill's voice is also classless. He has no public school accent. Like the Elizabethans, he speaks not as an Etonian but as an Englishman.[9]

Churchill's mother was American – from 'that craven nation of Jews and foreigners', as Morton had described it in his diary – but this part of Churchill's ancestry is put to one side. What is important here for Morton is that Churchill calls forth a response from the whole English people – the Scots, the Irish and the Welsh have vanished from this account – because he is not identified with sectional, class, regional or industrial interests. He rises above all the jarring elements of a potentially riven nation and speaks from, and on behalf of, the essential England that subsumes them all. This conception of Churchill's leadership appealed to Morton, I think, because it effaced both the realm of democratic political wrangling and the partnership in the war cabinet of socialists like Attlee and Bevin, and presented the war leader as if he had emerged from some deeper, profounder national tradition.

In late August 1941, Morton arrived back home, safe and sound. On 11 September, he and Mary took Brendan Bracken out to lunch at the Berkeley, maybe as thanks for the minister's having sent him off on his exciting mission. Morton recorded in his diary Bracken's saying (correctly as it turned out) that America would soon be forced into the war. Morton was himself sure that no such thing was likely. A month later he was writing in his diary that while he was in Placentia Bay he 'conceived a violent dislike for the Americans . . . I am convinced that they will never come into the War as fighters. They are sunk in sloth and luxury and bogged in Democracy, graft and greed, also ignorance.' The glowing reports of the American sailors – 'charming and virile young Americans' – that he had written in *Atlantic Meeting*[10] were, it seems, the exact opposite of what he had felt.

After their lunch with Bracken on 11 September, he took Mary to Bond Street and bought her an emerald ring for £475. He was, he reported, a bit horrified and ashamed to be spending so much money at such a time, but 'still, after our recent cerebral disturbance, I was determined to make some sort of atonement; and there it was. If it pleases her, that is all I ask.' He does not explain what this 'cerebral disturbance' was, but there is an entry for a few weeks earlier in his list of sexual encounters that probably explains it. Mary may have caught him out, yet again.

In October, for the first time in his diaries he started tentatively to envisage the possibility of victory, and of what would be needed in Britain's post-war reconstruction. 'The Jewish question', as he put it, would need looking into. 'I am appalled sometimes to discover how many of Hitler's theories appeal to me. I am also certain that if we win this War we shall find ourselves devising our own brand of what we should now call Nazism.' No doubt he had prudently chosen not to recommend this programme to Churchill when they had met from time to time on the deck of the *Prince of Wales*. Privately though, Morton's anti-Semitism and his conviction that fascism was a promising system were incorrigible:

It is a fearful tragedy that the German philosophy, or rather Nazi theories of life and conduct – their attitude to Jews, to the cult of hardness, to discipline, to service – to money – could not have been peacefully spread. Unfortunately, he [Hitler] decided to spread them with the sword, and I often wonder what would have happened if he had been as determined to spread them in other ways . . . Such ideas expressed in public today would put me in prison. I can't help it. I simply do not believe that Nazism is all bad and all wrong. I believe it is the first stage of a spiritual revolution.

Meanwhile, before this spiritual revolution could get under way, he had to push on with earning a living. He accepted a commission from the Ministry of Agriculture to write a book about the future of farming, and at once set off on expeditions to Berwick on Tweed, to Cambridge and to Cardiff, staying with farmers and agricultural experts. The book came to nothing. But in his peculiar, ambiguous way, Morton was doing his bit for the war effort, although if his ideas had prevailed when victory was secured, the practical difference for the British people between victory and defeat would have been small: fascism would have had an English, rather than a German accent, but it would still have been fascism.

His 1942 diary does not open until the end of February, by which time air raids had eased, and America had entered the war. Morton was not a bit relieved or impressed, and even speculated that Germany might sever its alliance with Japan, and that America might suddenly join with Germany in a joint attack on Japan. He kept these bizarre speculations to himself: 'This is something one dare not breathe to anyone,' he wrote. On 14 March he took a friend and 'an exiled German Jew' to lunch in London. The entry raises hopes that he might at least record his conversation with the exile, but he mentions only the high price and the poor quality of the food.

In March, one of his earlier efforts for the war came to fruition. Back in April 1940, it will be recalled, he had accepted a commission from the Ministry of Information to write a short book on the likely consequences for the British people of a German victory. On 26 March 1942, Methuen published it as *I, James Blunt*, a pamphlet of fifty-six pages, priced sixpence, in flimsy covers and printed on cheap wartime paper. It was Morton's only frankly fictional work. It is set two years in the future, in 1944, and takes the form of a diary kept by a sixty-one-year-old man who records his experience of life following the successful invasion of Britain by the Germans, in 1942. Not surprisingly, given Morton's attachment to the English myth, the locale of the book is a quiet little Georgian town in Surrey where, until the Germans invaded, 'everything blends beautifully, as English things do'.[11] But now a swastika flies over the town hall. Jews, socialists and trades unionists have been rounded up and herded off to concentration camps. Blunt's grandchildren have been corrupted by Nazi indoctrination at their school. In the bar of his local pub, the sporting prints have been taken down and replaced by pictures of Hitler. In London, Trafalgar Square is being remodelled as 'Hitler Square', and the Führer, when he is in town, lives in Buckingham Palace. The novella ends with the writer of the diary breaking off half-way through an entry as a sinister knock on the door comes in the dead of night. As a novel, *I, James Blunt* is no great shakes, but it works well as propaganda: it was, after all, unashamedly designed to chill the complacent. The prospect of a German victory is made to look uncompromisingly grim.

How could Morton, the secret Nazi sympathiser, have written a book that presents Nazis as brutes – as the literal enslavers of the British? How could he have made his book's hero a man who, before the war, had made speeches in defence of democracy? There are two answers. First, no matter how fervent the admiration expressed in his diary for aspects of fascism and Nazism, Morton never swerved from his determination to die at Binsted crossroads with his Home Guard unit, rather than let the Germans invade. Below the level of admiration of features of German ideology there was a more powerful hatred of the prospect of invasion by foreigners. It may seem slightly odd of him to have wanted to fight to the death to prevent the imposition of a political system that he quite liked, but, in the last resort, British democracy was a lesser evil than an invasion by Germans. For buried beneath British democracy, which never made Morton's pulse race, was an enduring, mythic England of fields and woods over which German control simply could not be contemplated. The second answer is more mundane. First and last, Morton was a professional journalist. He could write to order, quickly and effectively. It helped if he was not obliged to write things that he did not actually believe to be true, but if it came to the push, he could do it. And in the case of *I, James Blunt*, he had to say very little that he didn't believe to be true, and a great deal that he believed to be the grim, unwelcome truth. The book was a success. It ran to three editions within a month of publication, and in May he broadcast selections from it for the BBC.

Life at South Hay settled into a routine of feeding the rabbits, chickens and goats, supervising the Home Guard, and moaning in his diary about the interminable war. Nothing seemed to cheer him up. On 4 July 1942 he reported having just been to a passing-out parade of new army officers at Sandhurst. The problem, he wrote, is that 'there are not enough gents now in England to go round. It's true our officers are ghastly because they come from the wrong class.' He was, he went on, 'horrified to look at hundreds of common faces – the faces of our new officers'. The faces of the American troops who started to arrive in Britain during the summer were just as discouraging. On 28 July he wrote that they are 'obviously untrained. I hope they are not fighting units for they look a pretty dud lot.' On the same day, he recorded that he and Mary had been discussing the social revolution that they were sure would follow an allied victory. 'The malice, the envy, the tearing down of anyone who has managed to possess anything is going to be the new England.' Perhaps they would do well to sell South Hay while the going was good, and buy 'a less pretentious place elsewhere, a place that won't attract envy'.

Morton's wartime writing is so depressing that it comes as a surprise to find something that was written with a bit of zest. It is a little pamphlet entitled *Travel in Wartime*, written by him for BSA Cycles Ltd with the aim of encouraging the nation to save precious petrol by taking to its bicycles. It seems that BSA had presented him with a 'glossy new machine'. Astride it, he rediscovered the pleasures that were associated with his youthful ventures into the Warwickshire countryside:

> I soon found myself spinning along to a sound that will always remind me of my schooldays and my youth: the peculiar crisp and rubbery crackle of tyres moving over road grit. I learned again the joy, not of rushing downhill – that came later – but of moving in exquisite pleasure

along a country lane that was sufficiently inclined to require from me nothing more than an occasional downward push of the pedal in order to send me briskly along.

In 1943 he and Mary carried through their plan to sell South Hay and buy something smaller. In July, they bought Little Park House in Farnham, across the border into Surrey, just a few miles away from Binsted. They moved in September and stayed there for the remainder of the war. Throughout 1943 his commentary in his diary on the progress of the war was generally as mournful as it had been since the war had broken out, but he did brighten up on 9 September, when Italy surrendered. 'I rushed out and found Mary on the lawn on her way to get in the goats. I told her and she could hardly believe it. It is wonderful news. It is now only a matter of a year or so until Germany is beaten.'

This new, hopeful note continued through 1944, although he reported some terrible setbacks. The offices of Methuen were bombed in March, and he and Mary offered beds in their new house to staff who cared to come down from London for a few days of relative peace and quiet. On 17 May, Dorothy died. There is no mention of her death in the 1944 section of the diary, but a year later, he noted simply that 17 May was 'the anniversary of poor Dorothy's death'. He wrote nothing further.

The Normandy landings came in early June, but at the same time, German flying bomb and rocket attacks began, reviving the terrors that the Blitz had induced four years earlier. At home, Morton added a pig to his livestock and was pleased to discover how easy it was to fatten it up. In October he was commissioned by the BBC to deliver a weekly ten-minute broadcast on the Africa Service on 'Life at Home'. The Africa Service went out to what was then called Rhodesia (now Zimbabwe), and South Africa, where Afrikaner opinion, which was inclined to be sympathetic to the Germans, was courted on behalf of the Allies. The audience, though, was chiefly made up from expatriate British.[12] What they heard from Morton, as they huddled round their radios on the veld, were chatty accounts of the privations of wartime England and of the good humour and stoicism with which the British were responding. Unlike his diary entries, Morton's talks were generally upbeat, and from time to time, he said things on air that contradicted his private views. His view on the dismal quality of new, non-gentlemanly army officers, for instance, was suppressed in favour of an anecdote that he had heard from a young officer about the social composition of the occupants of his army hut: the hut includes 'a peer, the heir to a dukedom, two young Etonians, three cockneys from Whitechapel, and a Lancashire lad, the son of a grocer – a good mixed bag. And that, I might add, is typical of the admirable social mix-up of this war.'

In December, with the prospect of a German invasion now finally receding, the Home Guard was stood down, and Morton went back to Binsted to attend a commemorative dinner with his old platoon.

By now, Morton's activities had shrunk to the daily domestic round. He tended to perceive himself as an old man wearing his declining years away by feeding chickens and doing the washing up. Sometimes he wondered if he was doing his bit for the war effort; he wrote, on 13 January 1945: 'at the age of 52 I suppose I am entitled to slack like this but I can't help feeling that it is bad for my character. I feel like a little boy who has faked a cut on the hand to get out of gym at school.' The shortages of commonplace household items, and the price and inadequacy of meals in the smart restaurants that he had taken for granted before the war, still got him down. He meticulously described the contents of the 'filthy' meals he ordered and the high prices he had to pay, and he recorded, in January, a humiliating hunt around London shops to buy lavatory paper. He was cheered by news of the Allied armies' sweep from Normandy towards Germany, and was cheered too by commissions that were starting to come through for post-war writing projects. Organisations such as the London County Council were asking him to write up their plans for reconstruction.

In April he recorded his sadness at the death of President Roosevelt, and characterised his successor, Harry Truman, as 'a real little American Yid. A hard mouth, glasses and a business face.' A few weeks later, he recorded his response to news of the liberation of German concentration camps: 'the papers are full of pictures of corpses in high stacks, great big hay-cocks of death. I am glad these stories are being told.' The principal story of the camps, of course, was that most of the people in those grisly stacks were Jews, but Morton does not register it.

Victory in Europe came on 8 May. Celebrations in Farnham were strangely muted:

> The bearing of the crowd was amazing. This was the end of the war. It was VE day: the day we all longed for for nearly 6 years. Yet, to look at the crowd, not a smile anywhere. You might have thought it was a funeral. We are an astonishing nation. We prayed and we sang hymns and the Bishop gave his benediction. The sober Sunday bearing of the crowds was everywhere the same. The only people a bit lit up were Canadian soldiers.

To Morton's regret, the wartime coalition government ended and party politics resumed. A general election was called. He and Mary went to the poll on 5 July: 'I shall vote Conservative,' he wrote. The difficulties of collecting ballot papers from troops overseas meant that the result was not declared until the end of the month. On 27 July, by which time the Labour landslide had brought Attlee into office, Morton made a remarkably conciliatory entry in his diary: 'the country seems to be fed up with the Tory Party and perhaps it's time for the Labour Party to see if it can do any better . . . I have an open mind.' I doubt if his mind was as open as he professed. His trips to his old London haunts, now bombed and ruined, depressed him. The prospect of years of austerity and socialist direction of the economy appalled him. He seems not to have seriously considered that he might have an obligation, having come through the war with himself, Mary, all four of his children, and his property all intact, to put his shoulder to the wheel of national reconstruction. By November, he and Mary were beginning to talk about leaving Britain. On New Year's Eve he stood back and made his customary survey of his prospects:

> I have never felt so saddened and depressed about the future of my country as I do today . . . To me now, England seems ruined: sold financially to the US and at the mercy of 140 million Russians. What the future will bring, none can say: I personally think the ruin of European civilization. As I can't have very much longer to live I feel I would like to live my remaining years away from Europe and in a good climate. I keep thinking of Jamaica.

In the event, he lived for a further 35 years, and did not go to Jamaica. But the hold of England on him was definitely slackening. And it slackened further, and perhaps decisively, when he scanned the New Year's Honours List next morning and found no mention of H. V. Morton. He affected a disdain for such trivia, but he could not resist a stab of resentment: 'I think my contribution to "party funds" is worth at least a knighthood, for the royalties of *I, James Blunt* (which I foolishly gave to the Ministry of Information, not wishing to make money out of the War) have brought them in over £5000.'

He concluded his New Year's Day 1946 entry by writing, 'What I suppose is really the matter with me is that I have had to stay put for six years. I long to travel again.' He soon had an enticing offer, and it led to his eventual, permanent departure from Britain.

8

1946–1979

THE LONG, SLOW DECLINE

In February 1946 Morton and Mary, accompanied by Morton's old colleague, the photographer James Jarché, flew off to South Africa for a month, at the invitation of the Prime Minister, Jan Smuts, and the South African authorities, who were keen to publicise their country. On their return, Morton told listeners to his 'Life at Home' broadcast for the Africa Service how much he had enjoyed the trip and how eagerly he looked forward to a second, more leisurely visit. This second visit came in October. This time he went alone, and spent over four months travelling around the country. The visits had two results. He produced *In Search Of South Africa*, which Methuen published in September 1948. The second result was that he and Mary, neither of whom now felt any allegiance to post-war, austerity Britain, decided that they should sell up in England and move, lock stock and barrel, to the Cape.

A little notebook that Morton kept during his second visit has survived and it chiefly records an encounter that never found its way into the pages of the published book. On the flight out to Johannesburg he met a woman. By the time the Skymaster plane was flying through the night, across desert and jungle, towards its refuelling stop in Kenya, they were sitting next to each other, kissing and holding hands.

'What is this going to lead to?' I asked.
    'I don't know.'
    'I think I do.'
    'Yes, I think I do too.'

Morton had always been quick off the mark and adept at locating willing partners. This potential partner, however, left the plane in Kenya, bound for Nairobi, although she and her husband lived in Johannesburg. She promised to contact Morton again, and in his notebook, interleaved with his scribbled notes about the places that he was visiting in and around Johannesburg, are entries that record his impatience at the time it was taking for her to call him.

> No word from Nairobi & I think of her day & night. I am hurt, angry and fed up. To me, it meant a lot; to her, nothing. Well, it just proves that I am just a silly old man and richly deserve this ache. I now sincerely hope I never see her again.

But he could not get her out of his mind. Soon he was writing again: 'I thought that I had put sex in its place once and for all, & here I am like a boy of 17.' He was, in fact, fifty-four. Exactly two months after his encounter on the Skymaster, the call came, and 'on the 19th of Dec my dear love came to me'. Stolen afternoons in hotel rooms followed. ('We met at 11.30 in the hotel after her golf lesson.') Outside, the sun blazed down. Just before Christmas, he had what he recorded as 'one of the strangest experiences of my life'. He took the woman and her husband, who seems to have been complaisant about his wife's affairs, out to lunch and went back afterwards with them to their house. At the end of the evening, the woman drove Morton back to his hotel and on the way, they stopped the car and coupled in the darkness. The affair had a further complication. The woman was also in love with another man, and he was due to arrive in a few weeks' time from Nairobi. (It had been in order to visit him that she had broken her plane journey in Kenya.) She was planning to leave her husband for this man, despite her having expressed her love for Morton. The tension was twisted yet tighter when Morton was invited to quit his hotel and spend the rest of his time in Johannesburg staying with the woman and her husband at their house. He accepted the invitation and spent an anguished time trying to be civil to the husband, trying to get the woman alone, and fearing that the arrival of the suitor from Nairobi would soon put an end to his own chances of further romance. He could not, however, keep up a constant attendance: he had a book to write and had to go off on excursions to gather material. Coming back from one such excursion, he met the woman at the station and they hurried off, not to a hotel, but to the cathedral where they 'prayed side by side'. He does not say what they were praying for. They managed a few more passionate afternoons, and he pondered his relationship with the Nairobi suitor, who was expected daily: 'If he tries to double cross my darling, I shall be so happy to think I have double crossed him.' The whole business ended, inevitably, in tears, though probably not Morton's. The man from Nairobi arrived, and was peeved to find that the woman hadn't told her husband that she was leaving him. She confided tearfully in Morton, who strove unsuccessfully to take her, just once more, to bed. He then more or less retired from the fray, finished off the research for his book, and flew back to England.*

In Search of South Africa was dedicated to Timothy. It maintains the convention of the lone traveller making a single, continuous journey, the route of which was governed only by the carefree whim of the moment. But here and there, the convention creaks. Mary's and Jarché's presence on part of the trip is implied by the acknowledgement of their photography in the list of the book's plates. And the official help that Morton received is implied by incidents such as the narrator's casual-sounding, but evidently pre-arranged breakfast with Jan Smuts, and by his having a luxurious carriage to himself on the train that took him to the Kruger National Park.[1] The book was written and published at a momentous time in South African politics. During the early 1940s, black and coloured† people had only derisory political rights, but they were not utterly excluded from constitutional politics. The chief political battle, however, was between the Afrikaans-speaking descendants of the Dutch colonists and the English-speaking descendants of British colonists. From the mid-1930s up until 1948, the United Party, which bridged the two traditions, held power, with Jan Smuts as Prime Minister. Morton arrived just as this consensus was breaking down. In May 1948, just three months before his book was published, the Afrikaner-dominated National Party was elected. The remaining

---

*Twenty-seven years later, in February 1974, Morton recorded that Mary and he had just taken the woman's husband, who now had another wife, out to lunch in Cape Town. The entry makes no back reference to the events of 1946–7.

†'Coloured' was the regime's official term for the descendants of the slaves from the East Indies that the Dutch colonists of the Cape had brought over during the late seventeenth and eighteenth centuries.

political rights of black and coloured South Africans were extinguished, and the desolating, paralysing apparatus of apartheid was constructed and clamped in place.

Morton's book did address the underlying problems of South African society, but his chief aim was to leave the reader – who of course is assumed to be white – with a sense of a beautiful, bountiful country, full of friendly people and exotic wildlife, and bursting with opportunities. It is scarcely possible, however, to read the book now in the way that Morton's intended audience read it. There is plenty in the book that is written in Morton's most engaging manner and which has no immediate political bearing, but politics are never far away, even when he's watching lions in the Kruger National Park. It is Morton's handling of the ramifications of South African history and politics that is bound to command a modern reader's attention.

In his books on the Middle East, Morton had often been quite successful in entering imaginatively into the lives of the Arabs, Turks, Greeks and Egyptians that he met. But in South Africa, he was incapable, it seems, of seeing things from the point of view of the black and coloured inhabitants. The controlling perspective is that of the steady, rightful conquest of savage Africans by civilised Europeans. Blacks and coloureds, despite their overwhelming numerical presence, are marginal figures in the book. They perform colourful tribal dances in the Zulu homelands, they work in the gold and diamond mines (living in sealed-off compounds where 'life is made as comfortable as possible for them'),[2] they labour on the farms, and they are plentifully on hand as obliging servants, but they are never presented as the equivalent of the native populations of lands such as Ireland, Scotland, Egypt or Syria, about which he had so effectively written years earlier. Nor of course could the Afrikaners, or the English-speakers, be presented as the alternative, authentic South African natives. The country could not yield up to Morton an archetypal figure who could stand as a harmonious symbol of 'the people', or 'the nation'. Such terms could scarcely apply in such an unfinished, colonial country. The only appearance of harmony that South Africa could exhibit came from neither ancient national tradition, nor authentic consensus, but from the complete mastery of blacks by whites.

Often, this fundamental mastery is obscured by the narrator. For example, he visits a beautiful old Cape farmhouse, exquisitely set among its great trees, handsome outbuildings, fields and vineyards. A few yards from the house 'stands a slender white arch with a bell – the slave bell – hanging in it'. The slave labour upon which the farm had been founded is thus acknowledged, but it quickly fades: the narrator continues, 'Those old Dutch farms impressed me by their solidity and their dignity. Life must have passed very pleasantly there; no one went hungry or thirsty, and agriculture and viticulture were pursued not at a run, but at a gentle walk.'[3] Exactly whose life passed pleasantly, at a gentle walk, isn't made clear. Another farm, high on a mountain north of Cape Town, produces a rhapsody from the narrator. Within a couple of generations, a plateau had been subdued and made fertile, a homestead created, and a road built, by the black employees of a European family. Having seen the farm and spoken to its owner, the narrator confidently concludes: 'In a world sick and discontented and at odds with itself, that little story of a South African family lifted high above the earth upon its mountain top has the authentic ring of the Golden Age.'[4]

In South Africa, Morton was seeking an Arcadian world where an affluent, benign white patriarchy effortlessly elicits a smiling, eager deference from its black servants. It is as if the myth of England had been transplanted to South Africa. Maybe the reassuring world that Morton sought was slipping away in post-war England but could be found at the Cape. In his searches in Britain during the 1920s, Arcadia had always been elusive, but in post-war Britain, with its high taxes, its egalitarian rhetoric, and its disobliging domestic staff, Morton felt that it was becoming a foolish illusion. In the pages of *In Search of South Africa*, Morton was trying out versions of the life he could imagine himself living if he and Mary were to quit England.

But he was not so besotted that he always obscured the problem of the relationship between black and white. His notebook makes clear that what he termed 'the skeleton in the South African cupboard' – the question of the political relationship between black and white – insistently rattled its way out of the cupboard and into dinner-party conversations wherever he went. And at the very outset of the published book, when the narrator is wandering around Johannesburg and notices, for the first time, that blacks and whites may not travel on the same bus, may not stand in the same queue, may not pass through the same public door, he concludes that 'the leading fact in South African life' is 'that every white person is by virtue of his whiteness an aristocrat and consequently burdened with the anxieties and responsibilities that should go with that status'.[5] Social justice, it is implied, is best achieved not by democracy, but by aristocratic paternalism, by *noblesse oblige*. Morton's wartime diaries show that he had himself no allegiance to democracy in Britain. It is not surprising, therefore, that his narrator does not advocate it as the way forward for South Africa. Indeed, the narrator is at pains in the book to say that, as a visitor to the country (he does not say that he was a subsidised guest of the authorities), it is not his place to tell South Africans what to do. His task is to report what he sees and hears. But his sympathies emerge as the book develops.

They are revealed, for example, in his staging of an encounter with a sweet middle-aged English lady, and with a fiery Englishman who, disenchanted with Britain, is touring South Africa with a view to settling there. The Englishman asks the narrator if he has been to the north of the country, to see how the Afrikaners handle affairs: 'those Dutch people may not like us, but I tell you they've got the right ideas. No nonsense about equality about them.' The lady's view, by contrast, is that South Africa is 'such a lovely country to live in if only one could close one's eyes to the misery around one. Yes, I mean the dear natives. They lead such hard lives, don't you think?' The man is presented as the realist; the woman as the sentimentalist.[6] By the end of the book, the narrator is speaking for himself, rather than putting words into the mouths of people he meets: 'Perhaps the most significant thing about the Afrikaner is that in a world which has lost its nerve, he is not afraid to be a master.'[7] And on the closing pages of the book, even the 'perhaps' has evaporated:

The story of South Africa is that of two fine European peoples, as alike as two races can be, who have established their civilisation at great cost and with courage upon the tip of Africa. In spite of their unhappy schism [i.e. the Boer Wars of 1881 and 1899–1902], they have managed to exert their sway over, and to accept responsibility for, a greater number of servants than any nation has been blessed or cursed with since the slave empires of antiquity. Most travellers who have moved about among them must go away with the feeling that to them more than to most people in a changed and threatening world the twenty-fourth verse of the third chapter of St Mark applies more than it ever did.[8]

The verse from St Mark is: 'If a kingdom be divided against itself, that kingdom cannot stand.' The message is clear. Afrikaners and English-speakers must unite and rule over the servants – the black and coloured South Africans – with whom they have been blessed, or cursed. The anti-democratic, fascist ideas that Morton had privately approved during the war, far from fading, were beginning to find muted expression in the public pages of his books.

In 1948, at the end of July, with *In Search of South Africa* in the press and due out in a month or so, and with a new, Nationalist government installed in Pretoria, ready to institutionalise apartheid, the Mortons were on board the *Warwick Castle*, bound for Cape Town. The London and Farnham houses had been sold, and other assets had been liquidated. Nearly £70,000 had been transferred to a Cape Town bank account. Installed in their cabin on board, Morton wrote in his diary:

> It is very difficult to believe that I am leaving England. I am surprised to discover in myself no sentiment or emotion. All my worldly goods, my books, pictures, furniture are in four great crates in the hold of this ship. I am glad to get away from Socialist England where the idle & the worthless & the lazy set the pace & where the industrious & the enterprising are plundered & insulted. I hope in S. Africa to find a land where life will be better. Neither Mary nor I feel the slightest regret.

This is so brusque and uncompromising that it calls into question both those fervent declarations he had made about wanting to plant his family in ancient English soil, and those passages in his books where he had expressed a seemingly unquenchable passion for England. One of his fears – and here he was certainly not alone – was that Britain stood a fair chance of being obliterated in a war with Russia. Another of his fears was that, even if this catastrophe could be avoided, Attlee's Labour government would make life too uncomfortable for him. He might disguise this particular worry by saying that the England of hedgerow, cottage and meadow stood in jeopardy, but, at bottom, his fear was founded on pure self-interest, dressed up as concern about the state of England. In common with many rich people, Morton didn't like paying high taxes, even though it was plain that if Britain were to recover from the war, the well-to-do would have to stump up in proportion to their wealth. And in any case, he believed, as he put it in a 1947 notebook in which he had been making financial calculations, 'the country is heading for a financial crash'. He reckoned that his capital was safer in South Africa. Overall, he sensed that his status, both economic and social, would never be as high again as it had been during the 1930s. Rather than experience the humiliation of downturns in his wealth and social standing, he chose to quit.

On their first trip out to South Africa, he and Mary had passed through a quiet little town near the coast, about thirty miles east of Cape Town, called Somerset West.

Coloured boys on bicycles were delivering the groceries, coloured nursemaids were wheeling out the children; here and there I saw people who ought to have been in Cheltenham – ex colonels with spaniels, English matrons, and a pretty English girl on horseback – and the place had, I thought, a pleasant, friendly air.'[9]

Somerset West became the Mortons' home in South Africa. They bought a tract of land, above the town, called Schapenberg, 'sheep mountain', with a trout stream, a vineyard, and views of Table Mountain to the west, and the Hottentot Holland mountains to the east. There, they built a large house. (See plate 18.) This took a couple of years, and while they were waiting, they lived in the town, in an old Dutch parsonage that they had bought.

A couple of months after their arrival, Mary went back to England with Timothy to complete the business of transferring the family's effects to South Africa. Morton wrote her devoted letters saying how much he missed her and how the plans for the new house at Schapenberg were coming along. At the same time, he started an affair with a young woman. This affair had the novelty of the active connivance of the woman's mother, who wrote regularly to Morton saying how good he was for her daughter. On her return from England, Mary found out about the affair and went to a solicitor in order to get personal control of some of the joint assets. Morton's affair carried on for a further year or so, with him meeting his mistress in England when he went back on business, in Holland, and covertly back in South Africa. In September 1949 Mary had had enough. She wrote to him (he was in London), saying that she wanted a divorce. She did not, however, pursue the matter. She backed off, and domestic life went on. So did Morton's affair, and it soon took a farcical turn. In the spring of 1950, Morton's mistress went to Cyprus. He was to join her there. She wrote passionate, longing letters to him, and sent reports of holiday life on the Cyprus beaches to her mother. One day in May she mixed up a letter to her mother and a letter to Morton, and posted them off in the wrong envelopes. When Morton read what the woman intended her mother to read, about the idle life of swimming, dancing and drinking, he concluded that the woman was consorting with other men. With an extraordinary sense of outraged honour and dignity – he really felt betrayed, although the offending letter does not show that the woman was sleeping around – Morton wrote a terse little letter to the woman's mother, complaining about her daughter: 'If she has not betrayed me physically, she has done so mentally and the whole tone of her letter appals me.' To the woman herself he sent £200 for her fare back to South Africa, and an equally terse little letter that said 'There is nothing more to be said now except that our life is over.' But it was not until 1951 that the woman, who insisted that her fidelity to Morton had not wavered when she'd been in Cyprus, was able to write a regretful letter to him acknowledging that the affair was indeed well and truly over. The dozens of letters that the affair produced during its two-year life were collected, along with lawyers' comments, in a file that survived among Morton's and Mary's papers. There was no divorce, and there are no entries on Morton's list of sexual encounters beyond 1948. Mary seems to have reconciled herself to life with Morton. They were, despite Morton's systematic programme of infidelities, fond of each other, and this underlying fondness, coupled with their desire to maintain the public illusion of a happy family, kept them together.

While all this was going on, Morton was researching and writing a new book on London. It was published by Methuen in May 1951, as *In Search of London*. To a great extent, it recycled material that Morton had used in his London books of the 1920s, but it was informed now by the lengthy perspective that nearly forty years of having lived and worked in the city gave him. His opening chapter is an elegiac reflection on the changes he has witnessed, from the Edwardian world of swells and toffs that he saw when he came down to London in 1913, through the jazzy inter-war years, and up to the bomb-ravaged scenes of the late 1940s. Throughout the book, as the narrator wanders the streets, he is frequently taken by melancholy surprise when he turns a corner and sees a blitzed building, its flapping bedroom wallpaper made brutally public by the collapse of the building's exterior walls. He remarks too on the swift colonisation of the bomb-sites by wild flowers.[10] He is reassured by the amazing survival, sometimes almost unscathed, of the greatest of London's buildings – St Paul's and Westminster Abbey, for instance – and he takes his reader on a characteristically well-informed and genial tour. The narrator gives no indication that the author has in fact left England to live abroad, but here and there he opens a window into Morton's state of mind as he made his return journeys to investigate the city he loved. One of his favourite places was the Inner Temple, and his narrator describes its now bomb-damaged state. He then reflects:

> We who live in an ancient country hallowed by many centuries of living rarely consider the effect upon us of this background of experience. It is only when we go to live in a new country . . . that we sense a spiritual vacuum and miss, sometimes, in the most poignant and heart-aching way, the background of England, of London.[11]

Perhaps his private assertions of his complete equanimity at having quit England for good were tinged with bravado.

On the other hand, when he came back to London, as he frequently did, on business, or to work on various writing projects, his letters home to Mary were full of complaints about the way things were going: 'If I felt homesick, a memory of the Strand, with its surging droves of lower middle class people without hats and in mackintoshes would cure me of it,' he wrote. He approved of the way in which smart restaurants and smart shops were beginning to re-attain their pre-war standards, but felt that things would never be quite the same again. In particular, he hated the way in which black citizens were beginning to find a place in London society: 'The natives,' he wrote to Mary, 'stroll about London like privileged human beings.' 'They are everywhere, hideous and arrogant.' 'Would you believe it, there is a native ticket collector on the Victoria tube.'

What were the projects that brought him regularly back to England? His trips to London were often timed to coincide with the final stages in the production of five entirely new books – one on Spain and four on Italy – that he published between 1955 and 1969. Methuen no longer courted him as their star writer, but they were happy to continue publishing his travel books; his large and loyal readership was intact. In London, he would spend a month or so in a friend's flat, and at the Methuen office, correcting proofs. From 1953 onward, he also had a profitable connection with the *National Geographic* magazine. The American magazine's first commission for him was the coverage of the coronation of Queen Elizabeth II in June 1953. Drawing on his vast knowledge of London and of national ceremony, Morton pulled out all the stops and supplied readers with a combination of hushed reverence, when he was describing the Abbey service, and sketches of the ways in which Londoners were celebrating the event. This commission led to others. Accompanied by *National Geographic* photographers, he wrote pieces on the Lake District, on Ireland, and, going further afield, the Pyrenees.[12] Visits to London also enabled him to see his three children from his first marriage. He never looked forward to these encounters and begrudged the money he had to spend on taking his children out. He wished them well, but there is little warmth in the reports he sent back to Mary in Somerset West. His social connections in London were becoming attenuated, but he kept up his membership of his club, the Garrick, and was always pleasantly surprised whenever members and staff recognised him.

The focus of his life had shifted decisively to South Africa. He delighted in planning his library and the garden of his new house, Schapenberg, in the hills above at Somerset West. It was a rather curious building. Its facade fronts straight on to the steep slope of a hill, so there is no sense of a grand sweep up to the front door. The grounds at the back are more impressive, and Morton designed a colonnaded, classical terrace. His library, which was meant to duplicate the space of his old library at South Hay (and which, at the time of writing, is intact), has a somewhat mournful air. Morton's discovery one day of a large and poisonous mamba snake in a corner – efficiently dispatched by the gardener, Willie – pointed up the unbridgeable difference between Binsted and Schapenberg. The library is full of valuable and rare things – Morton's collection of Roman and Egyptian antiquities, some eighteenth-century paintings, items of seventeenth-century furniture, some rare clocks – but the general effect is somehow rather disjointed and incoherent. Morton's failure to secure for himself an unambiguous place in his nation's life as a scholar and man of letters, coupled with his undoubted success in becoming both an expert on all sorts of unrelated topics and a wealthy man, is expressed by the room. But Schapenberg suited Morton and Mary well, and there they lived the comfortable expatriate life.

This sunny life was punctuated regularly by trips to Europe to work on new books. *A Stranger in Spain* was the result of a tour that started in June 1953, just after Morton had finished covering the British Coronation for the *National Geographic.* Mary went with him, and he was given a great deal of help by the Spanish authorities. Spain was then a fascist dictatorship, headed by General Franco. Given the sympathy for fascist ideas and the contempt for democracy that Morton had expressed in his wartime diaries, he should have found Spanish politics congenial. And, by and large, he did. As ever, politics are rarely discussed openly on the page, but when they do make an appearance, the only debate that the narrator records, as he moves round the country, is a discreet debate between supporters of Franco's dictatorship and supporters of the exiled monarchy. The voice of republicanism and democracy is heard only once, from a guide that the narrator inadvertently employed to show him round Barcelona. The guide hated Franco, the monarchy and the church. 'His bitterness was such that I began to wonder if he were a member of some subversive group. He was an unpleasant man and I was only too thankful to pay him off and see the last of him.'[13] Given the way that Morton now travelled, he tended to find himself in only those places where he would hear what his official host wanted him to hear. And he was not going to rock his comfortable new boat by going out of his way to listen to, and publish, views that would be unwelcome to the fascist government. The Civil War of 1936–9, therefore, is handled only obliquely. In Toledo, for example, the canon who was showing the narrator around the cathedral 'mentioned casually that seventy or eighty priests were murdered by the Communists'. But the narrator makes no comment, nor makes any attempt to balance this atrocity by seeking out testimony from republicans. He does not, for example, visit, or mention, Guernica, even though the town was close to the route he took.[14] And whenever the police or the army are noticed by the narrator, it is to record how smart and courteous they are. The Spain that the narrator presents is the Spain that the Spanish authorities – who, after all, were materially helping Morton – wanted to see advertised.

Politics aside, the book fails as a travel book. The narrator's journey has no clear *raison d'être*: it is never clear why the narrator goes where he goes. There is no sense of a passion or a purpose that might be propelling the narrator across the landscape. He is based in Madrid and takes three excursions, one a southward loop by car through Andalusia, one a northward loop by car through the Basque region, and finally a brief hop by aeroplane to Barcelona, where the book abruptly expires. The sense of spontaneity that Morton had conveyed in his early books had faded away, leaving a well-to-do, state-sponsored traveller who dutifully moved from castle to cathedral to medieval town to bullfight, on what looks like a pre-arranged itinerary, with letters of introduction smoothing his way. He does his best at evoking the atmosphere of the places he visits, but page after page is laboriously filled with indigestible historical background. Only occasionally is there a glimpse of a more rewarding journey that might have beckoned. In Avila, for instance, he comes upon a travelling theatre. He watches as the players assemble their tiny plywood auditorium, but he cannot stay for their performance, for his schedule requires him to investigate the birthplace of St Teresa. But, he writes, 'I often thought of those actors when I was living in comfortable hotels . . . To have known enough Spanish to have joined them for a week would, I thought, have been an irresistible adventure.'[15] The problem with the book, and with most of Morton's post-war writing, is that he found it easier and easier to resist such adventures.

Morton was sufficiently self-aware as a writer to know that his book on Spain was below his old standards. In August 1954 he was in London correcting proofs. Mary was in Somerset West correcting another set and posting her revisions to him. He invariably accepted her suggested corrections. He was depressed about the book and she tried to cheer him up. But he wouldn't be cheered. On 2 August he wrote:

> O Mary, I don't want to write any more books. I just want to pootle
> about the garden and enjoy the rest I've earned . . . You are wrong about
> this book, my dear, and it has been very sweet of you to encourage me.
> But it's bad. It's commonplace and dreary. I'm through with writing
> and I'm glad.

A couple of weeks later, and still at work on the proofs, he wrote to Mary: 'The book bores me unutterably. I also think it is badly written and confusing. I am not proud of it and it is a dismal reflection that I could not have done any better.' And a week later he wrote to her: 'I find the book worse and worse with no spirit or originality.' His diagnosis was sound. Morton had never enjoyed roughing it when he travelled, but his early books did have spirit, and they were original. He really had wanted to search for Britain, and his device of chugging from place to place in a little car was a winner. His Middle Eastern travels, although reliant here and there on some useful connections with the authorities, maintained the sense of passionate engagement with the people and places he visited. But now, in the 1950s, he was courted by the tourist authorities of countries that were keen to subsidise the travels of a famous writer, and his side of the bargain was to write enthusiastic accounts of what he saw. If he had not been paid to travel, and had not been accommodated comfortably when he did, I doubt if he would have ventured very far from home. He was a professional writer, not an incorrigible traveller. His professionalism made him always work hard at mugging up the historical background to the places he was commissioned to visit, and he always tried to turn in a respectable piece, but it was a job, not a passion. When he was preparing for his *National Geographic* commission to do a piece on the Lake District, he wrote to Mary; 'I got to bed soon after ten with bloody Wordsworth.' The encounter wasn't very rewarding. A day or so later, he told Mary: 'Wordsworth? You can have him, and Dorothy Wordsworth, and the daffodils.' But in the published piece, Wordsworth and Dorothy are reverently included. No doubt the daffodils would have been included too, if his visit had been when they were in bloom. And when he was in Ireland, working on his piece for the *National Geographic*, he wrote to Mary: 'I am not interested in Ireland, which irritates me, but I shall be able to write the sort of thing they want.'

This slide into cynicism was not inexorable. His next book, *A Traveller in Rome*, was much better than his lacklustre book on Spain. His first visit to Italy had been during the early 1920s, and he had made a number of return trips. He had come to know Rome well, and had made contacts in high places who gave him assistance with his book. Even so, it was more a labour of love than had been some of his commissions during the 1950s. It suffers a bit from the sheer quantity of historical background with which Morton supplies the reader, but the narrator manages to keep it just about under control, leaving himself plenty of room to record an encounter with the city that happily combines spontaneity and depth of knowledge. For example, at the opening of the book, the narrator is staying at a *pensione* with an unreliable lift:

> I often preferred to walk up the five flights of beautiful stairs. The exquisite steps of Rome are among my first memories: steps of marble and travertine, shallow Renaissance steps, so much kinder to the leg muscles than the steep steps of ancient Rome: steps curving left, right and centre from the Piazza di Spagna, as if to show you what steps can do if given a chance; noble steps up to S. Maria Aracoeli; elegant steps to the Quirinal; majestic steps to St Peter's and to innumerable churches. Fountains and palaces – the most wonderful steps in the world. Even the stairs in my pensione were poor relations of the Spanish Steps, and their marble treads and gentle gradient compensated me for those moments when the lift was cantankerous.[16]

Deft little turns of phrase show that Morton hadn't lost his touch. The statues sculpted by the school of Bernini, on the parapet of the Ponte S. Angelo, call forth this description: 'Even on the stillest of mornings, when there is not a breath of wind and you can see every brick of the castle reflected in the glassy Tiber, these angels stand in some terrific seventeenth century gale.' And of the extraordinary Victor Emmanuel monument, he says: 'It is as if the march from *Aida* had been carried out in marble.'[17]

Morton's earlier book on the journeys of St Paul and the early Christian church had taken him to Rome, and from early childhood he had been fascinated by Roman antiquities. Working now on a book devoted entirely to the city, Morton got his narrator up at six o'clock, eager to be out on the streets, soaking up the atmosphere of the city. The narrator walks everywhere, rather than taking trams and taxis. This enthusiasm for the feel of the streets, coupled with the decades of Morton's background knowledge, gives *A Traveller in Rome* a confident, engaging air of intimacy with the life and history of the city. Morton was justifiably satisfied with his efforts. In London during the summer of 1957, correcting proofs for publication in late August, he wrote to Mary: 'I have been reading and re-reading the book . . . I think it *moves*. I was worried when I was writing it by the fear that it was becoming stagnant, but this is not so. It is, I think, more readable than Spain.'

While he was in England in 1957, Morton spent time lobbying to get his son Timothy into Oxford University to read law. He wrote optimistically to Mary, after a meeting with a don at Lincoln College, to say that he'd been given the nod that Timothy's chances were good. He tried to consolidate his lobbying when he was invited to a summer reception at All Souls College in late June, but, in the press of guests, he was disappointed to have been unable to buttonhole the dons that he wanted to influence. In a letter to Mary he says how much he enjoyed the event, although he records that he was obliged to sit close to 'a tall Yid', and that 'to cap it all', one of the college's guests was 'a big fat native', an African prince who, to Morton's astonishment, was addressed by his college host as 'Your Highness'. Morton told Mary; 'I was appalled and disgusted.' His anti-Semitism and racism were ingrained. A few days later, he bumped into his Lincoln College contact on a train, and was, he told Mary, snubbed. The don would give him no assurances about Timothy's chances, and was altogether very stand-offish. 'This sort of thing upsets me,' he wrote to Mary.

'I was so anxious to be friendly & after all I have got a certain standing.' Morton was always somewhat touchy about never having been to university himself,* and this encounter on the train, coming so soon after what he had assumed were successful visits to Oxford, bruised him. He simply was not being acknowledged by the Oxford don as the distinguished man of letters that he felt himself to be. Timothy did not go to Oxford. He went to Stellenbosch University, and then went to work in the advertising department of the *Cape Argus*.

Morton's next commission came from the American publisher Hawthorn. A book aimed by them at the Roman Catholic market, and entitled *This is Rome*, was to be prepared by a team that comprised Morton, the Canadian photographer Yousuf Karsh and the Catholic Auxiliary Bishop of New York, Fulton Sheen. The idea was for the bishop to take a young American boy around Rome, showing him the sights, with Karsh photographing their progress, and Morton supplying a supporting text. The result was a rather mawkish book, dominated by photographs of the boy and the very glamorous bishop, his fatherly hand on his young charge's shoulder, posing, in suitably reverent attitudes, in front of various ruins, churches and altars. Morton enjoyed the hectic few weeks in May 1959 working on the book, which was published in America later in the same year, and in Britain in 1960. Morton loved Rome, he was on ample expenses, and he was amused by the team he was working with. He even took his first pillion ride on a Vespa. He got on well with Karsh and Bishop Sheen. In a letter that he sent back to Mary in Somerset West, Morton reported that the bishop had remarked over dinner one evening that although Morton was not a Catholic, his books were of permanent value to Christians because they are 'reflections of a reverent mind'. Morton confessed to Mary: 'I felt rather shamed by this because you know what an irreverent bastard I really am.'

The success of this project prompted Hawthorn Books to apply the same formula to a book on the Holy Land. The team, changed only by the substitution of two new boys for the original single youth, met up again in 1960, travelled around the holy places, and produced another book, *This is the Holy Land*, published in America in 1961.

*See chapter 1, p. 20.

While Morton was in Europe in 1959 working on *This is Rome*, he applied to the Italian tourist authorities for funds and logistic support for a tour, with Mary, that would equip him to write a book about the country as a whole. 'I MUST have a car,' he wrote home to Mary, 'and if I can't be given one we shall go to Spain' – where he knew that he'd get a favourable response from the authorities. The best deal he could strike with the Italian tourist board was that they would prepare an itinerary, offer a reduction in the cost of their train fares, and make arrangements for them to be squired around by officials from local tourist boards. A couple of trips turned out to be necessary, but even so, the resulting book, *A Traveller in Italy*, which was published in 1964, described a tour that went only as far south as Assisi. It is a dull and indigestible book. In line with Morton's tried-and-tested procedure, it is a record of a tour by a lone traveller, who regularly digresses from his description of his travels to present the histories of the locations he visits. The twin problems, as with his book on Spain, are that the journey itself has no rhyme or reason – the narrator could hardly admit that its route was devised by the tourist board – and that the historical digressions are so lengthy and ponderous that they suffocate what little sense there is of a carefree traveller motoring along in the sunshine from Lombardy to Umbria. Morton always did his homework. His library was full of pamphlets and guidebooks that he'd picked up and quarried on his travels, and, as the bibliographies that he appended to his books indicate, he assiduously read up the histories of the places he visited. In his early books on England and Scotland, he had triumphantly managed to present a journal of a real quest, with historical set-pieces effortlessly emerging. But by the 1960s, he was losing his touch, probably because his travels were now turning into thoroughly commercial propositions, and because he was no longer writing daily instalments for newspapers – with their consequent demand for a sprightly sense of covering the ground. *A Traveller in Italy* is more of a history book than a record of a journey, but the structure of the book awkwardly constrains the history, for Morton is obliged to keep breaking into the past at arbitrary points, according to the particular demands of each of the historic sites his narrator visits, rather than relating the history of this part of Italy in one continuous sweep. But Morton found his touch now and then. His description of the view from his hotel room in Venice, for example, would have passed unremarked in his early books, but here, its sense of a direct response to the passing scene makes it stand out. This is delicately, even tenderly written, but even so, by characterising as 'Shylock' the otherwise wholly sympathetic figure that Morton observed across the alley, he taints him with a familiar, hostile stereotype of the Jew, although his characterisation here is far more respectful than those he delivered in his letters and diaries:

It was odd to glance from the window of such a chaste little room straight into the eyes of Shylock, who lived on the other side of the alley, a fork-bearded Rembrandtesque figure in a black skull-cap. We could have shaken hands from window to window across the narrow lane. The old man appeared to be independent of oxygen. The window was fast closed, and he would probably have gone without air all day but for his beloved canary. The bird lived in a beautifully-made cage of thin bamboo, which he placed out in the morning sun. It was the only sun the bird saw all day, and it did not shine for long in that narrow canyon. Sometimes a bright chain of song would bring Shylock from his shadows to whisper to the bird and smile, a sight Rembrandt would have enjoyed, then the sun went overhead and the little alley was dark until tomorrow.[18]

*

Back home in Somerset West, Morton was given another commission from the *National Geographic Magazine*, this time to tour South Africa itself. Starting in late 1961 and going through into the new year of 1962, he travelled around with an American *National Geographic* photographer. He regularly wrote home to Mary. Clipped to one of his letters is a cutting from the *Natal Mercury*, for 8 December 1961. Morton and the photographer had evidently given an interview to the paper in order to publicise their venture. The report reads:

Mr Morton said yesterday that the article would be entirely non-political, 'otherwise I wouldn't have done it.' It would, however, indicate obliquely that the non-whites of South Africa were not as ill treated as

people overseas seemed to think . . . 'When I came to South Africa about
15 years ago I came for peace and quiet and I intend to keep it.'

The photographer, Kip Ross, is quoted as saying, 'The whole article
will be propaganda for South Africa, although not deliberately so. We
felt it was time to present South Africa.' But the article never appeared.
Perhaps the *National Geographic* had second thoughts about publishing propaganda for a country in which the violent repression of
non-white opinion was standard practice. The Sharpeville massacre, in
which 69 people were shot dead and 178 injured during a demon-
stration against apartheid, had taken place in March 1960, eight
months before Morton gave his interview to the *Natal Mercury*. And
back in America, the home of *National Geographic*, the Civil Rights
movement was gaining momentum. This was not the moment for an
article that tacitly supported white supremacy.

Morton's next book took him back to Rome, a city that he was
beginning to know almost as well as he knew London. During a trip to
the city in the autumn of 1964, to do research for his new book, he
became intrigued by a service that was to be held at St Peter's for the
canonisation of twenty-two black Africans, martyred for their faith
during the 1880s. He secured a ticket, watched the ceremony closely,
and gave his impressions in a letter to Mary. He viewed the congregation with disdain: 'Every native in Rome was there and hundreds
flew in even from the US. Some were in show-off robes . . . Others –
hundreds – did not look as well-dressed as our servants on a day off.'
(How odd, incidentally, for him to have criticised people at a service in
St Peter's, of all places, for wearing 'show-off robes'.) The Pope was
attended by the Church's only black cardinal, and Morton told Mary
that 'the sight of the Pope receiving the Sacrament from the hands of
an African made "Apartheid" seem rather strange!' Strange or not, the
reporter for the *Natal Mercury* had probably been accurate in
representing Morton as an apologist for apartheid. It is clear from his
letters to Mary from Rome that he found the Church's inclusion of
blacks distasteful. He sent Mary a newspaper clipping describing the
ceremony, and in the margin he wrote 'Saint Mumbo Jumbo'. He
dismissed the whole business of the canonisation as cynical politics – a
'suck-up to the native' as he termed it – saying that it was all of a piece

with 'Martin Luther King and the Nobel Prize'. (King was awarded the honour in 1964.)

The project that had brought Morton to Rome on this occasion originated back in 1959, when he was working on *This is Rome*. He had managed to go behind the scenes, so to speak, of the Trevi Fountain with one of the city's civil engineers to see how the fountain worked. This had set off an interest in Rome's water system. Finding that no book on the subject had been published in English, he decided to write one himself. He cultivated his connections with the city's water engineers and was conducted by them around the complicated ancient network of aqueducts that brings water to the city. Morton had never learned to speak Italian fluently though, and in a letter to Mary he said how difficult it was to follow the English of the engineer who was explaining the water-supply system to him. Often in his letters he lamented having always to find interpreters as he travelled around the country. But he didn't let this disability hold him back, and never confessed it in his books on Italy: they are presented as if the narrator could effortlessly converse with anybody he met.

His book on Rome's aqueducts and fountains is called *The Waters of Rome*, and was published in 1966, when Morton was seventy-four years old. It is a handsome book, published not by his old firm Methuen, but by *The Connoisseur* in association with Michael Joseph. It is lavishly illustrated, both with reproductions of old maps and engravings, and with superb photographs, by Mario Carrieri, of Rome's many fountains. The book brought out the best in the elderly Morton. He freed himself from his self-imposed convention of loading assorted historical information on to the back of the narrative of a journey, and wrote instead a systematic, chronological history of Rome's water system, followed by chapters on each of the city's six aqueducts and the fountains that they feed. The history of a city's water supply might seem a somewhat unenthralling topic, but Rome is special. From the earliest times, right through to the time when Morton was writing, water was brought in not from reservoirs, but direct from springs in the surrounding hills, conducted along aqueducts that run for the most part underground, but for part of their journey supported on magnificent arches that stride across the intervening valleys. And at the ancient public termini in the city, the water is not shut off with taps, but runs continuously, supplying two things. First, in the days before water was piped to each household, residents came to the terminus for their household water, and secondly, the steady continuous stream flushed the drains, which, in turn, discharged into the River Tiber. These continuous supplies of water, which reach the centre of Rome only a few hours after welling up from the springs in the hills, discharge from quite separate aqueducts (six during the 1960s, but eleven in ancient times) into public supply points. Many of these supply points were turned into grand fountains. During the Renaissance, succeeding popes outdid each other in their patronage of architects and sculptors who rose to the challenge of transforming the utilitarian business of the delivery of fresh drinking water into the high art of spectacular civic monuments. Rome's water supply is a topic that brings together civic government, hydraulic technology, the patronage of art and the practices of architecture and sculpture, all set against two thousand years of the city's development. Morton's book frankly depends on already published sources, but he grasped the interconnections within the topic, and, with the aid of the superb illustrations, produced one of his best books. He follows each stream of water from its mysterious bubbling up from underground, along its eight-hour journey in its aqueduct, to its arcing fall from the mouth of a baroque lion, or dolphin or cherub into a basin that sparkles in the centre of the piazza. And he vividly explains the extraordinary political, artistic and technological vicissitudes that beset the development of the aqueducts. During the 1960s, Morton's career was declining: he was producing formulaic, rather dull travel – or pseudo-travel – books. But with *The Waters of Rome* the decline was arrested. It is a fresh and attractive book.

In the late spring of 1966, with the manuscript of *The Waters of Rome* safely in the hands of the publisher, he was off on his travels again. This time, again with the help of the Italian tourist authorities, he was chauffeured south from Rome to Bari in order to reconnoitre a book on southern Italy. He still enjoyed such trips, but he sometimes had doubts about whether he could keep on producing books. He wrote to Mary: 'I have been wondering whether I can still do another "traveller" type of book. I don't think I can face the rushing about.' And a month later, in June 1966, he described a typical, tiring day in his life on the road with his Italian driver, following an itinerary prepared by the tourist board: 'mountain roads, sudden stops, a church, a castle, a priest, a local historian – and then on again'. But despite these bouts of weariness, he pressed on, making two or three trips to the south – accompanied on at least one of them by Mary – and produced his final book, *A Traveller in Southern Italy*, which was published in 1968, when he was seventy-six.

The manner in which he was now accustomed to travel gave his narrator little to work with when he came to recording the business of getting from place to place. As usual, the narrator presents himself as a lone traveller, but he has few of the wayside encounters that solo travel produces and which give travel writing one of its characteristic charms. An exception is his meeting with an old man in S. Stefano, near Aquila in Abruzzo. 'While I was admiring the picturesque flights of steps that led to some of the houses, I saw an old man watching me. He wore a battered felt hat, and he looked a cheerful kind of person. I spoke to him . . .' The old man, who turns out to have once worked in America and therefore speaks some English, takes him round the village and introduces him to a family who invite him in for a glass of wine. Contact with the locals has been made. The actual origin of the encounter, however, was rather different. In a letter to Mary, Morton said that his chauffeur spoke little English. Needing information about Aquila, and speaking very little Italian himself, Morton had, as he told Mary, 'a brain wave': 'I told the driver to go into the mountain villages about 40kms from here and in every one ask if anyone lived there who had worked in America.' The chauffeur's enquiries turned up a helpful seventy-two-year-old man who had worked as a coal-miner in Pittsburgh. This was the narrator's old man in the battered felt hat. The convention that Morton adopted in his books, of the lone traveller effortlessly conversing with everybody he met, required that this episode be presented as if it happened quite by chance.[19] But behind the narrator is Morton, being chauffeured swiftly from first-class hotel to first-class hotel, indigestibly taking in notable churches, Roman ruins and local festivals along the pre-arranged way. He had never been one to rough it, but he makes his narrator somewhat wistfully confess, as he pulls in to a smart, modern hotel, that 'I wished, and not for the first time, that I had the courage to try a fourth-class hotel' in order to see if they were as rough as the earlier travellers, whose books he was using, had said they were. But the lure of air-conditioning and an en-suite bathroom is too great.[20]

The result, though, is a satisfactory book. It lacks the zest of his earliest books, but it manages the intrinsic problem of loading historical, guide-book information on to the narrative of a journey pretty well: the narrative does not buckle under the weight. It does, however, bear the marks of its origin. This is no carefree, random journey, undertaken by a free spirit. It is a dutiful tour on behalf of the Italian tourist board.

A Traveller in Southern Italy more or less brought Morton's writing career to a conclusion. Further books were issued, but they tended to be repackagings of earlier material. The old books were given larger page sizes, shortened texts, and new, lavish illustrations, sometimes in colour. Morton was never one to turn away the chance to squeeze some royalties out of his back catalogue, and he was pleased to see the publishing life of his books extended. But the re-issues lack the charm of the original editions. Bits of text pulled from various books written in the 1920s sit rather uneasily next to colour photographs taken half a century later, during the 1970s.[21]

The final decade of Morton's life, from 1969 to 1979, was spent quietly at Somerset West. 'Mary & I live very quiet, satisfactory lives,' he wrote in his diary in July 1974.

> I can't believe we have been married for over 40 years. It's fantastic. We share half a bottle of pop [champagne] every morning at 11. We have become very rural. Our lives are entirely on our own land with the dogs, Riley and Flora. So we live together in an age of anarchy.

He seems to have taken a mournful pleasure in writing entries in his diary that say how dreadful things are outside his precious house and garden. In 1974, in one of his customary New Year's Day *tours d'horizon* diary entries, he wrote, 'The whole world is in the grip of anarchy & this leads either to dictatorship of the Right or the Left. I cannot see how Democracy (much as I loathe it & its bumbling ignorance and self-approval) is to survive in England.' His political acumen had grown no sharper as he grew older. He lay in bed at night listening on his headphones to the BBC World Service and noted in his diary next day any bad news that he heard about Britain. In November 1974, for example, he wrote, 'Awful news from England of bankruptcies etc. & now clear that the country is ruled by the TUC.' Perhaps his prophesies of impending disaster in Britain were an expression of a need to keep reassuring himself that he'd made a wise decision in moving to South Africa nearly thirty years earlier. He did occasionally yearn for England, but appears never to have contemplated moving back. In September 1974 he wrote, 'I should like to see England again – the countryside, the cathedrals,' but he blew this wistfulness away with doom-laden entries that describe England as 'a sinking ship'. There are no equivalent entries in his diaries about South African politics. It's plain that he believed in white supremacy, but he never explored the disturbing implications of his belief. Perhaps the implications were too disturbing, too momentous. He never felt himself to be confronted by an inescapable moral and political challenge: the brutal world of apartheid politics scarcely impinged on the placid lives that he and Mary lived at Schapenberg.

The most immediate threatening cloud in their tranquil sky was the health of Timothy. Morton's dreams of a brilliant career for him in law, following an Oxford graduation, came to nothing. Timothy worked for the *Cape Argus*, although not as a journalist, and lived in Cape Town. But his mental health was shaky. He had a number of breakdowns that necessitated lengthy spells in nursing homes where he was treated for what Morton called 'paranoia' and 'mental delusions'. Eventually, he had to give up work and move back to Schapenberg to live with his parents. The presence of a delusional son, in his midthirties, in the household of elderly parents is bound to be stressful, but Morton's diary entries record irritation, rather than anguish:

T. seemed almost himself. I try to hide the anger that smoulders in me when I remember that this is the third time since he left the University that we have come to his rescue in an emotional-alcohol crisis. And I am now 81 & his mother is 74. It is shocking.

With encouragement from Methuen, Morton started writing his memoirs, but progress was desultory. He had bursts of activity, but for weeks he would write nothing. He came to realise that, at the rate he was going, and as old age overtook him, he would never finish them. This caused him no grief: he was happier, it seems, doing other things: 'Am messing about again with my "memoirs" which are good in parts. But my old fire & energy have gone. I am more interested in my field mice & in taming my doves.' Ever since he was a boy, Morton had loved animals. The houses that he lived in as a child, back in Birmingham, had always been full of cats and dogs – and even a tame owl. In all his books his narrator affectionately and acutely notices animals – a dog in Syria, cats in the Forum at Rome, donkeys in Spain, mice on Mount Sinai. Now in old age he could unaffectedly indulge his fascination. He and Mary always kept cats and dogs. She liked Dalmatians, and he was very fond of a Siamese cat that sat on his shoulder as he wrote. (See plate 19.) But the creatures that lured him away from writing his memoirs were mice and doves. Every morning he would open his bedroom window and tempt in a dove that he eventually tamed to eat corn from his hand. More absorbing still for him was a family of field mice for which he spent a couple of contented days building a castle out of the polystyrene packaging from a new short-wave radio. He would spend an hour each evening in the Italian garden that he had designed, watching his family of mice in their castle. He devised gadgets to discourage rats from preying on them. His diary entries recording his fascination with and affection for his mice recapture something of the self-deprecating charm of his early books: 'This morning was delighted to observe (9 A.M.) a mouse leave the Dungeon Restaurant & enter the castle itself – the first to do so.' He also found model soldiers absorbing. He ordered hundreds of them, painted them in period uniform and deployed them in battle formation. He was particularly pleased with a recreation of the Battle of Borodino, between Napoleon's army and the Russians in 1812.

And thus Morton lived out the last years of his life. He meandered on until he was nearly eighty-seven, rarely leaving home, spending his days sitting in his garden in the sun with a glass of local champagne, grumbling about the food whenever he and Mary were invited out by other expatriates to lunch, observing his field mice, marshalling his model soldiers, and making gloomy prophecies about the state of the world. He died, alone in his bedroom, on 17 June 1979. He was cremated, and, a year or so later, Mary wrote to his daughter Barbara (from his marriage to Dorothy), saying: 'You may like to know that I have Harry's ashes here, in an urn, amongst his model soldiers in his cabinet in his room upstairs. I know this is where he would like them to be.'

CONCLUSION

I set out with three aims: to examine the travel writing of H. V. Morton, to look at the myths he deployed, to find out more about the Harry Morton who invented H. V. Morton. What has been the result?

First, it is plain that Morton's travel books were not autobiographical in any simple sense. The beguiling mode of first-person narration, in which a solitary traveller tells his readers about a journey that he has undertaken, is a literary device. Morton certainly undertook the journeys that his books describe, but he did not travel in the way that his narrator says he travels. As a matter of historical truth, this is of little importance. The point of discovering the gap between Morton's life and the testimony of his narrator is to prompt analysis of how his books work. He was working in a vast, ancient tradition of travellers' tales, and he made no startling innovations. What he did do, after an apprenticeship in newspapers where he experimented with version after version of a persona who might narrate his travels, was to come up with the perfect, modest English amateur – witty, well-informed (but not intimidatingly well-informed), charming, flirtatious. He could be intrepid enough to go to sea in a trawler, or tramp across the Highlands, he could be self-deprecating enough to describe taking off his braces to bind round the jaws of a braying Egyptian donkey, yet he could effortlessly rise to the hushed rhetoric demanded by a description of a cathedral or an ancient battlefield. Morton was a clever, hard-working writer first, a restless traveller second.

His best books are his early books on Britain. The narrative voice that he had been searching for in his London books finally spoke clearly and distinctively. Having found a voice, his shrewd journalistic instincts directed him not to the uttermost ends of the earth, to bring back stirring tales of danger and privation, but to England, a country lying at hand, ready to be explored on behalf of people sick of war and ready to follow the narrator, either in their imaginations, or in their new Austin Sevens, out into the empty country lanes. The formula worked like magic, and Morton was not slow to apply it to the rest of the British Isles. His commercial instincts were keen.

When he had completed Britain, and made a great deal of money in the process, he adapted the formula in order to cater to the religious market. But his books on the Middle East show that although Morton's travels were generally subordinate to his writing, he did have a real passion for the landscapes, the people and the history of the region. There is no mistaking the thrill he felt when he saw the Nile for the first time, and there was very little slackening in his evident enthusiasm as he completed his journeys round the eastern Mediterranean and into the deserts of Syria, Iraq, Jordan and Egypt. Indeed, one of the puzzling things about his Middle Eastern trilogy is his decision to key it to the Judaeo-Christian story, and thus to raise expectations of piety. His biblical titles guaranteed him a market, and he was far too canny to have allowed any overt scepticism to creep into the text ('you know what an irreverent bastard I really am'), but the titles scarcely did justice to the range of topics that he covered in the books. He was probably more interested in ancient Rome, Greece and Egypt than he was in Judaeo-Christian history, and the books amply display this interest. He managed also to avoid the gross stereotypes that fall readily to hand whenever Europeans write about the Orient. In his books on Britain he blithely characterised people he met as Saxons or Celts or Vikings; the Middle East opened up a suite of equivalent stereotypes – wily Jews, noble Bedouins, crafty Greeks, fanatical Moslems, and so on. But, surprisingly, Morton used them less than might have been expected. And in places – his accounts of the Copts and of the Abyssinian priests, for example – he is remarkably sensitive.

His books on Spain and Italy are not nearly as interesting. The formula was becoming a bit threadbare, chiefly because he was no longer an independent traveller. He was now a hired hand. And this meant that the gap between him and his narrator widened, for he could not reveal, on the page, the exact circumstances that governed the journey. Additionally, he was less successful than formerly in managing the balance between, on one hand, keeping up the momentum of the narrative of the journey, and, on the other, of wheeling out background historical information about the sites his narrator passes through. Morton was a good popular historian, and the one book in which he freed himself from the constraints of the 'traveller' mode, and wrote straight history, *The Waters of Rome*, is a success.

What of the myths he deployed? Chief among them is the myth of England – the England of hedgerow and cottage. His formulation of this fundamental English myth is as potent as any that were produced between the wars. J. B. Priestley, one of Morton's rivals in the business of describing the nation, must have acknowledged the potency of Morton's formulation, for when he prepared a little anthology of inspiring writing on *Our Nation's Heritage* at the beginning of the war, he included, under the sub-heading 'What is England?', the passage in which Morton, sick in Palestine, conjures the vision of 'the village street at dusk . . .'[1] Morton, though, was not entirely enslaved by this myth. His books on Britain celebrate urban, industrial culture, often as enthusiastically as they celebrate the countryside. But when it came to the push, the rural parish was more powerful than the urban borough: when he needed a symbol for the England that was imperilled during the Battle of Britain, he found it in the prospect of the Hampshire fields, viewed from the tower of Binsted church. This mythic England exerted great power in his books, but little in his life. Even when it was accompanied by his ownership of seemingly precious acres of English soil, the myth exerted only a weak pull on him personally: he left England for South Africa with hardly a backward glance.

As a writer, Morton knew how to deploy myths to great effect. But he did not reach for them automatically. His Middle Eastern trilogy, for instance, largely avoids the obvious conventions that lay in wait for it. Nor is his book on Ireland mired in Irishness: uncharacteristically, he made his narrator confront the issues that Ireland was currently facing. This feat notably was not performed again in *In Search of South Africa*, a book that is politically anodyne – and which does not have uncontentious myths to fall back on.

Finally, what can be concluded about the man who constructed the persona who narrates the books? Starting with his politics, what is revealed is a heap of thoughtless prejudices. He liked to think that, as a newspaper man who had been close to the political pulse, he knew a thing or two. He was forever writing in his diary what he clearly considered to be an insider's analysis of events. The common herd, he thought, might believe one thing, but he knew better: Britain would be defeated by Germany early in the war, the Americans would never join the battle, Britain's economy would crash into ruins, there would be a war with Russia . . . There is not one passage of political analysis or prophecy in his diaries that shows any insight at all. He hadn't a clue. Moreover, the prejudices that passed for his politics were thoroughly crude. He was anti-democratic, anti-Semitic, racist. He was also hypocritical, for he was careful to let none of these prejudices leak into his books. Indeed, he was perfectly capable, if necessary, of writing things that he did not believe to be true. In his wartime propaganda books he declared that Britain was 'as sound as a bell', but privately he was moaning that the lower orders were ignorant and insolent, that the officers' mess was no longer the exclusive province of the gentleman, that the nation's finances were in the hands of treacherous Jews, and that unjust taxes were driving him to ruin. What was needed, in his view, was a bracing dose of fascism, coupled with a taxation policy designed to let him keep all his money.

His decision to move to South Africa expressed his selfishness, his lack of political savvy, and his prejudices. It was prompted by urgent, if mistaken, fears of Britain's imminent financial collapse, and by the allure of sunshine, low taxes and obedient servants. He never became a raging public defender of apartheid: he much preferred the quiet life, and the life that he and Mary designed for themselves never brought them sharply up against the injustices that were fundamental to the system – or, if it did, they looked the other way. But whenever views on race relations were expressed in his letters, they are not the views of a liberal who is too timid to make a public stand. On the contrary, they are the views of a white supremacist. And if he was ever worried that his comfortable life in Somerset West might not go on for ever, he fortified his belief that he had made a wise choice in going there by gleaning every scrap of news he could find of the tensions between black and white back in Britain. There was a sort of grim glee in his letter home to Mary that reported the defeat of a Labour candidate in the 1964 election by a conservative whose supporters were reported to have campaigned with the slogan 'If you want a nigger neighbour, vote Labour.' 'I was delighted,' Morton told Mary.

How important were women in his life? In his notes for his *Memoir* he wrote: 'Women have played the largest part in my life & anything I have done I owe to them.' His mother, certainly, was more encouraging to him than was his father, although his father, after despairing of his son's poor school record, did take him on as a reporter and thus got him started on the road to fame and fortune. But this generosity never produced real affection in return: it is always Morton's mother who is given pride of place in his affectionate memories. Perhaps his father was a philanderer. If so, maybe Morton's coolness towards his father was the result of seeing a reflection of himself, and of not liking what he saw. 'I remember Mother once saying to me,' he wrote, ' "If you treat Dorothy as your father treated me, I'll haunt you." And I did that.'* Morton's own relentless sexual opportunism, and his making a list of the hundred or so women with whom he'd had sex, indicates, at least, a sort of obsession. But although many – perhaps most – of these sexual encounters were designed to be ephemeral, he often spoke of love, and of the inspiration he drew from his various women. The pattern was established early in his life, when as a young man in Moseley, he would declare his love to two women on successive days, while, at the same time, keeping his eye open for any chance encounter with a shopgirl. Later, his dedication, albeit disguised, of his first book to a mistress, and her exalted appearance later in *In Search of England,* testifies to the encouragement she gave him and his recognition of it, at some personal risk.† He seems to have needed the constant approval of women, and was extremely touchy when he didn't get it. And it almost goes without saying that he expected a fidelity from them that he would never have dreamed of observing himself. His extraordinarily pompous response to the farce of the misdirected letters from Cyprus, during one of his later affairs, indicates that he expected devotion from his mistresses.‡ And even when he was in his seventies, travelling around Italy, he wrote very hurt, petulant letters to Mary if he was not receiving daily letters from her.

---

*See chapter 6, p. 165.
†See chapter 3, p. 100.
‡See chapter 8, pp 204–5.

Although he became a highly successful author, he never seems to have felt absolutely secure of his standing. At the height of his success in the late 1930s, despite his yeoman's house in Hampshire, his smart town house in a Chelsea square, his membership of the Garrick Club – despite all the appurtenances of wealth and fame – he never felt confident that he had been properly accepted as an English man of letters and that he had been accorded a suitable place in the nation's life. The denial of an honour in the 1946 list rankled. His being snubbed when he tried to get Timothy into Oxford upset him. He was aggrieved to have been given only cursory mention by the historian of the school he'd attended. Maybe he feared that in the opinion of those he wanted to impress, he was perceived as no more than a jumped-up reporter. And sometimes he defiantly described himself as exactly that – as a man who knew his way about the racy world of Fleet Street and who knew the smell of printer's ink. He certainly never moved in the circles of writers such as J. B. Priestley, Evelyn Waugh or George Orwell, and he would, equally certainly, have moved very uneasily in their circles in the unlikely event of his being invited in. During the war, when he was invited a couple of times by the BBC to be on the panel of the 'Brains Trust', he made rather a poor showing, judging by the transcripts of the programmes. He seems to have been overawed by the other panelists, and timidly gave way to them or deferentially expressed his agreement with them.[2] His own assessment of his character, set out in his *Memoir*, was clear and shrewd: he was a man who was at his most comfortable standing on the edge of a crowd looking in, rather than standing at the focus of attention. This was not the whole story though, for he dearly wanted to be acclaimed as the brilliant writer of superb books, written from this edge-of-the-crowd vantage point. When he was snubbed by the Oxford don, he wrote, 'after all, I have got a certain standing'. The problem was that in the Britain of the late 1950s, he hadn't. The status of a pre-war travel writer and journalist who had never been part of the Oxbridge establishment, and who was temperamentally and politically out of sympathy with Britain's new multi-racial, iconoclastic, youth-oriented culture, was bound to plummet. Morton had nothing more to say that anybody but his old readers wanted to hear. He was becoming a crotchety old relic. He was made a Fellow of the Royal Society of Literature in 1965, and was thereby accorded a mark of esteem by the world of letters, but by then he was seventy-three years old, and was more and more the expatriate, visiting London only on business, and grumbling when he did so. A couple of years later, he was agreeably surprised to be recognised by a few of the staff and members of the Garrick, but his commitment to England and its institutions was waning fast.

The British establishment may never quite have offered him the veneration that he felt was his due, but millions of his readers did. To be more precise, they did not venerate Harry Morton, for they knew nothing about him, and would have been disappointed if they had gone behind the scenes to meet him. If they had, their response would have been akin to that of Little Beaver – the young H. V. Morton – when he met his own hero, 'the Chief'. The object of Morton's readers' veneration was H. V. Morton, the urbane, charming writer who had persuaded them that he had searched for, and found, the essences of the countries he wrote about.

NOTES

INTRODUCTION

1. Methuen have reissued paperback editions of most of his books.
2. A representative sample: R. Colls and P. Dodd (eds.), *Englishness: Politics and Culture, 1880–1920* (Croom Helm, London, 1986); M. J. Wiener, *English Culture and the Decline of the Industrial Spirit, 1850–1980* (Cambridge University Press, 1981, repr. Penguin, London, 1985); P. Wright, *On Living in an Old Country* (Verso, London, 1985); J. Giles and T. Middleton (eds.), *Writing Englishness* (Routledge, London, 1995); A. Calder, *The Myth of the Blitz* (Cape, London, 1991); R Hewison, *The Heritage Industry* (Methuen, London, 1987); R. Lumley (ed.), *The Museum Time Machine* (Routledge, London, 1988).
3. Chatto, London, 2000.
4. D. Matless, *Landscape and Englishness* (Reaktion, London, 1998), p. 63.

CHAPTER I

1. *A Traveller in Rome* (Methuen, London, 1957, repr. 2001), pp. 271–3; *Blue Days at Sea* (Methuen, London, 1932; 4th edn., 1933), pp. 159–63.
2. T. W. Hutton, *King Edward's School, Birmingham* (Blackwell, Oxford, 1952), p. 168. Italics mine.
3. Jeanne Mackenzie's *Cycling* (Oxford University Press, 1981) is a lovingly-assembled anthology of evocative fragments, many from Morton's period.
4. *I Saw Two Englands* (Methuen, London, 1942), pp. 152–6.
5. 25 May 1931.

CHAPTER 2

1. Morton later published an affectionate account of Lawrence's shop. See *In Search of London* (Methuen, London,1951, repr. 2001), pp. 16–19.
2. Paul Fussell's *The Great War and Modern Memory* (Oxford University Press, 1975) is a good place to start in the vast literature on this topic.
3. PRO. WO374/49185.
4. H. A. Adderley, *The Warwickshire Yeomanry in the Great War* (Warwick, n.d.).
5. Ibid., p.213.
6. Cf. *A Traveller in Southern Italy* (Methuen, London, 1968, repr. 2002), p. 61.
7. P. Warner, *The Zeebrugge Raid* (Kimber, London, 1978), p. 30.
8. *The Call of England* (Methuen, London, 1928), p. 146.

CHAPTER 3

1. H. V. Morton, *Through Lands of the Bible* (Methuen, London, 1938), p. 255.
2. Ibid., pp. 267–9.
3. For an account of the Tutankhamun episode, told from the point of view of *The Times*, but which does not substantially challenge Morton's version of events, see O. Woods and J. Bishop, *The Story of the Times* (Michael Joseph, London, 1983), pp. 253–6.
4. See G. Pawle, 'H. V. Morton – Fleet Street and After', *Blackwood's Magazine*, vol. 326, July–Dec 1979, pp. 120–8.
5. V. Williams, *The World of Action* (Hamish Hamilton, London, 1938), ch. 26.
6. *In Search of England* (Methuen, London, 1927, repr. 2000), pp. 1–3.
7. B. Baxter, *Strange Street* (Hutchinson, London, 1935), p. 210.
8. S. P. B. Mais, *All the Days of my Life* (Hutchinson, London, 1937), p. 128.
9. Collie Knox, *It Might Have Been You* (Chapman & Hall, London, 1938), pp. 318–9, 360.
10. 'Embankment lovers' appears as 'London Lovers'. 'Madonna of the pavement' appears with title unchanged. See *The Heart of London* (12th edn., Methuen, London, 1931), pp. 86–8, 121–4.
11. *The Heart of London, The Spell of London* and *The Nights of London* formed a trio. All three romped away in edition after edition, and were eventually united, in 1940, within a single binding, entitled *H. V. Morton's London. A London Year*, which was based on the idea of the fashionable London 'Season', went out of print quickly. Morton issued a second, revised edition in 1933, explaining, in his introduction that he felt that the first edition voiced 'a delight in the gaieties of London life, now, alas, quite out of touch with our times'. He now considered that his record of the London season might be of 'archaeological interest'. See *A London Year* (2nd edn., Methuen, London, 1933), p. vii.
12. *The Nights of London* (8th edn., Methuen, London, 1935), p. 44.
13. *A London Year*, pp. 11–17.
14. *The Heart of London*, p. 11.
15. *A London Year*, pp. 99–100.
16. *The Nights of London*, pp. 158–162.
17. *The Spell of London* (10th edn, Methuen, London, 1932), p. 15. There are, too, faint echoes here of the St Crispin's Day speech in *Henry V* (iv.3), in which Henry honours those who shed their blood for England.

CHAPTER 4

1. Wood borrows Morton's title for his own book of essays. See M. Wood, *In Search of England* (Penguin, London, 2000), ch. 10, pp. 189–202.
2. *Daily Express*, 28 April 1926. Reprinted in *In Search of England*, p. 10. I have corrected what I take to be a misprint in the last sentence quoted: the text reads 'search of England'.
3. *In Search of England*, pp. 173–4.

4. B. Bryson, *Down Under* (Black Swan, London, 2000), p. 24.
5. *In Search of England*, pp. 78–81.
6. Ibid., p. 180.
7. *Daily Express*, 25 May 1926.
8. *In Search of England*, pp. 125–6.
9. Ibid., pp. x–xiii.
10. Ibid., p. 241.
11. Ibid., p. 55.
12. Ibid., pp. 196–200.
13. Ibid., pp. 186, 203–4, 98.
14. Ibid., pp. 22–5.
15. Ibid., pp. 32, 73, 223–4.
16. A. Howkins, 'The Discovery of Rural England', in R. Colls and P. Dodd (eds.), *Englishness: Politics and Culture 1880–1920*, pp. 62–88.
17. *In Search of England*, p. 180.
18. Ibid., pp. 111–14.
19. Ibid., pp. 263–70.
20. The Methuen Archive.
21. *In Search of England*, p. 2.
22. Valentine Cunningham's *British Writers of the Thirties* (Oxford University Press, 1988) gives an excellent survey of this ruralist impulse as it later developed. See pp. 226–40.

CHAPTER 5

1. *The Land of the Vikings* (Richard Clay, Bungay, 1928), p. 18.
2. Ibid., p.79.
3. *The Call of England*, pp. vii–viii, 191–3.
4. Ibid., p. 17.
5. Ibid., p. 24.
6. Ibid., p. 64.
7. Ibid., p. 65.
8. Ibid., pp. 82, 161.
9. Ibid., pp. 113–33.
10. Ibid., pp. 144–58.
11. Ibid., p. 172.
12. Ibid., pp. 175–96.
13. *The Call of England*, p. 201. In fact, the 'Old England' of the eighteenth-century aristocracy understood industry very well. Many a lord was keen to dig out the coal that lay beneath his rolling acres.
14. Ibid., pp. 203–4.
15. J. R. and M. M. Gold, *Imagining Scotland: Tradition, Representation and Promotion in Scottish Tourism since 1750* (Scolar Press, Aldershot, 1995), pp. 130–2; A. Taylor, *Scotland on Sunday Colour Supplement*, 30 April 2000, p. 7.
16. *In Search of Scotland* (Methuen, London, 1929), p. 6.
17. Ibid., pp. 48–51, 142. In later editions, Morton added an introduction in

which he asserted that Scott 'created the modern conception of Scotland'. (17th edn., 1932, p. viii.)

18. Ibid., pp. 28–30.
19. Ibid., pp. 98–106.
20. Ibid., p. 137.
21. Ibid., pp. 255–6.
22. Ibid., pp. 32–4.
23. Ibid., pp. 59–63.
24. *In Scotland Again* (Methuen, London, 1933; 10th edn., 1943), pp. 377, 305.
25. Ibid., pp. 210–23, 298–313.
26. In his book on Wales, he writes of the 'hearty men with whom I have climbed mountains'. One of them is 'the wild doctor who sweeps through the Larig like an angry clan'. Presumably, Morton knew this because he had swept through the Larig in the company of the wild doctor. *In Search of Wales* (Methuen, London, 1932), p. 152.
27. The Larig Ghru episode is further evidence of the rather cobbled-together nature of the book. The narrator's account of his route from Blair Atholl to Aberdeen (p. 313) does not correspond with the map of the route, which, following Morton's standard practice, is printed in the endpapers of the book.
28. *In Scotland Again*, pp. 147–53.
29. Ibid., pp. 314–33. The 1929 diary records that between 16 September and 20 September he went from Blair Atholl to Aberdeen, and thence to Arbroath. This accords with the route that the narrator of the book says he took. How many days he spent at sea is unclear.
30. *In Search of Ireland* (Methuen, London, 1930), p. 19.
31. Ibid., p. ix. The treaty gave the Irish Free State, as it was termed, dominion status, equivalent to that of New Zealand and Canada. Six counties in the predominantly Protestant north of the island were partitioned from the rest of Ireland, remained British and were given their own assembly. Between 1922 and 1923, a civil war was fought in the Free State between those who accepted, albeit reluctantly, the terms of the treaty and those who held out for a sovereign republic for the entire island. The Free State renamed itself Eire in 1936, and declared itself a republic in 1949. The six counties comprising Northern Island have remained part of the United Kingdom.
32. Ibid., pp. 263, 295–6.
33. Ibid., p. 50.
34. Ibid., p. 203.
35. Ibid., p. 42.
36. Ibid., pp. 90, 169–70, 313.
37. Ibid., p. 76.
38. Ibid., pp. 67, 80,180–5. See also pp. 8–9, 75, 179–80.
39. Ibid., pp. 133–6.
40. Ibid., p. 145.
41. Ibid., pp. 196–219.
42. Ibid., pp. 175–9.

43. Ibid., p. 136.
44. Ibid., pp. 170–5, 273–5.
45. Ibid., p. 76, 211–15.
46. 19 September 1983. Methuen Archive.
47. *In Search of Wales*, p. ix.
48. I.e. gin and Italian vermouth. Ibid., pp. 125–8.
49. Ibid., p. 135.
50. Ibid., pp. 16, 217, 189.
51. Ibid., pp. 73–6, 300–2.
52. Ibid., pp. 297–300.
53. Ibid., p. 304.
54. H. V. Morton, *What I Saw in the Slums* (Labour Party, London, 1933), pp. 8, 29.
55. Ibid., p. 9. Cf. pp. 35, 40.
56. Ibid., p. 43.
57. Ibid., p. 40. *The Road to Wigan Pier* (1937; Penguin edn., Harmondsworth, 1966), p. 16.

CHAPTER 6

1. M. Duffy, *A Thousand Capricious Chances: a History of the Methuen List, 1889–1989* (Methuen, London, 1989), pp. 108–9.
2. *In the Steps of the Master* (Rich and Cowan, London, 1934), pp. 21–2.
3. Ibid., pp. 244–9.
4. Ibid., pp. 239–41, 267–71.
5. Ibid., p. 6.
6. Ibid., p. 18.
7. Ibid., pp. 221–2. Cf. p. 109.
8. Ibid., pp. 340, 37–41, 38–9, 11–14, 195–201, 324–6, 335–8.
9. Ibid., pp. 18, 341.
10. Ibid., pp. 106–7.
11. Ibid., p. 292.
12. Leonard Wooley to Morton, 10 and 15 October 1937.
13. *In the Steps of St Paul* (Rich and Cowan, London, 1936), p. 1.
14. Ibid., pp. 56–7.
15. Ibid., pp. 51–3, 172–5.
16. The house was described by Christopher Hussey for *Country Life*, 20 February 1942, pp. 348–51.
17. *Through Lands of the Bible*, pp. 31–41.
18. Ibid., pp. 168–77.
19. BBC Written Archives Centre, Caversham.
20. *Women of the Bible* (Methuen, London, 1940; 3rd edn., 1941), p. 68.
21. Ibid., p. 12.

CHAPTER 7

1. *In Scotland Again*, p. 4.
2. Morton file, BBC Written Archives Centre, Caversham.
3. 26 June 1939. Morton file, BBC Archives.
4. *I Saw Two Englands*, pp. 31–2, 65, 97.
5. Ibid., p. 282.
6. Ibid., p. 215.
7. Ibid., pp. 283–91.
8. *Atlantic Meeting* (Methuen, London, 1943), p. 125.
9. Ibid., p. 80. Churchill went to Harrow School, not Eton.
10. Ibid., p. 95.
11. *I, James Blunt* (Methuen, London, 1942), p. 8.
12. See A. Briggs, *The War of Words*, vol. 3 of *The History of Broadcasting in the United Kingdom* (Oxford University Press, 1970), pp. 512–14.

CHAPTER 8

1. *In Search of South Africa* (Methuen, London, 1948), pp. 64, 332.
2. Ibid., p. 270.
3. Ibid., pp. 60–1.
4. Ibid., pp. 92–6.
5. Ibid., p. 3.
6. Ibid., p. 186.
7. Ibid., p. 295.
8. Ibid., pp. 352–3.
9. Ibid., p. 97.
10. *In Search of London*, pp. 42–5.
11. Ibid., p. 133.
12. *National Geographic Magazine*: Coronation, vol. 104, no. 3, September 1953, pp. 291–342; Pyrenees, vol. 109, no. 3. pp. 299–334; Lake District, vol. 109, no. 4, pp. 511–46; Ireland, vol. 119, no. 3, March 1961, pp. 293–334.
13. *A Stranger in Spain* (Methuen, London, 1955, repr. 2002), pp. 350–1. Cf pp. 7–8.
14. Ibid., p. 93. On 27 April 1937, German aircraft, supporting Franco's Nationalists, bombed the Basque town, killing 1,600 people.
15. Ibid., pp. 247–8.
16. *A Traveller in Rome*, p. 16.
17. Ibid., pp. 25, 228.
18. *A Traveller in Italy* (Methuen, London, 1964, repr. 2001), p. 334.
19. *A Traveller in Southern Italy*, pp. 23–7.
20. Ibid., p. 351.
21. See, for example, *H. V. Morton's England* (Book Club Associates, London, 1975); *The Splendour of Scotland* (Eyre Methuen, London, 1976); *The Magic of Ireland* (Eyre Methuen, London, 1978); *In Search of the Holy Land* (Eyre Methuen, London, 1979).

CONCLUSION

1. J. B. Priestley (ed.), *Our Nation's Heritage* (Dent, London, 1939), pp. 157–9.
2. 25 April and 4 July 1944, BBC Archives.

INDEX

References to Morton's diaries and the *Memoir* (his unfinished, unpublished autobiography) refer only to the composition or textual characteristics, not citations which are too numerous to be usefully indexed
n=footnote/endnote